CASE ANALYSIS AND
BUSINESS PROBLEM SOLVING

CASE ANALYSIS AND BUSINESS PROBLEM SOLVING

KENNETH E. SCHNELLE, Ph.D.

Head, Economics Section
Department of Business and
Engineering Administration
Michigan Technological University

McGraw-Hill Book Company

New York   St. Louis   San Francisco
Toronto   London   Sydney

CASE ANALYSIS AND
BUSINESS PROBLEM SOLVING

To FRANK KEREKES
and JOHN ROBERT VAN PELT
Dean of Faculty and President,
respectively,
of The Michigan Technological University

On the occasion of their retirements
after ten years of devoted service

PREFACE

This book was originally written as a chapter in the author's proposed text on human relations in industry. Inasmuch as the author views human relations as an applied field of problem solving, he regards the technique of complex problem solving to be basic to his approach. A sound grounding in problem solving was therefore taken to be an important and urgent objective in human relations training, and a full chapter on complex problem solving was contemplated.

As the problem-solving chapter developed, however, its length grew out of proportion to the remainder of the book. Hence the author was faced with a dilemma. On the one hand, an adequate treatment of complex problem solving seemed too long for inclusion in the text on human relations; on the other hand, no suitable text on complex problem solving was available to which students could be referred.

Therefore consideration was given to the publication of a separate little book to describe the nature of complex problem solving as it applies not only to human relations situations but also to business problems in general. Such a book would meet the author's need for a collateral text in the human relations course. More important, it would, hopefully, go far in filling the need for text material in business problem solving itself. Each year, critics of business education clamor for more and better courses in problem solving, but teaching materials, especially at the introductory level, are woefully deficient.

In the course of development of this book, many of the author's associates urged its expansion into a general treatment of business case analysis and business problem solving. It was argued that although case analysis and problem solving are not the same, they have many points in common, and a combined treatment would make good pedagogical sense. In addition, it was pointed out that no full-scale treatment of business case analysis is available to teachers or students who are increasingly using the case method in business school education. As matters now stand, each teacher who uses the case method and each author who prepares a case book devotes a little, but not enough, time to the subjects of case analysis and the case method of instruction. The result is that most students get inadequate instruction on the subjects, and they get it over and over again. Therefore it would seem more practical as well as more effective to teach case analysis and the case method of instruction once to each student, and to teach it well, than to teach it a dozen times but never in the depth it deserves.

Hence the evolved objectives of this book are threefold. First, it is a description of the case method of business school instruction. Second, it is a text on business case analysis. Third, it is an introduction to complex business problem solving. As already mentioned, all of these have many points in common, but they are not the same. Therefore, although all three will be discussed in this book, the student must be careful not to confuse them. In his exposition, the author will try to be explicit about which of the three he is discussing. He also wishes to make clear at the very beginning, however, that the central interest and the primary emphasis in this book are problem solving.

This book may be used in many different ways. Primarily, it is intended as a text for introductory courses, at the college freshman or sophomore level, in business problem solving. Depending on the amount of collateral reading assigned, the extent of independent research demanded, the number of written reports required, and the number of practice cases introduced, the course would require one, two, or three quarter or semester hours. Students completing such a course should be better prepared, in terms of both motivation and understanding, to handle upper-division courses in quantitative methods and business research techniques, and all courses using the case method of instruction.

In schools which do not have a lower-division course in case analysis and problem solving, the book may be used to introduce the difficult materials to be presented in operations research courses. Again, in schools which do not have a lower-division course which covers the present material, the book may be used as a collateral text in courses using the case method of instruction. Finally, the author believes the book may be used as either a primary or a collateral text in schools of engineering where a broader than usual approach to problems of engineering economy is desired. Outside the classroom, the book should be both interesting and useful to business managers and military field commanders who spend their lives in complex problem solving.

The book is both short and easy. The analytical concepts are simple, and no previous knowledge of business administration, economics, or mathematics is needed. Indeed, most of the ideas dealt with in this monograph are so simple that no one heretofore has deemed it necessary to pay any particular attention to them. Most of the writings in the field are contained in the introductory statements to case books. There as elsewhere, however, the treatments are casual and offhand. Such treatments are faulted on two counts: First, the reader is not forced to a realization of the importance of the analysis techniques, and, second, the difficulties of analysis are neither detailed nor solved.

Most of the materials contained in this text are so old and so obscure in their origins as to be considered parts of our useful folklore, and for these materials only general acknowledgments are made. Some parts of the text, however, are new, and these represent the author's personal contributions.

The author wishes to extend his thanks to two of his colleagues at Michigan Technological University, Paul W. Eaton and Lawrence J. Remington, who encouraged the project, made recommendations while the research was in progress, and read the final draft of the text. His affectionate thanks are also extended to his wife, Louise, who read the complete manuscript and offered valuable suggestions.

Special thanks are also extended to Professor L. L. Rakestraw, Michigan Technological University, for his valuable suggestions in connection with the author's discussion of historical research.

The author's thanks are also extended to the many publishers who have granted permission to quote from their publications. These publishers are recognized both in the footnotes and in the references. Finally, the author wishes to thank his many students who have used the materials contained in the text and who have criticized them liberally.

KENNETH E. SCHNELLE

CONTENTS

LIST OF EXHIBITS

CASE ANALYSIS AND
BUSINESS PROBLEM SOLVING

chapter 1

THE NATURE OF
COMPLEX PROBLEMS

The student who is just being introduced to business problem solving has in store for him a great deal of excitement but also some unexpected and rude awakenings. He will find that business problem solving is quite different from the kinds of problem solving he has encountered before.

In his previous classroom experience, most of the problems the student has encountered have been of the mathematical variety, and they have usually been chosen to illustrate a particular mathematical operation. In such problems, all of the elements are clearly stated, and all of the elements are needed in the solution. In addition, each of the problem elements, whether fixed or variable, is measured in cardinal terms,[1] and all of the associations between and among the elements are, or may be, specified by mathematical relationships (formulas).

---

[1] A *cardinal scale* may be either an *interval* or a *ratio scale*. In the former, a real number is assigned to each position on the scale in such a way as to specify the magnitudes of the intervals between positions. These conditions are met by the use of a common and constant unit of measurement. In a ratio scale, there is the additional requirement that the scale have an absolute and not an arbitrary zero point of reference. The ratio scale is more powerful than the interval scale because the ordinary operations of arithmetic can be applied both to the scale values themselves and to the differences between scale values. In contrast, with interval scales ordinary arithmetic operations can be applied

We shall describe problems of this variety as simple problems, [2] and problems which do not conform to this description will be termed complex. Most business problems are complex. Characteristically, in complex problems, the problem itself is not clearly defined, the crucial fixed and variable elements may not be identified, and even where they are identified, they frequently will be either unmeasured or measured in ordinal terms only. Finally, even where elements are both identified and cardinally measured, the relationships between and among them may be obscure.

Now some students (and teachers) who have sweated over the problems we have classified as simple will be offended by such off-

---

only to the differences between scale values. The centigrade thermometer is an example of an interval scale, while an ordinary ruler is an example of a ratio scale. An *ordinal scale* is very much less powerful than either the interval or the ratio scale, for the ordinary operations of arithmetic, such as addition, subtraction, multiplication, and division, cannot be applied either to the scale values themselves or to the differences between scale values. On the ordinal scales which are usually encountered, numbers represent rank ordering throughout the scale. For example, the teams ranked first, second, third, and so on are placed on an ordinal scale which states that the first team is better in performance than the second, but the scale makes no statement of how much better first is than second or fifth than sixth. Moreover, the scale does not imply that the degree of superiority of first over second is equal to the degree of superiority of fifth over sixth.

The subject of measurement scales has an extensive literature. One of the best brief discussions is given by Clyde H. Coombs, "Theory and Methods of Social Measurement," in Leon Festinger and Daniel Katz (eds.), *Research Methods in the Behavioral Sciences,* The Dryden Press, Inc., New York, 1953, pp. 471–488.

Another good discussion of measurement scales is to be found in Russell L. Ackoff's excellent text *Scientific Method: Optimizing Applied Research Decisions,* John Wiley & Sons, Inc., New York, 1962, pp. 177–216. This book is also highly recommended as a companion volume to our present book. Ackoff's discussion uses much more sophisticated mathematical analysis, but his problems have a much narrower scope, and he almost completely neglects the areas of problem selection, fact-finding, and selection of alternative courses of action for analysis. Nevertheless, students who wish to pursue their studies of complex problem solving beyond the elementary levels considered here should put Ackoff's book very high on their lists.

[2] This definition of simple problems does not exclude mathematical relationships which are expressed in terms of probabilities. Systems of stochastic equations, for example, would be classified as simple.

hand treatment of their professional occupations, but let us hasten to reassure the reader (if he be an engineer, scientist, statistician, or mathematician) that we do not imply that solutions to simple problems are easy. Let us hasten to add, moreover, that our dismissal of simple problems is not motivated by contempt. Instead, we dismiss these problems because, on the one hand, their detailed consideration is beyond the scope of the present book, and because, on the other hand, they have been given ample and competent attention elsewhere.

The complex problem, by definition then, is the problem which is not precisely stated. The problem elements are neither clearly nor completely identified. The variables are either poorly measured or even completely unmeasured. And the relationships between or among variables are unknown or exceedingly tentative.

Typically, the complex problem involves an almost infinite number of facts. Most of them are unknown. Those which have been identified are seldom quantified. Even the quantified variables are frequently stated in ordinal terms of rank order, or perhaps simply by statements of the presence or absence of the element. Finally, the relationships between or among variables are usually matters of wild conjecture rather than certain knowledge.

Obviously, with such crude data to work with, the solutions to complex problems will lack the precision and the elegance which are expected in solutions to simple problems.[3] Different practitioners, equally competent, may, from the same set of facts, choose different problems to solve, and even when the same problem is undertaken, different results may be obtained. In short, complex problem solving is extremely frustrating because one can never, even after the most conscientious analysis, be sure one's solution is correct. In fact, one may state that if an analyst should happen to hit on the very best solution to a complex problem, it would be a miracle in the first place, and the analyst would never know it in the second place.

---

[3] When we speak of solutions to complex problems, we mean deliberately selected courses of action and not, necessarily, optimizing solutions. Hence a solution to a complex problem may be more what Herbert A. Simon calls a "satisficing" solution (*Administrative Behavior*, 2d ed., The Macmillan Company, New York, 1957, p. xxvi). It is even possible under the terms of our definition of a solution to leave the situation in a worse condition than it was before the problem was solved.

Stating the present definition of complex problems in another way, one may assert that most of the problems we face are complex. A young man is trying to decide which college to attend. A businessman is considering the establishment of a new business, or siting a plant in a new location, or deciding on the feasibility of an addition to his product line, or determining which, among four or four hundred young men, to train for his own replacement. An elected official is trying to decide how to vote on a new piece of social legislation, or a bishop is trying to determine his posture on the problem of alcohol.

Let us consider one of these problems in detail. For example, how will or how can a young man select the college he should attend? Immediately, we observe that we are not even certain that we are tackling the right problem. Perhaps we should go to the more fundamental issues of whether he should (1) go to college, (2) join the army, (3) take a job in his father's factory, (4) get married, (5) bum his way, for a couple of years, around the world, (6) commit suicide, (7) become a professional loafer, (8) apprentice himself to learn a trade, and so on through the almost infinite number of possible roads from high school to the grave. Hence, in the very beginning of the investigation, we observe that we have a complex problem on our hands.

In this illustration, we haven't even identified the problem, and this lack of identification is itself a most significant complex problem.[4] How does one go about solving it? Simple models (mathematical) are silent from the very outset. They do not give even a clue toward the determination of the basic practical issues. They do not tell us which alternatives should be selected for analysis or what the variables of the problem are.

Suppose we have somehow solved the general problem of choice of the route which will be followed from high school to the grave, and suppose, also, we have decided the best road lies through a college curriculum. Now we can proceed to choose the college our young man should attend. Or can we?

[4] C. West Churchman, Russell L. Ackoff, and E. Leonard Arnoff, *Introduction to Operations Research,* John Wiley & Sons, Inc., New York, 1957, p. 67. These authors state, "There is an old saying that a problem well put is half solved. This much is obvious. What is not so obvious, however, is how to put a problem well. It has become increasingly apparent that the most productive formulation of a problem is itself a complex and technical problem."

No, we cannot. Before we start fooling around with the selection of a college, we should decide what road the young man hopes to follow after he graduates. Here, again, the simple, mathematical approaches fall short for, if anything, there are more roads from college to the grave than from high school (and no college) to the grave. Hence we are back, in the problem-solving sense, at the point from which we started before the young man made the decision to go to college.

Suppose, again, we have somehow solved the problem of what he wants to do after college. Now, perhaps, we can go to work on the matter of which college to attend. Here, at last, is a problem in which we can identify all of the possible alternatives. We can list all of the colleges there are (not forgetting all those located outside the United States). We can list these colleges by name, and we can proceed to gather all of the facts about each.

Well, this is a pretty big order! The *World Almanac* lists about 1,400 senior colleges in the United States alone.[5] For present purposes, we don't have to bother to determine how many colleges would appear on a complete list of all the colleges in the world. It is apparent there are far, far too many even to consider an investigation of them all.[6]

So what should we do now? Well, we could follow the suggestion of a statistician and draw a random sample of these thousands of colleges.[7] In following such a procedure, we could select a smaller number than the whole population and assume that the colleges selected for the sample would be a representative cross section of the universe. But good judgment in choosing the colleges to be selected would probably be better than random sampling. Plain horse sense suggests the elimination of all colleges which can be rejected on

---

[5] *1966 World Almanac and Book of Facts,* Newspaper Enterprise Association, 1966, pp. 705–718.

[6] This difficulty is one of the commonest features of complex problems. For example, the businessman who is trying to select a plant site, if he is to do a thoroughgoing job of analysis, would have to investigate every possible site. The number of site possibilities would far exceed even the number of colleges our hypothetical young man is faced with.

[7] A good statistician, of course, would recommend a stratified sample and not a simple random sample. To identify his strata, however, he would follow his judgment in the same way we follow ours in the techniques described here for complex problem solving.

cursory rather than detailed examination. For example, if the curriculum desired is simply not offered at particular colleges or groups of colleges, they require no further consideration. By such a selection procedure one might, depending on the curriculum alone, eliminate all foreign colleges and, perhaps, half of the domestic ones. This would leave about seven hundred still to be investigated, but progress has been made by the application of judgment rather than by mathematical techniques.

Still further reductions are necessary before the list of colleges can be cut down to manageable size. How this reduction is to be accomplished is one of the major aspects of the problem. In many of the complex problems which are encountered in everyday life, the difficulties of identifying problem elements are much more severe. For example, when a firm is considering the expansion of its product lines, the number of different products which might be added is virtually infinite. Under such circumstances, how can the number of alternatives be cut down to manageable size? We will talk much more about this later, and we will try to give at least partial answers to the questions.

Suppose, now, that we have narrowed the problem down to one of selection among a manageable number of alternative colleges. The next step is to discover all of the relevant facts about each of the colleges as well as all of the details concerning the road the young man wishes to follow after graduation from college. The statement itself is its own proof of further complexity. As soon as one says, "All of the facts," about anything, one is defeatist by definition, for one could not, in a thousand or a million lifetimes, get all of the facts about, or related to, anything. So again we must either declare the problem cannot be solved or we must find some way to approach the difficulty of the "open-ended" list of facts. Here again, mathematical techniques which are used in simple problem solving are silent, and some kind of judgment technique must be employed. More will be said on this point later.

Returning to our main theme, and supposing for the moment that we have somehow selected the facts which will be used in the analysis as well as the alternative courses of action to be analyzed, the next step is to consider each fact in terms of its effect on each course of action. For example, the costs of education at diverse colleges would, for most people, be a set of relevant facts, and it is probable that, again for most people, the costs would all be listed as unfavorable. Thus every fact must be assigned to its proper position on the decision ledger. Some facts will favor the selection of college A, while some will disfavor college A. Other facts will favor or disfavor colleges B, C, D, and so on through the entire list of colleges under consideration. This assignment of the *direction* of influence of each fact should proceed pretty smoothly, but about the time one decides he's making real progress, troubles develop. The analyst discovers some facts which are certainly relevant, but he doesn't know for sure whether, for a particular college, they are favorable or unfavorable. Take, for example, the fact that college A is located in a city of 2 million people. On the surface, it is hard to tell whether this is good or bad. On which side of the ledger does it belong? How does one decide? And, finally, will mathematical analysis furnish the answer?

Again we observe the tricky nature of complex problem solving. We have a problem, and we have facts. We have alternative courses open to us, but we have now encountered a problem of determining the effect of an element on other parts of the problem. This is essentially a difficulty of measurement. And it is not a *little* problem in which we are uncertain whether the measurement value is, say, 40 or 140. This is a big, fat problem in which we don't even know whether the value is plus or minus. And if this kind of thing can occur, what kind of mathematical problem-solving technique can help us at all? The answer, of course, is that no mathematical method can solve a problem in which measurements are so uncertain.[8]

In the present illustration, we need techniques which will directly attack the problem of measurement itself, and this is a major aim of this book. We will have a great deal to say about the difficul-

---

[8] Professor L. J. Remington, Michigan Technological University, in a private communication to the author, dated February 20, 1965, wrote, "I object to this use of the word mathematical as if it were restricted to computation. I view mathematics as a language and quite applicable even in those cases where computation is impossible. Any complex problem that can be discussed in English can be discussed in mathematical terms." The author agrees, in principle, with Remington. He is in particular agreement if Remington calls symbolic logic a branch of mathematics. For practical discussion in this book, however, the author uses the more restricted definition of mathematics.

ties of evaluating or measuring facts and their relationships among one another. For the present, however, we are content to demonstrate the difficulty itself.

Frequently, when there is no doubt about whether a fact is favorable or unfavorable to a particular course of action, there may still be doubt about the *degree* of favorableness or unfavorableness. For example, we may have no doubt that location of a college in a large city is unfavorable—for students of agriculture, for example—but we may have considerable doubt about just how unfavorable it may be. The fact is certainly relevant, and it is certainly unfavorable, but the question of whether it is only slightly or very unfavorable remains. How does one measure degrees of unfavorableness? Is such measurement really necessary?

The answer, of course, is yes. Suppose, in a given analysis, we have six facts favorable to action A, and we have only one fact unfavorable. Can we assume that action A will produce agreeable results? Certainly not. The six favorable factors may all be frivolous, while the single unfavorable factor may be tremendous. The single unfavorable fact may outweigh in importance all six of the favorable facts put together. Hence the question of quantification is crucial, and detailed attention should be given to it. Mathematical problem solving does not even consider the question, for it assumes the difficulty away. In mathematical problem solving, measurement is the task of someone else, but the measurement problem is far more difficult than the application of mathematical logic to measurements which have already been obtained.

So where do we stand in our definition of a complex problem? It is a problem which has not yet been defined. The facts surrounding the problem have not been identified. Even when facts are known to be relevant, they have not been measured in a manner suitable for mathematical manipulation. And even when the measurement magnitudes of variables are adequately known, their relationships to each other and to the alternative courses of action are unknown. For all these reasons although mathematical techniques may and often will be applied within the framework of complex problem analysis, they are subordinate to and dependent on the broader and more inclusive procedures of complex problem solving.

The essential characteristic of complex problem solving is its emphasis on the collection of data for defining the problem, determining the problem-solving objective, measuring variables related to both the problem and the solution goal, and determining relationships between and among variables. It is, to a large extent, what researchers call "dirty work" as opposed to the "clean work" which is characteristic of mathematical problem solving.[9]

In some cases, the investigations of complex problem solving will yield a sufficient amount of information to permit formulation of the formerly complex problem into simple problem terms which will allow mathematical solutions. More often the results of complex problem-solving investigations will produce data which are too crude for fancy mathematical manipulation, and the techniques of complex problem solving will be not only sufficient but even necessary to avoid the illusion of greater accuracy than the data themselves allow.

The techniques of complex problem solving, then, are fairly primitive. This is distressing to us all, but it is devastating to those who must have their analyses neat and clean. People of this bent should not enter the field of business management, for the problems encountered there do not lend themselves very often to sophisticated mathematical analysis. Most practical problems are complex, and the more significant the problem, the more complex it usually is. Therefore people who wish to succeed in management positions must learn to "make-do" with second-best methods of analysis.

From these remarks it is argued that whenever mathematical methods can be used, they should, by all means, be applied. Moreover the developers of mathematical techniques should be congratulated on their progress to date in their efforts to extend the range of applicability of their techniques. They should be strongly encouraged to continue these efforts so that fewer and fewer problems will remain for the older, less exact, and less elegant methods.

At the same time, it is neither necessary nor desirable for the rest of us to sit on our hands while waiting for the mathematical programmers to solve all of our problems. In the first place, they never will, and, in the second place, we can't wait until tomorrow for today's decisions.[10] With a little effort, we can greatly improve on the

---

[9] Cf. Churchman, Ackoff, and Arnoff, *op. cit.,* p. 621.

[10] In this connection, David W. Miller and Martin K. Starr (*Executive Decisions and Operations Research,* Prentice-Hall, Inc., Englewood Cliffs, N.J.,

older techniques for solving complex problems, and improvement will pay off in rich material and human benefits.

The primary purpose of this book is to describe a problem-solving model which has general applicability to all types of complex problems, without exception. The technique is easy to learn, for the concepts are simple and the routines are standard for all problems. The problems themselves, on the other hand, are the most difficult the world can present. Therefore, let the reader be of good cheer. He will be able to attack the most difficult problem with the assurance that *he will always get a solution*. The solution will probably not be the best of all possible solutions, but nobody will ever achieve best solutions in the area of complex problem solving. And let him be further encouraged, for as he gains practice with this technique his solutions will improve throughout his problem-solving lifetime.

1964, pp. 409–411) write as follows: "The major models of operations research are inventory models, waiting-line models, allocation of resources models, and competitive models. The mathematical models are particularly applicable to simple situations in which costs can be measured accurately and where the number of different cost factors is few. In addition, the mathematical models require the development of mathematical interrelationships between and among the pertinent variables. Where these are unknown, or only vaguely realized, mathematical solutions are impossible. Generally speaking, knowledge of interrelationships is best in situations which can be controlled and subjected to systematic investigation by the problem-solver. Hence, the more complex the problem becomes, the less likely it is that sophisticated mathematical problem statements and problem solutions will be found. The mathematical procedures, nevertheless, are useful in many areas of problem-solving, and they should be used wherever applicable."

The Miller and Starr book is impressively comprehensive and authoritative. Therefore, it is recommended, and it is especially recommended for students who want a mathematical treatment of problem solving but who are themselves mathematical neophytes.

chapter 2

THE CASE METHOD IN BUSINESS EDUCATION

In a recent report, the Associated Press carried the story of a very large contribution made to a prominent university. The gift was made for the purpose of medical education and research, and it was made by a graduate of the business school of that university. Shortly after the medical research gift was made, the business school of the same university solicited a very small gift from the same donor. He replied that he could not contribute because he was opposed to business school education. He said that his business school training had been a waste of time. Finally, he stated that the only thing worth learning in business school is *decision making,* and *this cannot be taught in school.*

This man's attitude is extreme, but it emphasizes the recommendation made in a series of recent studies on the subject of business education. Most critics assert that greater effort should be expended on teaching specific skills, such as reading, writing, speaking, quantitative methods, and on problem solving. Proportionately less effort should be spent on functional fields, such as marketing, finance, and labor relations.

Some schools have, for years, followed the

modern recommendations. Foremost among these is the Harvard Business School, and the high reputation of that institution rests, to a considerable extent, on the ability of its graduates not only to make decisions but also to act on them.

The Harvard Business School uses the case method of instruction. Typically, a new student is presented with a case book in every course, and each day, from the very first, he is expected to solve real business problems. For students who have never previously used the case method, and especially for students who have never studied business administration in any form, the first few weeks may be somewhat frustrating.

In the case method, students will be called on to report in class on their own solutions, and oral discussions, with argument, will normally be encouraged. In addition, several times a week, written case solutions may be required. In short, case method teachers have long supported the modern argument that reading, writing, and speaking, together with problem solving, are the best forms of business instruction.

In this book we shall, in large measure, use and illustrate the case method. In fact, one of our purposes is to teach the student how to go about solving cases. The basic technique was developed at Harvard, and the next chapter will detail the Harvard principles. The same principles, however, have a much earlier origin in political and military writings. Machiavelli's *The Prince* [1] is an early example of complex problem solving, and the methods used there have a surprisingly modern ring. Von Clausewitz' *On War* [2] is a more recent example of complex problem-solving techniques. And today the instructions issued by the United States Army for field decision making are substantially the same as those given at the Harvard Business School.

Hence the problem-solving techniques which will be described here have a long, well-tested history. The methods have survived for the very good reason that they work, and the case method started at

---

[1] Niccolò Machiavelli, *The Prince,* The Harvard Classics, vol. 36, P. F. Collier & Sons, New York, 1910.

[2] Karl von Clausewitz, *On War,* Combat Forces Press, Washington, D.C., 1953.

Harvard has spread throughout the world. Today upper-division courses in most schools of business use the case method as the basic instructional tool.

One approach to the learning of case analysis is trial and error. Another is to demand a maximum of student participation in the learning process. Both approaches are combined in our present requirement of the reader. This is to turn now to Exhibit 1, The Hayden Tool Company Case, and proceed, without further instruction in complex problem solving, to analyze and solve the case.

EXHIBIT 1 THE HAYDEN TOOL COMPANY CASE

The Hayden Tool Company is located in a large manufacturing center in southern Connecticut. It is a small, family-owned corporation with the majority stock ownership in the hands of Mr. Hayden, the founder and active manager of the business. The company is engaged in the manufacture of machine tools and dies and of machine parts and subassemblies, all on contract for other manufacturing concerns. The shop consists of one large building and, except for a small office at the front, it is completely unpartitioned.

The total staff consists of Mr. Hayden, who spends most of his time out of the office as salesman and customer-contact man, Miss Holman, who handles all of the office work, and Mr. Becker, general foreman and shop superintendent. The company employs two die makers, four master machinists, and six apprentice machinists.

Paul Keller and Jack Edwards, apprentice machinists, had been assigned to a job order under the supervision of one of the master machinists. Both had been with the company for slightly over one year and, up to the time of the present incident, they had been regarded as eminently satisfactory by the general foreman and the master machinists. On the day in question, Keller and Edwards were working on a rush order for small machine parts which were to be turned out by two simple operations on the turret lathes. After the machines had been set up, both men had received the necessary directions for accomplishment of the task. They had both been working hard, for they had been impressed with the need for speed, and the work was begun by 7:30 A.M. Wednesday. No difficulties were encountered, and both Keller and Edwards worked without assistance or supervision until shortly after ten o'clock. At this time, Mr. Becker, on his way through the shop, stopped behind Keller, looked over his shoulder, frowned, and uttered a somewhat disturbed "Tsk, tsk." No words were spoken, however, and Becker soon passed on to other duties. Some ten minutes later he returned and repeated his first performance. Then again, a short time later, Mr. Becker appeared for the third time and repeated his two previous routines.

Keller turned abruptly and, shaking his clenched fist in Mr. Becker's face, cried out above the noise of the running machinery, "I'm warning you, Becker, if you don't stay away from me, I'll punch ya' in the kisser."

Mr. Becker looked startled, but said nothing and walked away. He went to the office and instructed Miss Holman to make out a discharge notice for Mr. Keller and to deliver it immediately. These instructions were carried out, and Mr. Keller left the shop within thirty minutes.

In the early afternoon, Mr. Curley, president of the machinists' union, called on Mr. Hayden and protested Keller's discharge. He repeated the facts as told to him by Keller and exactly as they had happened.

Unless the reader has spent at least three hours preparing his solution to the Hayden Tool Company case, he should not be reading these lines, and he is cheating. In the author's own instructional efforts, he passes out the Hayden Tool Company case on a separate mimeographed sheet on the first day of class, and students are required to submit written solutions at the next class meeting.[3] The reason for this practice is to try to get the student to participate in the learning process by requiring him to wade in and get his feet wet on a real, complex problem before he has received any formal instruction. What we desire of the student is a personal commitment to induce a condition of "cognitive dissonance" which will require active resolution or adjustment.[4] So if the reader has come this far without having prepared a solution for the case, he should turn back here.

For those who have done an honest job of solving the case, a few general remarks on the nature of case materials are in order. The first is the observation that the problems contained in cases are very different from those which students have previously encountered. Until now the teacher has clearly stated what the problem is. In case materials, the problem is buried beneath and intermixed with large

[3] Instructors who wish to follow this practice are hereby authorized to reproduce the Hayden Tool Company case, for classroom use, without writing for permission to the copyright holder.

[4] Leon Festinger, *A Theory of Cognitive Dissonance,* Stanford University Press, Stanford, Calif., 1957. A state of dissonance exists whenever a person receives two pieces of information which are incompatible. Dissonance is a daily occurrence. One usually feels compelled to do something to reduce it. In the present context, the student is expected to defend his solution vigorously but finally to concede the merits of the points made in class by the instructor. Hence participation in learning is increased.

numbers of facts and circumstances which confuse and complicate problem identification. This is as it should be, for in the world of affairs, as opposed to the classroom, events flow in an unrelenting stream, and problems are easily misidentified or even overlooked entirely. In the "real world," therefore, business practitioners must be on a constant alert to discover problems and problem areas. Hence, for instructional purposes, the case writer tries to detail a stream of events, just as it happened, and the reader is supposed to become almost as much a part of the situation as he would be in the world of affairs. Of course, the student in the classroom does not have to "put his money where his mouth is," but even this condition is approximated, for the student is usually concerned about his grade in the course. Also, in case presentations, it is impossible to include all of the intangibles which are present in real life but which are too difficult to catch and record. These intangibles will often affect real-world case solutions, but their absence from written case materials does not affect the problem-solving procedure.

A second difference between case problems and other problems used in the academic field is the way in which the former present their data. The case itself, as we have said, is nothing more than a chronology of events, and these events are the problem data. Again, as in the real world, facts are incomplete and, what is sometimes even more disconcerting, they are frequently impertinent or superfluous or downright misleading. In studying a case, the student must not merely recognize the existence of a fact, he must also determine its *meaning*. He may question whether the fact is accurately reported, and he will almost always recognize the need for facts which are not contained in the case. These difficulties over facts contained in or absent from the case are exactly the same as those which arise in business life. The management practitioner is constantly reminded of the need to recheck certain facts, to initiate research to obtain missing facts, and to guess at facts which are needed but which cannot be obtained in time for their practical use. In solving case problems, students should do the same things.

A third feature of case materials is their insistence on action. A case solution leads to a student commitment. In other kinds of academic instruction, the student usually ends his consideration by stating what he *thinks* about the situation. In the case method, the student is required to *do* something about it. Psychologically, there is a wide gap between thinking and acting. Thinking is usually concentrated on what the student believes is the "big picture." His thoughts tend to be large, and he winds up by spouting high-sounding platitudes which rarely have anything to do with the problem. In contrast, the case method demand that the student take or recommend action forces him to pay very close attention to detail. Students soon learn that cases which look almost alike may require very different solutions because a few of the details in one are different from those in another. Students also learn that solutions to real problems depend on accommodations among conflicting demands or even conflicting business principles.

For example, the mangement principle that the supervisory span of control is fairly limited is well established. It is also established that multiple layers of supervision should be eliminated wherever possible. Students can learn these principles without much difficulty, but when faced with a case which involves industrial organization, they learn that if one decreases the span of control, he will probably also increase the layers of supervision.[5] To solve this kind of problem, it is not sufficient for the student to report that a problem exists. He must commit himself, and he will learn that the only help is to study, in very much greater detail than we have given here, the exact circumstances of the situation. A few small details, one way or the other, make all the difference between emphasis on span of control or emphasis on layers of supervision.

To be acceptable, a case solution must state in detail the precise action which is recommended, and it must include details not only on what to do but even, in most cases, on how to do it. In short, the complex problem-solving teaching technique insists on recommendations for *completed action.*

A final feature of the case method is a special difficulty of the classroom situation. In business practice, a manager never has any doubt about his own identity. In the classroom, however, the case does not state who the analyst is. In the Hayden Tool Company case, for example, the analyst might be Hayden, Becker, Edwards, Keller, Holman, Curley, or even some other person such as the rush-order contractor who is not specifically named in the case.

---

[5] This same illustration has been used by Simon, *op. cit.,* pp. 20–21.

Now it is possible to analyze any case from as many points of view as there are interested parties. And at least once during the course of instruction it is useful to analyze a case from at least two points of view, for it is highly educational to observe that case solutions by different persons differ widely among themselves. If goals or objectives differ, solutions will usually be different. It is not, however, recommended that students do this as a regular practice. In the first place, more benefit is derived, from available time, if a student solves a larger number of different cases from a single point of view. In the second place, complex problem solving doesn't need to be complicated any further by the introduction of schizophrenic confusion. Hence we recommend that as soon as a student reads a case he should identify himself with the person in the case with whom he feels most sympathetic. Such practice will invite much greater interest.

In passing, one should note that instruction in case techniques holds no institutional bias. It is not a technique which is suitable for businessmen only. The method can be equally applied by any actor in the stream of events. The technique is equally valuable to businessmen, labor leaders, independent operators, government officials, army field commanders, clergymen, physicians, lawyers, beggarmen, and thieves.

chapter 3

THE PROBLEM—SOLVING MODEL

As we have already stated in the Preface, this book is concerned with three similar, but different, subjects: First, the book contains a description of the case method of instruction. Second, it is a text on business case analysis. Third, it is an introduction to complex business problem solving. All three subjects have many points in common, but they are not the same. Therefore, it is our intention to describe each of these subjects, to point out their similarities, and to demonstrate their differences. Following this, we shall set forth the problem-solving model which will be used in the balance of the text.

THE CASE METHOD OF INSTRUCTION

In the preceding chapter, we have described a case as a description of a sequence of events. Virtually all observers insist that cases must be records of events which actually happened.[1] Such a sequence is illustrated by the

[1] Cf. F. K. Berrien and W. H. Bash, *Human Relations,* Harper & Row, Publishers, Incorporated, New York, 1957, pp. 525–558. Edward C. Bursk, *Text and Cases in Marketing,* Prentice-Hall, Inc., Englewood Cliffs, N.J., 1962, pp. 10–22. Richard P. Calhoon, E. William Noland, and Arthur M. Whitehill, Jr., *Cases on Human Relations in Management,* McGraw-Hill Book Company, New

Hayden Tool Company case which the student has already read. In this, as in all business cases, the problem is not stated. The events described are the immediate data with which the student must work, but the facts given in the case are never complete. Finally, the case does not state who the case analyst is. For different purposes, cases may differ widely. Some cases are short, while others are long. Some contain a wealth of detailed information, while others are skimpy.

Objectives of the case method

Probably no two writers would agree on a list of case method objectives, and many would argue violently over the order of importance in an agreed-on list. Therefore, our discussion presents only a tentatively complete list of objectives, and it makes no judgments concerning their relative priorities.

1. One of the most frequently stated objectives [2] of the case method is to present descriptions of actual business situations to familiarize students with business principles and methods as they are employed in the world of affairs. In pursuit of this objective, a case should be rich in detail to enable the student to discover the primary and secondary goals of the firm, the reasons for its particular organizational structure, the rationale behind its operational procedures, the personalities and motives of the principal actors in the situation, and the factors which influence or have influenced its current or past decisions. If a student reads a large number of cases of this variety, he should learn what has been and is being done in many different firms, in many different industries, in many different situations, and in many

---

York, 1958, pp. 9–12. John Desmond Glover and Ralph M. Hower, *The Administrator*, Richard D. Irwin, Inc., Homewood, Ill., 1963, p. xviii. Harry L. Hansen, *Marketing*, Richard D. Irwin, Inc., Homewood, Ill., 1961, pp. 6–8. Alva F. Kindall, *Personnel Administration*, Richard D. Irwin, Inc., Homewood, Ill., 1961, p. xi. Paul R. Lawrence and John A. Seiler, *Organizational Behavior and Administration*, Richard D. Irwin, Inc., Homewood, Ill., 1965, p. viii. George R. Terry, *Marketing: Selected Case Problems*, Prentice-Hall, Inc., Englewood Cliffs, N.J., 1956, pp. v–vi. J. Phillip Wernette, "The Theory of the Case Method," *Michigan Business Review*, University of Michigan, January, 1965, pp. 21–24.

[2] Kindall, *op. cit.*, p. xi. Terry, *op. cit.*, pp. v–x. Lawrence and Seiler, *op. cit.*, p. viii.

different stages of organizational development. In addition to learning what is done, the student should learn both the how and the why.[3] In most cases of this kind, the student will also have the opportunity to judge the effectiveness of past decisions and the demands for new decisions in the current situation. Hence the objective of case materials of this variety is to teach the business facts of life as well as the principles of effective administration. Cases may be selected to cover the general field of management or they may be chosen to illustrate a specialized field such as marketing, finance, or industrial relations.

2. A second objective of the case method is to introduce realism into formal instruction.[4] In the textbook-lecture method of instruction, students frequently feel they are being overstuffed with theory, and they sometimes wonder how the theories would work out in practice. Teachers often hear students and business practitioners complain that things which look good in theory might not—even would not—be practical. It is well known, for example, that real-world situations are complicated and not simple. No event stands alone, but rather is surrounded by a multitude of simultaneous events. In a total complex of events, a multitude of theories may be called on to explain what is happening, and a similarly large number of principles might be required, in concurrent or sequential application, to accomplish the mission of the organization. Moreover, theories and principles may be, and in practice frequently are, in conflict, and a nice balance among their applications may be required. This condition may call for ignoring some theories and principles in favor of applying others which, in the total complex, are more important. Finally, the textbook-lecture method is sometimes too dry to hold the interest of students, and in this event they even fail to learn the theory.

Using the case method, the student develops his own theory, and he has confidence that it will work because it was first observed in a practical situation. He also learns that practical situations are complex and usually require a balanced application of many theories in a carefully considered, sensitive manner. As he becomes more experienced in the subject matter of the course, the student tests the theories he has induced from previous cases by applying them to new

---

[3] Glover and Hower, *op cit.*, p. xi. Wernette, *op. cit.*, p. 22.
[4] Cf. Terry, *op cit.*, pp. v–x.

cases as he studies them. Thus, concurrently, and on a continuing basis, he learns to apply the knowledge he has already gained. In addition, the case method is seldom dry, for cases are living, moving events which are peopled with real personalities who have personal goals, skills, and defects. As the student reads an increasingly large number of cases, he gradually develops a sense of having been through the world of affairs on a carefully conducted tour with a first-rate guide.

3. A third objective of the case method is to teach, by demonstration, the infinite variety of goals, problems, facts, conditions, conflicts, and personalities which occur in the business world.[5] The student learns to expect complications and to deal with them with cautious confidence. He learns that no two situations are ever quite the same, that perfect solutions will never be achieved, and that as soon as one problem is disposed of, another will arise. When cases are used for classroom discussion, in the give-and-take exchange of ideas and arguments, students learn to think on their feet, to take and defend action-decision positions, and to remain flexible enough to change positions as events change or as feedback from their decisions indicates error. In short, students who are taught by the case method learn to expect complicated situations, and they learn to anticipate decision error, but they also acquire the ability to react to situational feedback in a calm but decisive manner.

4. A fourth objective of the case method is to teach decision making.[6] Most cases present situations which can be improved by new action. This is another way of saying that most cases present current problems which demand solutions. In such cases, the student, is required to discover the problem or problems, to analyze them, and to recommend action to be taken to correct or at least to improve the situation. In pursuing this objective, it is not enough for the student to criticize what has been done or to speculate on what is likely to happen in the future. Instead, he is required to decide in detail what he would do to improve the current position of the organization or to meet the anticipated difficulties of the future. In short, the student is required to get out of his academic ivory tower, to make an action

[5] Glover and Hower, *op. cit.,* p. xi. Kindall, *op. cit.,* p. xi.

[6] Bursk, *op. cit.,* p. 19. Lawrence and Seiler, *op. cit.,* p. viii.

decision, to be prepared to defend his position, and to be ready to suffer the consequences of his errors. (Bad decisions will be torn to shreds in the classroom.)

To many teachers this is the most important objective of the case method. It brings instructional realism to its ultimate conclusion, for in the world of affairs the final object of business analysis is to reach a decision on some problem or problem complex. In addition, the problem-solving, decision-making aspect of the case method leads easily and naturally to what educators call participative learning and what psychologists call ego involvement. When students are required to make specific decisions and to prescribe detailed actions, they do become personally involved. They get their feet wet clear up to their groins and their hands wet clear up to their armpits.

5. A fifth objective of the case method is to teach the student the importance of business research as a tool for use in problem solving.[7] No matter how detailed the case report may be, students quickly learn that it will always be deficient in terms of the facts which are given and especially deficient in terms of relationships between and among the facts which are given. Shortly after a student begins to analyze a case, he will discover the need for facts beyond those which have been given. Until these facts are supplied, the analysis will be impaired.

There are two ways to handle the deficiencies of facts. The best way is to defer analysis until the necessary information is obtained in the actual, real world in which the problem arose. The other way is to make note of the factual deficiencies, to determine the research methods which could be used to obtain them (if time and money permitted), and, finally, to make frank assumptions about the missing facts as though they had been given in the case or as though they had been obtained by the recommended research procedures. In making these assumptions, the student should avoid a willy-nilly selection of wild possibilities. Instead, he should try to make reasonable inferences which tie as closely as possible to the facts he does know. In ordinary courses taught by the case method, neither time, money, nor convenience will permit the actual research of needed facts, and in such courses, it is usual and proper to make assumptions as they

[7] Cf. Berrien and Bash, *op. cit.,* pp. 525–558. Lawrence and Seiler, *op. cit.,* p. viii.

are needed to permit the analysis to proceed. In courses which are oriented more toward problem solving than case analysis, at least some actual research in the world of affairs is recommended. In either event, the case method cannot but alert students to the demands which are constantly made, in real-world situations, for the performance of business research as a prerequisite for business problem solving.

6. A final objective of the case method is to teach students to think independently but at the same time to work cooperatively in teamlike situations.[8] The objective is to teach both individualism and cooperativeness. These are logical opposites, and from the teaching point of view, it is like telling a novice horseman to be gentle but firm. Nevertheless, it is not only possible but commonplace to teach the gentle-but-firm technique, and it is possible to teach students both the importance and the technique of individualistic cooperation.

More and more frequently, business decisions are made in group meetings. Boards of directors, executive committees, and group conferences are used increasingly for decision-making purposes. In such conferences, the most valuable men come prepared with their own analyses and their own action recommendations, but they are anxious to hear other points of view, other interpretations of the facts, and other recommendations for action. They come to the conference with a full grasp of what the problem is, what the facts mean, and how the future should be shaped, but they have not hardened their positions. They are flexible and receptive. They are prepared to make their own valuable suggestions, but they are ready to accept anything better that might be presented by somebody else. This does not mean they are prepared to compromise either their minds or their souls, but it does mean they are able to incorporate the contributions of others into their own thinking or even, on occasion, to abandon their positions completely in favor of those of others.

Advantages and disadvantages of the case method

ADVANTAGES   The advantages of the case method are implicit in the discussion of case method objectives which we have just completed. They may be summarized as follows:

[8] Terry, *op. cit.*, pp. v–x.

1. Students learn the what, how, and why of business organization and operation by observing, from case materials presented, a large number of reported business organizations and operations.

2. Students learn, by personal induction, by exchange of ideas among students, and by careful teacher guidance, the principles of business administration. Students acquire confidence in these principles (theories) because they were derived from practical situations.

3. Students learn quickly, easily, and naturally, for they are constantly required to apply the knowledge they have already gained to new situations as they are presented in newly assigned cases.

4. Student interest in learning is increased and learning reinforcement is enhanced by the ego involvement of students in the learning situation.

5. Students learn the complicated nature of business, and they learn to cope with complex problems containing conflicting goals, personalities, and theories.

6. Students learn the ultimate objective of business analysis is business decision making. They learn to take the bull by the horns and to recommend specific action. Once they have committed themselves, they learn to defend their decisions and to risk the consequences of their errors.

7. Students learn the importance of business research in business decision making.

8. Students learn to think independently but to work cooperatively.

DISADVANTAGES The disadvantages of the case method center mainly on the quality of the teacher and of the students.

1. For the case method to be successful, the instructor must be a skilled discussion leader. To get the most out of case material, the teacher must also be thoroughly trained in the subject matter of the course.[9] As a discussion leader, the teacher must force students to start mutual deliberations as soon as the class begins, to keep the discussion moving forward without bogging down on a minor or unre-

[9] Cf. Calhoon, Noland, and Whitehill, *op. cit.,* pp. 15–17. Roger M. Burke, "What I Am Learning at HBS," *Harvard Business School Bulletin,* June, 1958, p. 19. Leonard S. Silk, *The Education of Businessmen,* Committee for Economic Development, New York, 1960, p. 23.

solvable point, to achieve participation in the discussion by every member of the class, to maintain a permissive attitude to avoid discouragement of discussion because of fear of ridicule or censure, to avoid premature projection of the instructor's viewpoints, to keep careful track of time to assure the covering of material prescribed for the class session, and to summarize from time to time, but especially at the end of the session, the consensus which has been expressed. To achieve all of these objectives in every class session is probably too much to ask of any teacher. Moreover, it is probably not desirable for a teacher even to try to achieve all of these goals in every class period. Different cases present different conditions in terms of both teaching objectives and student reactions. To accommodate these changing conditions, good teachers will frequently break all of the rules to win a particular advantage which presents itself in the particular situation. Therefore the so-called rules of policy are highly idealized, and they must be used as guides only to teacher behavior. Nevertheless most writers agree that case method success depends more heavily on teacher competence than most other teaching methods. Therefore this aspect must be counted as a disadvantage of the method.

2. The success of the case method also depends heavily on the quality of students.[10] The best student is one who is highly motivated to learn, who is mature in his social relationships, and who has had some previous business experience. Of course, the more intelligent the members of the group, the better. Students who neglect their case preparations will be not only a drag on the class but also a bore to themselves.[11] They will not understand what is going on, and they will regard the discussion as a bull session concerning trivia. At best, they will get very little out of the course and, at worst, they will become disciplinary problems.

Students who suffer from personal adjustment problems present difficult situations. Some are too sensitive to enter the discussion for fear of being made to appear ridiculous. Some enter the discussion

[10] Cf. Calhoon, Noland, and Whitehill, *op. cit.*, pp. 12–14. Burke, *op. cit.*, p. 19. Silk, *op. cit.*, p. 23.

[11] Cf. Edward E. Werner, "One Variation of the Use of the Case Method in Marketing," *Collegiate News and Views,* South-Western Publishing Company, Cincinnati, October, 1959, pp. 5–8.

with their minds closed to suggestions from others. Some fly into anger easily if anyone disagrees with a position they have taken. Some become sarcastic and engage in personal attacks on others. All of these reactions slow down the progress of the class and place enormous burdens on the discussion leader. Nevertheless, if the leader is expert, the case method is one of the best devices for teaching students the flexibility of mind and the emotional maturity which will be required in the world of affairs. Therefore this disadvantage is not without its compensations.

Students who have had considerable practical background in business make ideal subjects for teaching by the case method. As we have stated, students will learn more from each other than they will from the instructor. It follows, therefore, that when the students themselves are knowledgeable, they will have more to share with others. Hence if the group is made up of regular college students, it is better to postpone use of the case method to upper-division courses to permit the class participants a couple of extra years not only to mature emotionally but also to learn more of the facts of life. Again, if students have not had previous business experience, cases which are selected must contain more detail of an informative nature to enable students to get a more realistic picture of what is going on. Finally, with inexperienced students, the teacher must interfere more often in the discussion, to interject business facts which would ordinarily be commonplace to experienced men.

All in all, therefore, the case method places heavy burdens on students, and these must be rated as a disadvantage of the case method.

3. A third disadvantage of the case method lies in the claim of some writers that it is more appropriate in some subject areas than in others.[12] The method is said to be best in subjects like personnel management, business policy, and human relations. It is said to be inappropriate in subjects like accounting, statistics, and economics. Presumably, in the former group of subject areas the principles are less rigid, and there is more room for disagreement and discussion. In the latter group of courses, the subject matter is better organized and solutions are more specific.

[12] Cf. Silk, *op. cit.*, p. 23.

The present writer tends to disagree with these propositions, but he believes that case method courses in the latter subjects suffer from lack of good case materials. What is needed, he thinks, are more and better cases to illustrate the subjects which remain resistant to the case method of instruction.

4. A final disadvantage of the case method has been cited by Alan P. Trei.[13] He objects to the drive for consensus in classroom discussion. He claims that consensus opinion is pedestrian. He believes students should be encouraged to be more daring and that at least some classroom time should be devoted to the examination of radical ideas. Failure to do so, Trei claims, leads students to lose initiative and to overvalue group agreement.[14]

These views are interesting, and they should stand as warnings to students and instructors, but they should not, we believe, be overdrawn. There is room, in classroom discussion, to accommodate the radical idea, but the radical person should not expect to be allowed to monopolize the discussion. Even the radical person, moreover, can be accommodated in his written work, for he is given complete freedom to express his own ideas as he chooses.

Classroom procedure

The preceding discussion of objectives, advantages, and disadvantages of the case method have already suggested the major procedures used in the classroom. The primary procedures are devices used by the teacher to encourage or even to force students to restate the pertinent facts in the case, to summarize the business principles illustrated, to evaluate actions which have been taken in the past, to specify organizational goals or individual objectives of persons or groups involved, to recognize and verbalize currently existing prob-

[13] "What I Am Learning at HBS," *Harvard Business School Bulletin,* June, 1958, p. 20.

[14] This claim is denied by other research findings (D. G. Marquis, "Individual Responsibility and Group Decisions Involving Risk," *Industrial Management Review,* vol. III, 1962, pp. 8–23, and Y. Rim, "Leadership Attitudes and Decisions Involving Risk," *Personnel Psychology,* vol. IV, 1965, pp. 423–430). These writers conclude that committee decisions, in areas involving uncertainty and risk, tend to be more risky than the average of individual decisions.

lems or problem areas which are likely to develop in the future, to interrelate facts and theories logically in order to predict the future course of events under existing circumstances, to formulate alternative courses of action to guide the future, to weigh the advantages and disadvantages of each course of action, to select a particular action alternative, and to predict the outcome of its implementation.

Inasmuch as the classroom experience is almost worthless to students who come unprepared, some teachers require brief written reports on all cases.[15] These reports, at the very least, should state the central issues of the case, the primary action alternatives, the recommended solution, and the relevant principles involved. The written report system assures not only case preparation but also the commitment of students to action positions. The combination of case knowledge and personal involvement goes far toward assuring a lively discussion in class.

In preparing for classroom discussion, students may work either alone or in small groups. Many teachers prefer the group preparation method because the interchange of ideas in small groups brings out a greater variety of ideas than could probably occur to any one individual. In either case, however, every student should be prepared to begin the discussion in the classroom. Usually, the teacher will lead off by calling on a particular student, asking something like, "Mr. Jones, what is today's case about?" [16] Mr. Jones should briefly restate the facts of the case. When he has finished (after two or three minutes), the instructor will probably ask, "Does anyone wish to add anything to Mr. Jones' statement?"

If the case describes past action decisions, the instructor might next ask, "Mr. Brown, why do you suppose the president (treasurer, sales manager, personnel director, or any other person concerned in the case) decided to produce and sell electric shavers (or whatever else might have been decided)?" The object here is to force students to examine past decisions and to induce from them the business prin-

---

[15] Cf. Werner, *op. cit.,* pp. 5–8.

[16] The exact procedure which will be used to begin and to pursue a class discussion, of course, will depend on the nature of the case and on the intentions of the instructor. Therefore the selection and order of questions which are used here should be regarded only as an illustration of how a particular teacher might proceed in a particular case.

ciples on which the decisions were based. When Mr. Brown has finished, there is likely to be a lively discussion, for usually other students will have different notions. This discussion will be allowed to continue until the instructor is satisfied that the important principles have been brought out, and at that time, he may move the discussion on to the next point. Before doing so, however, he may take it upon himself to summarize (or to have some student summarize) the theories which have been illustrated.

Inasmuch as business objectives or goals are the lodestones toward which all actions are oriented, the teacher will usually next ask, "Mr. Smith, just what do you think the president (or other person or group) is trying to accomplish?" This should lead to a statement of purposes, and a number of different students may wish to contribute. Someone, the instructor if necessary, should, at this point, question whether the apparent goals are the *proper* objectives. This question will almost always produce a lively discussion, and student participation should be active. The question is important, for if it should be agreed that the wrong goals have been pursued, the complexion of the whole case would change, for when objectives change, the actions required to achieve them will almost always change.

The discussion of goals leads naturally into a consideration of new actions which might be taken to further their future achievement. At this point, the instructor might ask, "Mr. White, what action alternatives look promising?" As White states his alternatives, the teacher may list them on the blackboard. After White has finished, other alternatives may be volunteered by other members of the class, and these may be added to the blackboard list. This listing of alternatives will be accomplished with little consumption of time.

With the list on the blackboard, the instructor may now ask, "Mr. Abbot, if alternative number 1 were implemented, what consequences would you anticipate?" This consideration of consequences is a forecast of events which would probably follow from the indicated action, and *it is the key to action-decision analysis.* When Mr. Abbot has completed his statement, the instructor will probably ask further, "Mr. Abbot, from your statement of expected consequences, what would you say are the advantages and disadvantages of this course of action?" These too might be listed on the blackboard. When Abbot has finished, other students will probably wish to challenge his forecast of consequences by denial or by addition. If volunteers challenge, they must be prepared to state why they believe Abbot's forecast is wrong and why theirs is right. In this part of the discussion, all students should try to be objective, and in no case should they engage in unkind personal attacks on others. At the same time, this is the place to get at the heart of a case, and discussion should be both lively and free. If a student's position is attacked, he must take the criticism in the spirit of mutual self-help, and in his reply, he must be equally careful to be objective. The instructor will usually try to stay out of these interchanges, but he will try to keep the discussion on an objective, productive, professional level.

After the advantages and disadvantages of alternative number 1 have been listed, the teacher may frequently ask, "Mr. Crane, on the whole, would you say that the consequences of alternative number 1 are generally good or generally bad?" Or, "Will we be better off or worse off for having taken this action?" This question forces Crane to evaluate the diverse advantages and disadvantages. A single disadvantage, for example, might outweigh in significance half a dozen advantages of less consequence. After Crane's evaluation, other students will doubtless wish to argue, and this will usually be allowed, but it will be hoped that before the discussion is ended a fairly good consensus may be reached.

With the temporary completion of consideration of alternative number 1, attention turns to the second, third, and subsequent alternatives. After the consequences of each are predicted and evaluated, it may be obvious which alternative is best. If the decision is close, a more careful evaluation may be required. The detailed procedures for more careful evaluation will be the subject of a later discussion, but it is well to note here that the essence of careful evaluation is cardinal quantification of advantages and disadvantages.

The final step in the classroom procedure is usually a statement by the instructor to summarize the important points of the discussion. It will emphasize the principles or theories which have been discovered, the business procedures and conventions which have been observed, and the points on which little or no agreement has been reached. It will also usually recapitulate the action decision which has been agreed on and the expected consequences from its implementation. At any rate, sometime during the course, most instructors will devote considerable time to the question of implementation, for a badly implemented, good decision may be no better than an expertly implemented, bad decision. The point here is this: It is necessary not only to determine what should be done but also how, in detail, it is to be accomplished.

This concludes our description of the case method of instruction. Before leaving it, however, we should repeat that there is considerable variation in classroom procedure by different teachers and by the same teacher in handling different courses and different specific cases. Therefore students should use our description of the case method as a guide to the fulfillment of their obligation to prepare their cases and to participate in the classroom discussion. At the same time, they should remain flexible enough to adapt themselves to their particular teacher and to their teacher's own variations in procedure from day to day.

CASE ANALYSIS

The discussion of the case method which we have just completed has already presented a fairly good idea of the steps one should take to analyze a case. If the student asks himself the questions which the teacher will probably ask in class, and if he carefully prepares the answers, he will be at least minimally prepared. Nevertheless there are a few additional points which can be suggested to assist in the analysis of a business case.

The first suggestion is that a case should be read, for the first time, as far as possible in advance of the time the student will sit down to do a serious analysis. The reason is to allow the facts to simmer in his mind for a while and to permit the subconscious to work them over. We will have more to say on this point later.

When the actual case preparation begins, the case should be reread. This time, it should be read carefully, and special pains should be taken to straighten out misconceptions arising from the first reading. This warning is more important than students may think, but it is a fact that when we read we have strong tendencies to comprehend what we believe or what we expect to find. Very often the case contains unexpected twists, and a failure to catch these can be disastrous to subsequent analysis.

After the second reading, a third perusal of the case is needed. This time the analyst usually works with a pencil and copious amounts of paper. The immediate objectives are to record the pertinent facts and to interpret their meanings. Now whether a fact is pertinent depends on its relationship to other facts in the case or its meaning in the total picture. This is probably the most difficult thing for students to learn, and it is also difficult to teach. Among the few suggestions which have been made by other writers are those presented by George R. Terry,[17] and the remarks which follow are a combination of his suggestions and the author's experience. The student is advised to proceed as follows:

1. Classify each fact in the case according to its category as (*a*) an organizational fact, (*b*) an operating fact, or (*c*) a past action fact. Under the organizational category, one should list the kind of firm one is dealing with (manufacturing, merchandising, financial, etc.). One should note the place of the firm in the industry and its relationship to other firms, especially its suppliers, competitors, and customers, and, if appropriate, its relations with government agencies. Third, one should note the organizational subdivisions within the firm, together with their lines of authority, responsibility, and communications upward, downward, and sidewise. Finally, under the organizational category, one should list the primary and secondary organizational goals. As the organizational facts are put into place, the relationships between and among them begin to emerge, and understanding is achieved when the image of the firm develops as a more or less unified whole. When this occurs, the student may have some confidence that he has grasped the meanings of the organizational facts. If some of the facts do not fall into place, greater effort is indicated; but if some facts are ultimately resistant to unification with the total picture, this is an event of major significance, for it may pinpoint a trouble spot in the organization, and such trouble spots may be major problems in the current situation.

Under the operations category, one lists the routine procedures which are followed in the organization. It is usually wise to approach the fact listing in this area in a systematic way. Terry suggests subcategories according to business functions such as planning, financing,

[17] *Op. cit.*, p. vii.

purchasing, manufacturing, warehousing, transporting, selling, and controlling. The object is to gain an understanding of how the firm carries on its regular business, and one way to do this is to examine each of its operations separately. If this suggestion is followed, one should always include, as one of the functional categories, the task of coordinating all of the other functions of the organization. Again, as the facts are classified, a more or less complete picture of each operating function and of the total operation should emerge. Still again, however, if the picture is incomplete or if it is confused, either more work by the student is indicated, or the firm is in trouble.

Under the past actions category, one begins to get into the moving events section of the case. In this classification, one should note what action decisions have been made, the reasons given in the case for their having been made, the time sequences of successive decisions, and the sequences of events following decisions. From the various time sequences, one should try to relate subsequent events to earlier decisions and to identify, tentatively, the consequences of decisions. One should then compare the consequences with the expected results which may have been given in the case as reasons for the actions. If more than one decision was made, one should check to determine their apparent congruities or conflicts. From these various observations, the student should try to judge whether past decisions were good or bad. In addition, he should check to determine whether, in the implementation of past decisions, appropriate accommodations were made in the organizational structure and/or in the operating procedures to have allowed past decisions some fair chances of success. Finally, in this moving events classification of the facts, the student should begin to develop an idea of what is likely to happen in the future.

2. After the facts have been classified, and after their interrelationships are understood, the student should appraise the current situation. He is led naturally into this appraisal by the last step in his classification of the facts. He has begun to develop an idea of what is going to happen next. These ideas should now be formalized in the listing of predictions. Then each forecast should be labeled as favorable or unfavorable, and, finally, the unfavorable predictions should be studied to determine the speed with which they are expected to develop and their importance to the achievement of the objectives of the

organization. In considering the importance of an unfavorable prediction it is usually wise to examine the extent of organizational involvement. This is not the same thing as importance, but it is related to it. For example, an evil event may be tremendously important as an obstruction to the achievement of organizational goals, but corrective action may be straightforward in the sense that only a small part of the operation or organization needs changing. On the other hand, a relatively unimportant evil consequence may be avoidable only by completely overhauling the organization and operating procedure. In the latter case, the risk involved in making extensive changes may be too great to warrant corrective action.

3. Before leaving this section on facts, one additional statement may be helpful. We determine the interrelationships among facts by observing the completeness and unity of the organizational and operational pictures. We also determine interrelationships by noting temporal sequences in moving events. An additional test of relationship among facts is that of imagining what would happen if a given fact were changed. If the change would have extensive repercussions on other facts so that it would be necessary to change the latter to accommodate changes in the former, the former is not an isolated fact. It is a related fact, and the nature of the relationship may be inferred from the accommodations which would be necessary if the fact were changed.

After the facts have been classified and after their interrelationships have been identified, it may be said that the analyst has a good understanding of the case. He is now prepared to note the lessons he has learned from it. Hence the next step in case analysis is to identify the business principles which the case illustrates. The student should note which principles were applied, which were neglected, and the consequences of application or neglect. When the student begins his course with the case method, he will probably have trouble with this aspect of the analysis, for he has not yet learned the principles. Still, even at the beginning of the course, the student should try to induce principles from the facts of the case. To clarify this statement, let us say what is meant by a business principle. It is the same thing as a simple theory. It is induced from the facts of the real world and not deduced from categorical assumptions of truth. It is a generalization of observations of relationships among facts or events. A principle is developed gradually from repeated observations in the natural world. At first, it is held very tentatively, for subsequent observations may fail to confirm it. As the principle is more and more often confirmed by observation, greater confidence may be placed in it. Finally, the value of theory is very great, for whenever the *essentials* of the observational conditions are presented in new situations, the theory may be used to explain past events and to predict future events. Hence the development of business theory is fundamental to the development of executive competence.

The next step in case analysis is to identify and list problems and problem areas. Almost every case one sees will present one or even many problems. Whenever things are going badly, there is a problem. Even when things are going nicely, there may be actions which could be taken to help them go better. Frequently there are so many problems that it is difficult to know where to begin. In a later chapter we shall devote considerable space to the question of problem identification and selection. For the present it is enough to say that the question of problem selection is very important, for unless the problem is wisely selected, a poor solution to the case will be almost inevitable.

In selecting the problem for analysis one must have primary regard for the goals of the analyst. People with different objectives will select different problems. Therefore the first step in problem selection is goal identification. Next, all of the problems observed in the case should be listed. They will be inferred from the previous analysis of the facts. Then problems should be classified as either primary or secondary by noting relationships among problems. A secondary problem is one which arises out of, or is caused by, a more basic one. Generally, the student should try to solve the primary problem, but sometimes he may instead elect to solve a problem of greater urgency or one which looks easier to attack.

After the problem has been selected, the next step is to list the alternative courses of action which might be taken to correct or at least improve the outlook for the future. The greatest difficulty here is to choose, from among the many, many alternatives, the relatively few which one has time to analyze. Again, we shall devote a whole subsequent chapter to this subject, but for the present we may advise the following: (1) choose three, four, or five alternatives for analysis;

(2) spread the alternative choices as broadly as possible over the entire spectrum of possible alternatives; (3) choose at least one conservative and one radical alternative; and (4) on the basis of one's understanding of the case, choose alternatives which show promise of success.

The next step in the analysis is to forecast the consequences of each alternative course of action. As this is accomplished, a list of advantages and disadvantages is developed for each alternative. The pros and cons for each are then weighed and the most favorable course of action is selected for implementation. The details of weighing or evaluating advantages and disadvantages is left for a later chapter. For the present it is enough to repeat that, in many cases, a gross evaluation is sufficient, but in close decisions more careful weighting may be required.

The final step in analysis is to select the best course of action and to plan for its implementation. We have already mentioned the importance of implementation. Later in the book, we shall devote more time to its details.

BUSINESS PROBLEM SOLVING

As we mentioned earlier, business case analysis and business problem solving are similar, but they are not the same. In business case analysis, a business situation is presented in a written case. Either the facts are fully contained in the case, or they must be inferred from materials which are presented, or they must be assumed. In business problem solving, we visualize a real-world situation. There is no classroom, no teacher, and no written description of the situation. In problem solving, we assume the analyst is an actual business practitioner who is in physical contact with the world of affairs, and it is his responsibility to record the facts for analysis and decision making. On the one hand, therefore, case analysis is primarily a clean, armchair occupation, while on the other hand, problem solving is a dirty, feet-wetting experience.

Case analysis is far more realistic than most other classroom procedures, but problem solving, at its best, is even more realistic. It is done in the real world itself. In teaching problem solving, the classroom is used for instructor guidance and for the sharing of experience by students. Hence problem solving is like case analysis, except that in problem solving the analyst must produce the case. Once the case is prepared, problem solving approaches an experience in case analysis. Problem solving is still not the same as case analysis, however, even after the case is prepared, for as the analysis progresses, the need for additional information will become apparent. In full-scale problem solving, therefore, additional returns to the real world, for research of additional facts, will be needed.

At the present time, many schools use the case method, and in many subject areas fine case materials are available. For obvious reasons, however, few schools offer courses in problem solving. As substitutes, many schools offer courses in business research. Presumably a student who has been trained in both business research and case analysis should be able to accomplish a problem-solving mission. This, however, is a questionable presumption, and the writer, from his experience with students who have had both case analysis and business research experience, believes that the combination of both in an actual course in problem solving should and will be the next important development in business school education. Ideally, students should first be trained with the case method. This experience will illustrate to them the need for training in business research. Then a formal course in business research should be taken, and the sequence should be topped off with a course in problem solving.

In the remainder of this book, our intention is to pursue the subject of problem solving. While many of the details of problem solving will apply to case analysis, as many of the details of case analysis apply to problem solving, the primary purpose in our subsequent discussion is to encourage students to attack problems which they themselves have observed. Our intention is simply to make the case method even more realistic by the natural progression to real-world problem solving. Our further intention, and indeed our primary purpose, is to present a problem-solving model, not merely for training in the classroom but for actual use in the world of affairs.

The problem-solving model

In our exposition of the subject of problem solving, it is convenient to use a systematic procedure to keep track of what we are doing. For this purpose, we use a problem-solving model. In its essentials, the model has been in use for many years. It was presented at the Harvard Business School as follows:

1. Statement of the problem
2. Statement of the pertinent facts
3. Statement of alternative courses of action
4. Advantages and disadvantages of alternative courses of action
5. Evaluation of advantages and disadvantages
6. Selection of the best alternative

The United States Army uses the same steps for problem solving with the following exceptions:

1. Instead of calling the procedure a problem-solving model, the Army calls it "the commander's estimate of the situation."
2. Instead of prescribing a statement of the problem, the Army prescribes a statement of the commander's mission.[18]

---

[18] The commander's mission is a statement of the objective desired in the solution. This has very close affinity to the statement of the problem in the present model. In fact, as we shall demonstrate in paragraph I, Exhibit 11, the statement of objectives is a restatement of problems. Objectives may be thought of as desires to set things "right," and problems are statement of things which are not "right."

The matter of objectives and goals is fundamental to every problem analysis, and most writers devote considerable space to a discussion of them. We have already discussed them in connection with our description of case analysis procedure, but in our problem-solving model no specific mention is made of goals, for the establishment of objectives is regarded as a precondition of analysis. In Chapter 2, for example, we pointed out that the same case solved by different people may yield different conclusions. For instance, if the problem analyst in the Hayden Tool Company case is Curley, his objectives may be divided into long-term and short-term goals. For the short term, he might desire the reinstatement of Keller, and for the long term, he might desire to extend the influence of the union. If the analyst were Becker, his short-term goal might be to get out the rush order, and his long-term goal might be to consolidate his position as foreman. If the analyst were Hayden, his short-term goal might be to settle Curley's complaint as quickly as possible, and his long-term goal might be to keep his organization intact.

The problem of objectives assumes particularly large proportions when the analyst is an outside consultant rather than a participant in the action. In such circumstances, one dares not assume the goals sought by one's principal. The

3. Instead of requiring a statement of facts, the Army prescribes a statement of enemy and friendly capabilities.

In the author's extension of the model, he has divided the task of evaluating advantages and disadvantages into two steps. In the first, we determine the value or the importance of advantages and disadvantages on the assumption that the proposed effect will occur with absolute certainty. In the second step, we evaluate the likelihood that the effect will occur. In addition, in our model, we take specific notice of the crucial importance of judgment in the solution of complex problems, and we have added a number of steps to assist the analyst to improve his judgment over time. Finally, we have given special attention to the implementation of the decision. Hence the model presented here will have the following steps:

1. Statement of the problem
2. Statement of the facts
3. Statement of alternative courses of action
4. Advantages and disadvantages of alternative courses of action
5. Evaluation of advantages and disadvantages
6. Certainty of occurrence of advantages and disadvantages
7. Selection of the best alternative
8. Implementing the selected course of action
9. Comparing expected with actual results of the decision

---

consultant must question his client very carefully and be very sure he knows what the principal wants to accomplish. For example, Ross Stagner ("Resolving Top-level Managerial Disagreements," *Business Topics,* Michigan State University, East Lansing, Winter, 1965, pp. 15–22), in an investigation of disagreements among top-level managers within a single company, found that some managers were primarily profit-oriented while others were concerned with the company's public image and still others were personally power-oriented. Under such conditions, different problem solvers will arrive at quite different problem solutions, and it is not surprising that disagreements arise. Hence, even when he is a participant in the action, the analyst must continually have regard for the goals of other people involved.

In any case, the objectives of analysis have fundamental influence on the selection of problems for analysis and the pertinence of facts in the situation. In the present treatment, the goals of analysis are established before the analysis is undertaken, but the problems and facts which are selected reflect the established objectives.

Each of these steps will be described in detail. As the reader makes his way through the book, he will be impressed by the mass of detail required for a full-scale application of the model. For instructional purposes, this detail is essential, but readers must not imagine that full-scale solutions must or can be accomplished on each and every complex problem encountered. The model can and should be used, under appropriate circumstances, in abbreviated form. When there is plenty of time, and when the problem is one of very great importance, a full-scale analysis should be made. For minor problems, or when time is pressing, an abbreviated solution must be substituted.

During the instruction period, however, all of the analytical details must be learned, and learned thoroughly. Students must accomplish their analyses with treatments as full as circumstances permit. The prescribed techniques must be so thoroughly learned that they become second nature. After the course is completed, students should do full-scale analyses at regular intervals to keep sharp edges on their analytical tools.

At the end of this course of instruction, the student's speed in analysis will be greatly improved over his first attempts. Even his fact-finding skills will be vastly more efficient. Finally, the tricks of short-cutting will be described. In Chapter 15, we shall discuss the manner in which the model may be used under various business conditions and in the face of diverse business limitations. Meanwhile, let the reader not anticipate the circumstances under which the model will be used in different situations. Neither let him look for shortcuts. Instead, he is urged to learn the technique in all of the detail in which it will be presented, and during the course of instruction the student should give every analysis the fullest treatment which time permits.

chapter 4

STATEMENT
OF THE PROBLEM

The most important step in complex problem solving is the selection of the problem one proposes to solve. Unless the right problem is chosen for analysis in the first place, one cannot hope to get a good solution. This statement is so obvious as to require little discussion.[1]

A few points, however, have important implications. As we shall presently demonstrate, problem selection is far from an exact science, and it is doubtful whether, despite our most meticulous efforts, we ever succeed in choosing the best. The nearest we can come is to *begin* our trials with that problem in which solution payoffs in relation to solution costs are *likely* to be greatest.

Second, we shall discover that so-called problems are really clusters of problems, or what we shall call problem areas. As we shall also argue, the present problem-solving model requires taking one problem at a time.[2] Finally,

[1] In this connection, Peter F. Drucker (*The Practice of Management*, Harper & Row, Publishers, Incorporated, New York, 1954, p. 531) writes, "The most common source of mistakes in management decisions is emphasis on finding the right answers rather than the right questions."

[2] Cf. Churchman, Ackoff, and Arnoff, *op. cit.*, pp. 157–190. Perhaps the most serious defect of the model presented in this book is, indeed, just this. In contrast, the more sophisticated mathematical models are capable of logically handling more than one problem at a time and of keeping track of interrela-

we shall state that the solution of one problem in a problem cluster will change all of the other problems. Some will disappear and others will be born. One measure of how well one selects his problem for analysis is the effect its solution has on the total complex. If the aggregate effect is to create a great number of additional serious problems while eliminating a few unimportant problems, one may suspect he has done a poor job of initial problem selection. Of course, this is not certain, for he may have selected a good problem for analysis, but he may have done a bad job of analysis or of implementation.

Third, even though optimal selection of the problem is only a remote possibility, the effort one expends on any problem in the total complex of problems will usually produce better understanding of the entire problem area. This means that further effort to select and solve problems in the problem cluster will probably lead to improved results. Hence, despite our pessimism about the ease with which one can choose correct problems for analysis, we are optimistic about the overall efficiency of the model.

Considering the length of time the basic procedures for complex problem solving have been with us, it is astonishing how little has been written on the subject of problem selection. No one would argue that selection is less than a matter of first importance, but writers seem to assume that selection is either unimportant or too simple to engage attention. Hence most of what follows in this chapter is based on the author's personal effort and observation.[3]

---

tionships between the problem under analysis and other problems in the complex. On the other hand, the present model is not intended for use where simple problem-solving models are applicable, so one can hardly argue that sophisticated models are superior to ours, for the former cannot be used at all on problems we define as complex. Moreover, as we shall demonstrate presently, even the one-problem-at-a-time defect can be somewhat attenuated.

[3] The author, of course, does not wish to imply that no attention has been given to the question of problem selection. Drucker (*op. cit.,* p. 354), for example, argues that problem definition must start with the location of the "critical factor." This is the thing which must be changed before anything else can be altered. Paul H. Rigby (*Conceptual Foundations in Business Research,* John Wiley & Sons, Inc., New York, 1965, pp. 96–102) concludes that problem selection is best guided by the development of a theoretical framework for the investigation. Professor Rigby admits, however, that theoretical problem indicators are somewhat difficult to find in applied business research and, especially, in problem solving. In his chapter on problem solving (pp. 37–71), Rigby as-

As a start, the novice in the use of this model should be conscious of the tremendous importance of problem selection, but he should recognize that the solving process cannot be permitted to bog down because of failure to select some problem to solve. The first great lesson here is that speed of action is sometimes of the essence. If one delays too long, the opportunity may be missed. In the world of affairs, the problem is a moving picture, not a snapshot, and the entire situation might change within a very short time. Finally, the novice must observe that failure to act *is* a solution in which the default is an implicit decision to do nothing.

Once the decision has been made to approach the problem area with determination to avoid default, the analyst should, on the simple basis of his best personal judgment, list all of the problems he sees and all of those he suspects in the situation complex. From this list, he then tries to choose for analysis the one which seems to him most suitable. His choice, therefore, is guided by personal judgment, but there are a few rules which may assist the novice.[4]

---

sumes that operational problems are self-evident. Edward T. P. Watson ("Diagnosis of Management Problems," *Harvard Business Review,* vol. 36, January–February, 1958, pp. 69–76) states that in attempting to discover problems, one first looks at trouble spots which are revealed in regularly submitted control information. These should be regarded as symptoms. Symptoms should then be examined to determine failures in management: (1) failures to set objectives, (2) failures in planning, (3) failure in organization, and (4) failure in control. In other words, the symptoms may point to deeper problems in the areas of these failures. Rensis Likert ("Measuring Organizational Performance," *Harvard Business Review,* vol. 36, March–April, 1958, pp. 41–51) has argued that our concern with measurement of managerial performance at the end-result level has obscured the importance of intervening factors which influence end results. He looks for problems in the "human assets area" and argues that these are usually overlooked. More attention should be given to problems of human loyalty, motivation, confidence, and trust. Churchman, Ackoff, and Arnoff (*op. cit.,* p. 107) point out that problems always contain four characteristics: (1) a decision maker, (2) a desire or goal which is something different from the present state, (3) an environment which contains the problem and resources which can be used to influence the present situation, and (4) a choice between at least two alternatives. Ackoff (*op. cit.,* p. 64) writes, "A problem was shown to consist of a decision-maker, one or more objectives, two or more unequally efficient courses of action, a state of doubt, and an environment."

[4] The so-called rules are not, unfortunately, based on experimental evidence. Essentially, they are based on the author's experience. This, however, is not entirely unscientific. The investigation of problem-selection procedures has

Choose the goals of analysis

Although goals and problems are the obverse and reverse of the same coin, most people think of goals in a broader sense than they contemplate problems. Moreover, when we speak of goals we frequently have reference to ethical as well as business objectives. Hence before one progresses very far in his selection of problems for analysis, he should examine the broader aspects of the business situation to determine the fundamental restrictions which may be placed on his freedom of action by social, religious, and ethical considerations.

It is beyond the scope of this book to dwell on these matters, but it is neither feasible nor desirable to neglect them completely. Therefore a few words on the subject seem to be in order. The first word is this: The problem solver himself is personally responsible for the moral consequences of his decisions. This responsibility has both private and public aspects. On the one hand, the analyst must satisfy himself that his conscience is clear but, on the other hand, he must be persuaded that others will agree that his motives are pure. While it is sometimes difficult to do both, a real effort in that direction should be made. If both cannot be achieved, most people elect to satisfy their private codes of morality and to hope that others will someday recognize their virtues.

Second, in choosing the goals of analysis, the problem solver will be oriented toward the ends he hopes to achieve. It is not enough, however, to be satisfied with ethically selected ends. It is also necessary to be satisfied that the means by which the ends are to be achieved are ethical, too. This requires that ethical judgments will not be confined to goal selection, but rather that ethics will be involved in the entire subsequent analysis to assure the good which is sought in

---

proceeded in much the same way that clinical investigation technique has developed in psychiatry. There is hardly any satisfactory technique for the diagnosis of mental disease which does not involve the judgment of a trained psychiatrist. Some of the theories of personality and psychiatry, after development by clinical observers, have been subjected to experimental investigation, and it is to be hoped that future research will be accomplished to confirm or reject and to extend the list of the so-called rules presented here.

the solution is not overbalanced by the bad which may be sustained in its achievement.

Third, whether one embraces the hedonic doctrine (the duty to select the more pleasurable and to reject the more painful course of action) or the perfectionist principle (the duty to cherish and protect one's God-given human attributes of mind, soul, and body and to reject any act which might sully or destroy them)—these are the two great "schools of ethics" from which many philosophers believe that all other ethical systems are derived, one must consider long-term as well as short-term consequences. One mark of wisdom as well as morality is the ability to project into the future and to be patient for its arrival.

Fourth, business objectives must conform to the demands of the morals of the analyst. Within this framework, the analyst seeks to guide the stream of events to produce salubrious consequences for all concerned in both the long and the short terms. This, of course, is a gigantic undertaking, and many obstructions lie in the pathway to its achievement. Very often, even usually, achievement of a particular goal will benefit some of the people concerned but injure others. Sometimes an event will produce undesirable short-term consequences but eminently desirable long-term results. Sometimes the ends may be entirely desirable, but the costs of achievement may be too high. Therefore, in selecting goals, one must almost always balance the good against the bad and select those goals which appear to be best from an overall point of view.

With these considerations in mind, let us proceed to the task of actually selecting the problem for analysis.

Solve one problem at a time

As we have previously mentioned, our complex problems come in bunches. One is frequently tempted to try to encompass them all in a single analysis. This should never be attempted with this model, and this rule is adamant. Some of the other rules which will be detailed presently may, and frequently must, be broken, but this one never.

In the Hayden Tool Company case, if we assume the point of view of Mr. Hayden, we might be tempted to state the problem in some such fashion as this: "What should be done about Becker, and what should be told to Curley?" This is a two-headed monster, and either head is repulsive enough alone. Both problems are complex, and they are *interrelated*. This is to say that the solution to either one of them would affect the other. If we were to try simultaneous solutions, the analysis would become too complicated even to keep track of what we were doing. Finally, if we solve one of these problems, there is a chance that the other will disappear.

Solve the most urgent problem first

We have previously stated that complex problems are streams of moving events, and delay is often fatal. Therefore it is necessary to act with dispatch, and the rule is to take the most urgent problem first. Unlike the first rule, to attack one problem at a time, however, the present rule may be, and sometimes should be, violated.

Let's review the procedure for problem selection which we have already stated. After examining the total situation, we list *all* of the problems, big and small, near and remote, urgent and postponable, primary and secondary, obvious and suspected, enduring and transitory, easy and difficult, personal and public, wide-ranging and narrow, genetic and symptomatic, practical and theoretical, and so on until as complete a list of problems as possible is made—within the time and expense limits imposed.

This listing of problems is so important to general technique that it is difficult to overemphasize it, for the better one's list, the better one's selection from it will be. Now again, from the author's experience, it usually happens that the tyro problem solver will produce a very short list, while the virtuoso problem solver will rapidly write out a surprisingly long one. Therefore, for the beginner, and as insurance even for the expert, the following procedure is recommended: Read the case or examine the business situation. Start writing the list of problems which come to mind without stopping to reflect on the *quality* of the list being made. In fact, use the shortest shorthand you know. Get the idea down, and get it down fast. Don't let anyone or anything interrupt your train of thought. Keeping things moving, and one idea will suggest the next. Hurry, hurry, hurry. After a few minutes, you'll run dry, but you'll have a great deal down on paper. Rest a few minutes by looking out of the window and thinking of absolutely nothing (if possible). Now reread the case, and start listing problems again. Don't try to remember whether you've listed a problem before. Just keep listing until you go dry again.

This procedure, as some people know, is a cross between brainstorming and head-shrinking. The aim of the brainstorming technique is to spawn ideas as rapidly as possible and to attempt to reach the full range of all possible problems. While ideas are being generated, one must try not to evaluate or to determine whether ideas are good or bad, for such interruption cuts off the flow. In the head-shrinking allusion, we have reference to the free-association methods which have been developed and successfully used in psychoanalysis. Much nonsense is generated, but sometimes deeply seated ideas of great value are produced.

After two or three attempts at this technique, if time permits, one should put the whole thing aside for a day or two and let the unconscious mind work it over. This procedure should not require either explanation or defense, for almost everyone has experienced the benevolent and astonishing facility of the human mind to work over problems during rest or even during occupation with other duties. Frequently a problem which defies solution comes easily the next day. Therefore, after a day of rest, try the procedure of listing a couple of times more. By now even a novice should have several pages of problems listed, and this is good, for *the greatest barrier to selection of the correct problem lies in failure to think of it.*

After the listing has been completed, it is time to read the list. What a mess! Three-quarters of the items are repetitious, frivolous, farfetched, or unrelated to the facts. Some of the writing may be undecipherable. Nevertheless, when all of the bad is thrown out, it is amazing how many good, sensible problems are left. These should be copied on a fresh sheet of paper.

At this point, the student should review the Hayden Tool Company case and try out the problem-listing technique.

After the chaff is separated from the grain, the list must be inspected to determine the relative urgencies of the problems. In this operation it is better to work on fresh paper rather than to mark up the problem list, for that list will have to be used many times and it is best to keep it uncluttered. In reviewing the list for urgency, it is sufficient to rate each problem as "VU" (very urgent), "U" (urgent), and "NU" (not urgent). Separate lists of these categories should be prepared, and on the "VU" list, the problems should be ranked in the order of urgency.[5]

It would be very nice if we could now tell the reader to solve that problem which analysis has ranked most urgent. Unfortunately, this cannot be automatically recommended. The reader will recall that the rule to solve the most urgent problem first may be, and often is, broken. By now, if the reader inspects his list of problems, he will discover that some of the most urgent problems may be among the least important. On the other hand, the most urgent are frequently of great importance, and deferment of urgent, serious problems seldom occurs. Hence it may be said that although the most urgent problem may not be the best to select for analysis, it *usually* is the best.

Solve the easiest problem first

Some problems are so difficult, because of uncertainties concerning facts or relationships among facts, as to cause the analyst serious misgivings. Most solutions to complex problems are more or less tentative, but implementations are usually irreversible. Hence if we make mistakes, they are never directly retrievable. After solutions have been acted on, if things fail to work out according to expectation, one cannot recall the action and start over again as though nothing had happened. The only thing one can do in such cases is to start a new study of the problem area from the very beginning.

[5] Professor P. W. Eaton, in a private communication to the author, dated February 12, 1965, stated that he prefers the "deadline" technique for the rating of problems for urgency. For example, problem A requires solution before 2:00 P.M., problem B before next Monday, problem C before February 18, and so on. This technique has not, to our knowledge, been tried in practice, but it has the face advantage of forcibly reminding the analyst to get on with his problem solving before solutions are thrust on him by his own default. Also, by using the deadline technique, it may appear that there is time to solve less urgent problems before the deadline for the more urgent. If the less urgent is more important or easier to solve, and if the more urgent is not defaulted in the process, the less urgent should be solved first. Professor Eaton also suggests a simplified, critical-path analysis might be useful for the determination of the proper order for sequential problem solving. For a brief description of critical-path analysis, the reader is referred to *A Programmed Introduction to PERT*, John Wiley & Sons, Inc., New York, 1963.

Hence, as a general rule, one should look for the problems which are most obvious and which appear to be the quickest and easiest to solve. They should also be those which will produce results at the earliest date. If this procedure is followed, one may learn a great deal about the total problem complex, and this new knowledge may be sufficient to clarify facts and fact relationships so that the more difficult problems can be approached later with greater assurance.[6]

Moreover, as always when acting on any part of the problem cluster, the other parts change. Hopefully, if one solves an easy problem with confidence at the start and with success in the result, some problems which appeared in the old complex will disappear in the new. Thus, by solving an easy problem, one may so change the total situation as to make it unnecessary to solve some of the formerly present, difficult problems.

To determine which of all the problems listed are easy, difficult, or very difficult, one must rely on personal judgment. In following his judgment in this operation, the novice is advised to determine relative difficulty on the basis of the degree of confidence he would have in approaching the problem. If the reading of the problem gives the analyst an uncontrollable urge to get things going, it may be judged easy. If, however, the reading of the problem leaves the analyst with "that tired, run-down feeling," it should be judged difficult. If the reading produces a feeling of downright illness, classify the problem as very difficult. In his early attempts at problem selection, the tyro will make

[6] Franklin A. Lindsay (*New Techniques for Management Decision-making,* McGraw-Hill Book Company, New York, 1958, p. 120) argues against selecting the easiest problem for first solution. He states that problems which are selected because they appear to be easy often turn out to be difficult. Moreover, if one deliberately sets out to solve easy problems first, he will frequently fail because the problem has been artificially restricted in scope and has become unrealistic. Lindsay argues, therefore, in favor of selecting problems of major importance. The author agrees with Lindsay that problems which appear easy have a way of developing into very difficult ones. Such developments, however, usually occur because the analyst fails to restrict the scope of the problem. Therefore, we argue that if problem scope can be limited without imposing artificial restrictions, the analyst may avoid Lindsay's second objection and not be hurt by the first.

Despite his disagreement with Lindsay on the present point, the author recommends Lindsay's book as an exceptionally valuable collateral reading text for this book. It is comprehensive, authoritative, and nonmathematical. An added advantage is the fact that it is available in a paperback edition.

many bad judgments, for some of the most difficult problems will sometimes appear, on the surface, to be easy, and vice versa. As one gains experience, judgment improves.

After the classification is completed, we would like to be able to recommend to the analyst that he immediately select the easiest problem of all to solve. Unfortunately, this cannot be done, for although the rule is a good one, it has exceptions. Hopefully, the easiest problem will also be the most urgent, but if it is not, one must decide whether to follow the rule of ease or the rule of urgency. This can be decided only on the basis of further and more detailed study of the situation.

Solve the primary problem first

In the Hayden Tool Company case, the firing of Keller and the protest by Curley are problems of great urgency. As such, they require prompt attention, and most students who have analyzed this case elect to handle the question of what to tell Curley. More mature students, while recognizing the urgency of Curley's presence, observe the firing of Keller to be a mere symptom of much greater difficulties. These students tend to analyze the problem of what to do about Becker.

The differences between primary and secondary problems are most significant, and readers are urged to pay strict attention to these differences. A primary problem is one which lies at the root of a whole tree of dependent problems. The secondary problems are the ones which are most obvious, but they are only symptoms of the more obscure but more important primary problem. Now the fact that secondary problems show up, like broken legs on a centipede, causes us to get excited about them and to attempt to cure them, one by one, as quickly as possible. This temptation is reinforced by the fact that secondary problems are usually the problems which precipitate crises. In the Hayden case, the firing of Keller precipitated the crisis of Curley's complaint. Nevertheless, if Becker had handled the situation correctly in the first place, the firing incident would not have occurred. Hence, to avoid all similar crises, one should do something about Becker.

It follows from the preceding remarks that if one diagnoses the primary problem, and if it is successfully solved, a single solution might automatically take care of a number of present, secondary problems. At the same time, solution of the primary problem might prevent the development of additional secondary problems in the future.

The relationship between primary and secondary problems is like the relationship, in medicine, between a symptom and a disease. A person suffering from hysterical blindness may be relieved of his blindness by hypnotic suggestion, but unless the etiology of the disease is discovered, and unless the cause is removed, the patient will probably be back in a week or so, suffering from deafness or paralysis or something equally distressing. A hypnotist could spend a lucrative lifetime removing one symptom after another, but never touching the disease. Similarly, the complex problem analyst might spend his whole life removing symptoms of business pathology without ever getting to the real cause of trouble.

In any event, the great lesson to be learned here is this: The discovery and solution of basic, fundamental, or primary problems will go further than any other action to remove all of the problems in a given problem area. If one fails to get at the root of the problem cluster, his efforts will be largely wasted, and his actions, in trying to solve secondary problems, will become confused and contradictory. This will lead eventually to a complete collapse of the situation which the manager is attempting to control.

Granting the proposition that primary problems are to be solved first, the next question is one of how to tell, from the list of problems on hand, which are primary and which are secondary. One way is to recognize that by definition only one primary problem can be present in each problem complex. Therefore, unless more than one complex appears in the case, there can be only one primary problem. Hence one may proceed by relating each problem to every other problem. Ask the questions: "Does A derive from B? Does B derive from A? Do A and B derive from some other problem, C?" If the answer to the first question is yes, then A is secondary, but B may be either primary or secondary. If the answer to the second question is yes, then B is secondary, but A may be either primary or secondary. If the answer to the third question is yes, then A and B are both secondary. If the answer to all three questions is no, then we are dealing with at least two and perhaps three different problem areas.

Following through with this analysis, it should be possible to identify all problem areas and, in addition, one should be able to identify the primary problem in each. When this is accomplished, one may list the primary problem and all of the secondary problems on separate sheets of paper for each problem area.

Then, at last, it would seem that one could select the primary problem and proceed with the analysis. Unfortunately again, no. In the Hayden case, we might decide that Becker is the primary problem, but what about Curley? Can we tell him that we're sorry about Keller, but we are not concerned with him because he has only secondary importance? No, of course not. Hence even though we may recognize the problem of Keller to be secondary, we do not belittle it. In short, while, generally speaking, we will solve primary problems first, we must not overlook the fact that secondary problems may, if neglected, produce other serious problems, and it may be necessary, as in the Hayden case, to handle a secondary problem first.

The universal approach to problem selection

All of the rules we have advanced for problem selection are designed to assist the analyst to choose the most important problem. To repeat, one must analyze one problem at a time. Other things being equal, one should select the easiest, the most urgent, or the most fundamental. Hopefully these will all be the same problem, but usually this is not the case. How, then, can one make the final selection?

How do we judge relative importance? The only safe way is to do at least a partial analysis of all of the problems on the list. This is what we mean by the *universal approach*. Usually it doesn't make much difference which problem is partially analyzed first, but the novice is advised to start with the one which seems easiest to him. After a partial solution is found to a couple of the easy problems, the novice is advised to try his hand at one or two of the problems he considers most urgent. Finally, he should do a preliminary analysis of *all* of the primary problems.

When these preliminary (partial) analyses are completed, the beginner may discover that solutions to the primary problems *require* particular kinds of solutions to secondary problems. In the Hayden case, for example, suppose, in analyzing what to do about Becker, we decide to keep Becker in his present position. Under these circumstances, it would probably be impossible for Hayden to rehire Keller. If Keller were to be rehired, Becker should concur, and, in fact, he should probably be the agency by which rehiring is accomplished. If, on the other hand, Becker is to be fired, Hayden might have a completely free hand in deciding what to do about Keller. Hence it is necessary to give timely attention to urgent problems, but one should always complete enough of the analysis of the relevant primary problem to assure that the solution to the urgent, secondary problem will be consistent with the expected solution to the primary problem.[7] If either or both of the urgent and primary problems are difficult and resistant to analysis, it is wise for the novice to "warm up," so to speak, on a few of the easy problems. In general, problems should be solved in the order of their urgencies, but preliminary warm-up on easy problems may be useful, and sufficient partial analysis of primary problems must be accomplished to assure that solutions to urgent problems will be consistent with expected solutions to primary problems.[8]

The problem statement

After the analyst has decided on the problem to be solved, it should be cast into a simple, concise, and unambiguous statement. During the course of the analysis, the problem solver will have occasional need to refer back to the statement to remind himself of what he is doing. To those who are unfamiliar with complex problem analysis this statement may seem unbelievable, for if the problem was as carefully selected as we recommend, it might appear that one could never forget it. Nevertheless, it is perhaps *because* we have weighed

[7] Drucker (*op. cit.*, p. 353) writes, "One of the most critical jobs in the entire decision-making process is to assure that decisions reached in various parts of the business and on various levels of management are compatible with each other." Churchman, Ackoff, and Arnoff (*op. cit.*, p. 56) argue in a similar vein.

[8] Remington (*op. cit.*) points out that our adamant instruction to solve one problem at a time is now violated by our so-called universal approach. In a sense this is true, but we assume that problem solving proper does not begin in earnest until the problem is finally selected. In any case, after the problem for analysis is selected, its solution must be carried through without attempting simultaneous solution of other problems.

the possibilities of so many problems that we sometimes become confused. If this confusion creeps into the analysis, the further investigation of the problem is likely to veer off in peculiar directions, and the result is complete incoherence. As we proceed with our description of the present problem-solving model, the point made here will become more apparent. There is nothing basically difficult about the model, but the material which we shall be simultaneously analyzing will become so voluminous that our greatest difficulty will be to keep track of what we are doing.

The second reason we should be careful about the way in which we state the problem is that, sooner or later, we will usually have to communicate it to other people, and it is best to nail it down at the very beginning.

One special point should be mentioned in connection with the statement of the problem; namely, although the wording should be simple, concise, and unambiguous, one should *aim for statements which are broad in scope.*[9] By this we mean that the statement of the problem should not restrict the range over which the analysis can be made. In the Hayden case, for example, it would be unwise to state the following problem: "Should I (Hayden) rehire Keller without consultation with Becker, and return him to the job as though nothing had happened?" With this kind of statement, one has restricted his analysis to an investigation of only two alternative courses of action. Either Keller will be rehired under the conditions stated, or he will not. Obviously there are a great many other alternatives (almost infinite). Keller can be rehired under a huge variety of circumstances, and the particular circumstances constitute different alternatives. If it were a simple choice between standing pat and rehiring under the stated conditions, one might be forced to a suboptimizing decision by backing Becker. If, however, conditions other than those which have been stated were allowed, a far better solution might be achieved by rehiring. Hence a better statement of the problem would be: "What shall I do about Keller?"

---

[9] Lindsay (*op. cit.,* p. 121) cautions his readers against too narrow problem statements for, as he points out, restrictive statements often lead to suboptimization in solutions.

chapter 5

STATEMENT
OF THE FACTS

In Chapter 1, we observed that one of the great differences between complex and simple problems is that simple problems contain all of the relevant facts; they are all taken to be true; they are all measured in cardinal terms; and they are all interrelated by mathematical formulas. In complex problems, on the other hand, we may not know all of the relevant facts; we may not know whether the facts on hand are pertinent; we may not have cardinal measurements; and we may not know what the relationships among the facts may be.

In a textbook case problem, the student is given some of the facts. In the Hayden case, for example, the bare bones of a situation are described, and the student is expected to analyze this case and to recommend appropriate action. As soon as he starts digging into this case, however, the student is struck by the paucity of information given. While the case states that the company is located in southern Connecticut, it would be much better to have a complete sociological study of the community. One doesn't get much feel or flavor from the bare bones, and a solution which might fit one "large manufacturing center" might not work at all in another.[1]

---

[1] A first-rate example of a sociological study of a factory town is con-

Another glaring defect of the Hayden case is the failure of the writer to give the date. Actually this case dates from 1931. If this had been known to the student when he first attempted the analysis, his attitude toward Curley, the union, and the whole situation would have been different, for in 1931 we didn't even have the National Industrial Recovery Act, to say nothing of the Wagner Act or the Taft-Hartley Act.

Again, we don't know how long each of the employees (except Keller and Edwards) have been with the organization, and we don't know anything about the informal organization. The group situation is a complete blank, but there is little doubt that its characteristics are crucial to both problem selection and problem solution.[2]

We would like to know what the responsible master machinist was doing while the events described in the case were transpiring. Why didn't Becker operate through the master machinist? Perhaps he did, but the fact was not reported. If he did, what did the machinist think of this peculiar state of affairs? What were the other machinists doing, and what did they think?

How rush is the "rush order"? In a depression situation in which business is hard to acquire, can we afford any delay in getting out the work? Or, if he were advised of the trouble, would the contractor be sympathetic to the point of urging Hayden to forget the urgency of the order and to resist the union?

In a similar vein one could keep posing questions for a very long time, and it would be quite a while before we ran out of *pertinent* questions. Actually, of course, there is every indication that, in any situation, all facts are related, either closely or remotely, to all other facts. Therefore one may argue that no statement of a complex problem is ever complete until all of the facts of the universe are known and recorded.

For practical purposes, however, no businessman can wait for

---

tained in W. Lloyd Warner and J. O. Low, *The Social System of the Modern Factory,* Yale University Press, New Haven, Conn., 1947.

[2] The literature in the field of group dynamics is huge and far too extensive to be discussed or even listed here. All students, however, should be familiar with the classical study in the field: F. J. Roethlisberger and W. J. Dickson, *Management and the Worker,* Harvard University Press, Cambridge, Mass., 1939.

the accumulation of all the facts. He must make his decision on the basis of the facts at hand or on the basis of facts which can be obtained within the time and cost limitations of the business situation. As a practical matter, therefore, no problem solution can take account of all the facts. Still, on a strictly practical level, what is needed is a reasonable effort to gather the most pertinent facts. Hence the businessman gathers facts to the point at which the cost of further investigation exactly equals the benefit which is expected from the additional information. This statement, of course, is the principle of marginal analysis which is taught in elementary economics.[3]

Although marginal analysis is clearly the profit-maximizing principle to apply, the businessman must use it in a rather horseback fashion. He may be able to estimate fairly closely how much it will cost to gather additional facts, but his estimates of how much benefit will be derived, when the facts are known, will be exceedingly rough. Hence, while the marginal principle is easily stated, its application is based on the businessman's judgment. Thus a clear mathematical principle applies, but facts are unknown, and measurements are too crude for direct application. Therefore we do not attempt the mathematical solution, but we are helped in our thinking by our knowledge of it. We know, at least, what we are trying to achieve.

When we are talking about gathering facts, we have reference to two separate aspects of facts. So far we have been talking about simple quantity. The more facts we have, the better off we are. Some facts, however, are better than others. Hence, while we are interested in the *quantity* of facts, we are more interested in their *quality*. A few carefully measured facts, directly relevant to the problem at hand, may be worth more than thousands of facts which are badly measured or remotely related.

The quality of facts is determined by three characteristics. The first is the degree of confidence one has that the so-called facts are indeed facts. In the Hayden case, is it really a fact that Becker fired Keller without even talking to the master machinist? On the surface, it would appear that the supervisor was not only not consulted but that he wasn't even informed. Disgraceful, if true. Again, is it a fact

---

[3] An excellent discussion of marginal analysis, at an elementary level, is found in George Leland Bach, *Economics*, 4th ed., Prentice-Hall, Inc., Englewood Cliffs, N.J., 1963, pp. 338–367.

that the entire working force was passive to the events described in the case? Impossible.

Suppose we investigate the latter so-called fact. There is no doubt that the rest of the community is aware of what happened, but it may be difficult to learn what the group thinks about the event. It is certain that the workmen's views of the situation are not only different from Becker's, but very likely that they differ among themselves. Hence we may get a general notion of an effect on the work force, but we may have great difficulty in measuring the effect or of measuring the future results of the effect. In short, the first problem of quality in a fact is the degree of certainty that it is a fact.

The second problem is to determine the direction and degree of the effect of a fact. For example, a fairly high quality fact concerning the effect of this incident on the other workmen would be one in which we could state that the effect is anticompany and that the feeling is exceedingly strong. A very high quality fact would be a measurement of the strength of feeling in terms of what it would cost to return workers' attitudes to the condition that existed before the incident occurred.

The third determinant of fact quality is its relevance to the problem situation. Obviously, the mean daily temperature at the Hayden Tool Company site can be both quickly and accurately determined. This is a high quality fact, in terms of measurement, but it has very little relevance.

How does one judge the relevancy of a fact? There are several ways. First, scientific investigation is the best-known method. It has been often demonstrated that productivity increases with improvements in labor morale.[4] Hence, in the Hayden case, we may assume that if morale has suffered in the course of the events described, productivity will be impaired. Productivity, in any profit-making institution, is certainly and highly relevant, for Hayden himself would doubtless admit that at least one of his major business goals, especially in a depression, is to make a profit.

A second important way to determine relevancy is to consult an expert. Experts may be people who are knowledgeable about scien-

---

[4] Cf. Rensis Likert, *New Patterns of Management,* McGraw-Hill Book Company, New York, 1961, pp. 26–43.

tific findings within particular disciplines, or they may be people who have wide and outstandingly successful experience. In the latter respect, the expert gives his testimony as a medical clinician diagnoses disease. He knows, from experience, what is relevant and what is not.[5]

The third way to establish relevancy is to rely on one's own experience. This is probably the least valid approach, unless one is himself an expert, and our immediate tendency is to decry it. Nevertheless, there is much to recommend reliance on personal judgment, and it will be one of the major purposes of this book to demonstrate ways to improve it. The reasons personal judgment should be respected are not difficult to find. In the first instance, one must remember that many decisions must be made quickly, and one frequently has no time to consult anyone's judgment but his own. Second, the analyst is usually best informed and most familiar with the problem complex. This is especially true of managers who have been in the same job for a long time and who have, over the years, used the present problem-solving model. They will have made many mistakes, but they will have learned a great deal about the problem situation, and their analyses will have been constantly improving.

Finally, relevancy of facts frequently develops from the continuing analysis of the problem itself. As one proceeds, he is repeatedly struck by the difficulties of ignorance. For example, Hayden may list as a fact the assumption that Becker wants to retain his job. If correct, the fact is relevant, but if Hayden suddenly realizes that he is working on assumption rather than fact, he will be immediately aware that a contrary assumption would have massive effects on his whole approach to the problem. Hence relevancy may become apparent from the analytical exercise.

Let's pause here to review our conclusions up to this point. (1) There is no limit to the number of relevant facts in a complex problem. (2) The practical limit to fact-finding is determined by the equation of marginal costs and marginal benefits involved in acquiring additional facts. (3) The marginal principle, in business practice, is a useful guide to action, but cost and return estimates are usually

---

[5] Cf. Harold Koontz, "The Management Jungle," *Journal of Academy of Management,* December, 1961, p. 174.

crude, and final reliance is usually placed on the analyst's judgment. (4) Fact gathering for problem analysis has two separate aspects: (a) the larger the number of facts provided, the better the analysis; (b) the better the quality of the facts, the better the analysis. (5) It is better to have a small number of high quality facts than a large number of low quality facts. (6) The quality of facts depends on three criteria: (a) the higher the degree of certainty of existence of the fact, the better the fact; (b) the better the measurement of the fact, the higher the quality; (c) the more relevant the fact to the problem situation, the higher the quality. (7) The relevancy of facts is judged by four methods: (a) scientific investigation, (b) opinions of experts, (c) personal judgment, and (d) demands of the problem analysis.

After all of this discussion and argument, we still have not touched on the matter of how to obtain the facts. In very large measure, this is the subject of Chapter 14 in which we shall discuss the need not only for research but also for the research attitude. If facts are needed, the best way to get them is to research them. There will always be time to do some research, but there will never be enough time or money to do a complete research. Therefore the amount of research which will actually be accomplished will vary greatly with the situation, and one will always compromise between his ideals and the needs of the situation.

Since compromise is inevitable, it is important that whatever time and money are available for research be spent in the most profitable way. To accomplish this, we lay down the following rules: (1) Make a preliminary analysis of the situation on the basis of facts which are immediately available at the time one first becomes aware of the presence of a problem. (2) On the basis of one's personal judgment, from clues furnished by the preliminary analysis, list the specific additional facts one would like to have before undertaking a final analysis. (3) By the application of appropriate research techniques, discover as many of the desired facts as time and money will allow. (4) Write up the situation in the form of a case, giving as many facts as possible and specifying the chronology of events. (5) Give the case to a friend, and ask him to list additional facts he would like to have before he attempted to solve the case. (6) At some point in the fact-finding process, because he will run out of either time or money, the analyst must make assumptions about the desired but still missing facts, for the analysis must go forward. Assumed facts should be explicitly labeled as assumed.

The reason for the initial step of making a preliminary analysis is to assure that the analyst directs attention to the facts of greatest relevancy. Remember that we don't want large numbers of facts for the sake of gathering facts. We want, so far as possible, the highest quality facts obtainable. The directions recommended here are designed to force the analyst to keep his mind on the principal issues and to gather the most needed facts first. The research for facts is urged for the obvious reason that research, as we define it in Chapter 14, is the only avenue open for the procurement of information. During the write-up of the case, one is forced to set down the facts as a stream of events. The first result is to suggest the relationships of the facts to each other and to the total problem complex.[6] A second result is to uncover gaps in one's knowledge. These will suggest additional research to close the gaps. After the write-up is finished, a qualified friend can give tremendous service because, approaching the case without preconceptions, he knows only what has been written down, and he will quickly lay his finger on additional gaps in the information.

Finally, when time or money runs out, one must proceed on the basis of the facts available. If one's knowledge is less than perfect, this must not disturb his composure, for if there is anything at all certain about complex problem solving, it is that one always operates in the shadow of ignorance.

[6] Although the chronological ordering of facts is suggestive of causal relationships among them, the analyst must carefully avoid the *post hoc, propter hoc* fallacy. This is the error of ascribing causality merely on the basis of antecedence.

chapter 6

ALTERNATIVE COURSES OF ACTION

Step 1 in the complex problem-solving model is selection of the problem for analysis, and step 2 is gathering of the facts. Actually it is more nearly correct to state that steps 1 and 2 are fact gathering and problem selecting, without assigning either to a position of superior rank. From the discussions in Chapters 4 and 5, it is evident that these steps are taken both alternately and simultaneously. One cannot settle on the problem for analysis until the facts are in, nor can one decide which facts to gather until the problem is known. In practice, therefore, by the time the analyst reaches this point in his study, he will have used up a great deal of scratch paper, for he will have proceeded by fits and starts. He will have retraced his steps over and over, adding and changing, until he is satisfied that the facts support his problem selection and that the problem can be solved on the basis of the facts collected.[1] If things have gone well, in the issue if not in the route, however, the problem for analysis is now fully decided, and the facts are at hand.

As we advised in Chapter 4, the problem

---

[1] Drucker (*op. cit.*, p. 358) puts problem selection before fact-finding, while other writers put fact-finding before problem selecting. Our view is more of an alternation than a compromise between these opposing positions.

has been stated in simple, concise, and unambiguous terms, and its statement has been made in broad language which will permit investigation of possible alternatives *over the entire range of possible courses of action.* The next step is to list the alternative courses of action. Before attempting to accomplish this, the facts of the situation should be analyzed in accordance with the procedures described in Chapter 5, under the heading of *Business Case Analysis.* In other words, before one attempts to list alternative courses of action, one should have not only a grasp of the facts but also a comprehension of their meanings, both in themselves and in their interrelationships.

For purposes of present discussion, let us carry forward the analysis of the sample case in Chapter 2, and let us assume the analyst is Hayden. Let us also assume that Hayden has identified Becker as his primary problem and Keller as his urgent problem. Let us finally assume that preliminary analysis of the Becker problem leads Hayden to believe that his decision will be to retain Becker in his present job.

Suppose, then, that the problem for immediate solution is stated as follows: "What shall I do about Keller?" (It might equally well be "How shall I handle Curley?") The next step is to list the alternative courses of action. By the time one gets his list up to ten or twelve, however, he begins to realize that alternatives are virtually endless. The first two alternatives are obvious. Hayden may tell Curley that Keller's dismissal must stand, or Hayden may rehire Keller and simply put him back on the job, without any comment to Becker or anyone else. These alternatives are extreme, and they lie at opposite ends of the alternative spectrum. In between these extremes, there is a limitless number of other possibilities. Keller can be rehired on condition that he apologize to Becker. He can be rehired if, on application to Becker, the latter will accept him. He can be rehired, with Becker's approval, after suffering a one-week suspension. He can be rehired if he quits the union. He can be rehired if he promises never to speak to Becker in the future, unless Becker speaks to him. He can be rehired if he promises to work four hours a day overtime until the rush order is out. And so on, ad infinitum.

Some of the alternatives we have listed look pretty good; some look silly. A great many more alternatives exist that have not been listed at all. The question is, can we ever really list all of the possible alternatives? Even if that were possible, could we hope ever to analyze them all? On both practical and theoretical grounds, the answers to both questions are no. These answers, obvious as they are, represent *major defects in the problem-solving procedure.*

Follow, please, this argument. Unless all possible alternatives are selected for analysis, the best alternative might escape selection. Then, inasmuch as we cannot determine until after analysis which alternative is best, we have no criterion for alternative selection in the beginning. This is a chicken-egg dilemma. We don't know which alternative is best until after analysis of all the alternatives, and we can't analyze all of the alternatives. Hence if we limit analysis to a reasonable number of alternatives, say four or five, the chances are probably a million or more to one that the best alternative will not be selected for analysis. Then, when the analysis is finished, we must choose from those we elected to analyze in the first place.

Therefore two difficulties arise. First, how many alternatives should be analyzed, and, second, which alternatives should be selected? The first difficulty is solved by practical considerations, but some theoretical principles may also apply. The practical limitations hinge on time and money. In the Hayden case, Hayden might judge that forty-eight hours is as long as he can afford to delay his decision to Curley. If he has already used up twenty-four of these hours, he must make his decision today, and that would limit the number of alternatives he would have time to consider. In terms of practical costs, many of the alternatives will be so closely similar as not to warrant differentiation (costwise) for analytical purposes. Remember that "a difference to be a difference must make a difference." [2] This is to say that true differences between alternatives may exist, but if the differences are very small, it may cost more than it is worth to discover them.

On the theoretical side, in complex problem solving, the identification and measurement of variables is so crude that any *apparent* differences among closely similar alternatives would be unreliable, for the ranges of error in analysis would greatly exceed the true differences in the solutions.

---

[2] This quotation is attributed to Robert S. Woodworth, for many years Professor of Psychology at Columbia University. We have, so far, been unable to identify where he said it. One of his best-known works is *Experimental Psychology,* Holt, Rinehart and Winston, Inc., New York, 1938.

Taking both the practical and the theoretical considerations into account, but also relying, in large measure, on the reported experience of many analysts,[3] we recommend selection of neither fewer than three nor more than seven alternative courses of action. Five frequently seems to be the best number of alternatives to investigate.

With this conclusion established, tentatively at least, we now approach the much more difficult task of deciding which alternatives, of all possible alternatives, to select for analysis. Remembering that if we err in this selection the damage can never be rectified, we proceed with great caution. After examining all possible criteria and all routes of procedure, we discover none that can assure successful selection of the alternative which, if all of them were analyzed, would turn out to be best.

Therefore, we take the coward's way out. If we can't be right, let's try to buy insurance against being too far wrong. This decision leads to the following recommendations: (1) Select one alternative from each of the two extremes of the alternative spectrum. (2) Select another from a somewhat central position in the spectrum. (3) Select other alternatives which lie approximately midway between alternatives which have been previously chosen. In considering the selection of alternatives in steps 2 and 3 above, one should also be guided by his analysis of the facts to attempt the selection of action alternatives which his judgment suggests would be logically and reasonably likely to produce the desired results.

In Exhibit 2, the full spectrum of alternative courses of action is

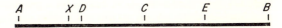

Exhibit 2   Recommended alternatives for analysis.

represented by the line *AB*. Our recommendation is to select, as a minimum, alternatives *A, B,* and *C,* which lie near the center and the extremes of the spectrum. If additional alternatives are to be considered, they should be chosen to lie at positions *D* and *E*.

The merit of this system of alternative selection is this. Suppose

[3] The problem-solving model recommended in this book has been used for six years in college classroom instruction. About 1,500 students have used it, and their experiences have been discussed in class.

the best alternative is the unknown action alternative X. If we analyze all of the alternatives indicated in Exhibit 2, we will, as expected, miss the best alternative, but we will select D which is within a cat's whisker. In contrast, suppose we choose to analyze alternatives indicated by positions on the spectrum in Exhibit 3. In this case, we would conclude

Exhibit 3   *Not recommended alternatives for analysis.*

by implementing alternative A, for A is the closest to the position of X, but we would have missed alternative X by a country mile.[4]

[4] Professor Eaton (*op. cit.*) suggests a selection of alternatives in accordance with Exhibit A. This procedure gives better coverage of the alternative

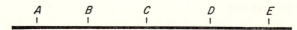

Exhibit A   *Eaton's recommended alternatives for analysis.*

spectrum with the same number of alternatives. We endorse this analysis in principle, but in the fuzzy world of reality the difficulty of approaching the extremes is so great that we are content to *try* to reach them.

Eaton also suggests that some problems do not lend themselves to one-dimensional analysis of alternative courses of action. For example, suppose there are three candidates, A, B, and C, for a particular job. Each has special qualifications which are not present in the other candidates. The problem is to select the best candidate. In this case, one would have three extremes, as in Exhibit B.

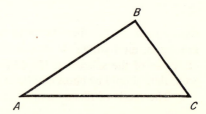

Exhibit B   *An illustration of three extreme alternatives.*

chapter 7

ADVANTAGES AND DISADVANTAGES OF ALTERNATIVES

In order to carry forward the analysis of the Hayden Tool Company case, it is desirable for us to make a few assumptions. It is reasonable to suppose that Hayden, in his investigation of the facts, would, at the very least, have interviewed Becker. In all probability, he would also have interviewed both the machinist supervisor and Edwards.

Let's assume that in these interviews Hayden has learned that Becker is somewhat confused by what happened, and he is not very coherent in his description of the incident. He appears to have the feeling that he handled the matter badly, but he doesn't know just where things went wrong. He likes Keller, and he holds no grudge toward him, but if he had to do the whole thing over, he doesn't see how he could act differently. He is *sure* in his mind that his own behavior was blameless, and he flatly insists that Keller's actions were so blatantly insubordinate that his continued employment in the plant was and is unthinkable.

Concerning the incident itself, Becker stated that he had no criticism of the way Keller was doing the job. Becker was merely watching the operation to see whether there might be a better or faster way to do it. His repeated returns to the scene were simply repeated attempts to explore an idea that had been going through his head.

The machinist supervisor reported that he did not witness the incident, and the decision to fire Keller was made without consulting the supervisor in advance. Becker did, however, report the trouble to the supervisor soon after Keller left the plant. The supervisor concurs with Becker's decision, even though he had no part in making it. The supervisor believes Becker acted properly. He stated that in some situations immediate action is necessary. One acts, and later he informs all who are concerned of the action taken.

With respect to Keller, the supervisor likes him, and he is sorry he had to be fired. So far as he knows, this was the first time since Keller came to work at Hayden's that he had been in any trouble at all. Concerning Becker, the supervisor reported that everyone knows Becker to be one of the top toolmakers in the city. He is still fairly young, and he is not set in his ways. He is always thinking of, and always looking for, better ways to get jobs done. Becker is, however, quiet and reserved. He's friendly enough, but he doesn't mix very often with other people in the shop.

Edwards reported he is a good friend of Keller's, and it was he who urged Keller to see Curley. Edwards feels Keller had plenty of cause to teach Becker a lesson, and if it had been he, Edwards, who had been involved, he would have "socked him instead of just yelled at him." When asked whether he had had any trouble with Becker, he replied negatively, and when questioned further, Edwards admitted that, although the apprentices were scared by Becker, he had never, until the present turn of events, treated them unfairly.

Regarding the social aspects of the work group, all persons interviewed believed Hayden's was a good place to work. Wages were standard, and working conditions were excellent. Becker stays pretty well to himself, and when he deals with others, he sticks to business. His approach is one of old-world formality. He calls everyone Mister, and everyone calls him Mr. Becker. The machinists and toolmakers have a high degree of shop communication with each other. There is a small amount of horseplay and considerable good humor. These men are continually playing practical jokes on the apprentices. Becker has never interfered with these activities, but he has never

joined in them. The apprentices feel overworked, and they do monotonous jobs. They feel they don't have the same freedom that is enjoyed by the toolmakers and machinists. They complain about some
of the tricks which have been played on them, and they resent their
pay of 35 cents per hour in comparison with the toolmakers' pay of
$1.32 per hour. They admit that the pay differentials are standard in
the industry, but they feel they should have as much freedom as the
others.

In view of these additional facts, let's assume that Hayden
judges the primary problem to be the morale of the apprentices and
the most urgent problem to be Keller. Because of the time limitation,
Hayden elects to analyze only three alternatives, but in his preliminary analysis he has decided his solution to the Keller problem must be
consistent with his expected decision to attempt improvement of the
apprentices' morale.

Therefore Hayden chooses to analyze the following alternative
courses of action: (1) Stand pat on Becker's decision to fire Keller.
(2) Rehire Keller without consultation with Becker or anyone else.
(3) Convince Becker he should rehire Keller. These alternatives, in
Hayden's judgment, are choices representing the middle (3) and the
extremes (1 and 2) of the alternative spectrum.

The next step in the analysis is to list all of the advantages and
all of the disadvantages of each alternative, and this is the subject of
the present chapter. The recommended procedure is simple. Take an
ample sheet of paper, and prepare analysis sheets somewhat like that
shown in Exhibit 4.

EXHIBIT 4 SAMPLE ANALYSIS SHEET
ALTERNATIVE:_____

Advantages	Disadvantages

Separate sheets should be used for each of the alternatives being analyzed. To facilitate this operation, the author has a stack of similar mimeographed analysis sheets, both in his office and at home. The author's sheets have room for eighteen lines of advantages and disadvantages, and since legal-sized paper is used, the lines are quite long. These analysis sheets are used up at the rate of fifteen to twenty per problem.

The next operation, unfortunately, is another weak link in the problem-solving chain. How do we determine advantages and disadvantages? Are there any rules for, or at least guides to, successful listing? The answer is that these listings rely on the judgment of the analyst. The better the analyst, the better the judgment, and the better the lists of advantages and disadvantages.

Despite this unfortunate state of affairs, however, at least two suggestions can be made. First, in listing advantages and disadvantages, one starts from a recognition that each course of action, if it were selected and implemented, would lead to a stream of consequences. Hence, when he is considering the advantages and disadvantages of a particular alternative, the analyst must try to visualize the consequences which would follow from its selection and implementation. Some of these consequences will be good and some not good. These are the advantages and disadvantages.[1] Therefore, in completing the lists of advantages and disadvantages, the first step is to try to imagine the consequences of each alternative.

The second suggestion for listing advantages and disadvantages is a familiar procedure. Recalling the brainstorming–head-shrinking procedure which was used to facilitate listing of problems in Chapter 4, we have been equally successful in using the same technique for listing advantages and disadvantages. The detailed procedure works as follows: Don't be fussy about grammar, spelling, punctuation, handwriting, or even content. Consider the alternative at issue. Write down all of the *known and suspected advantages and disadvantages*. Do it as

---

[1] Simon (*op. cit.*, pp. 67–68) defines rationality in decision making as a three-step process: "(1) the listing of all of the alternative strategies; (2) the determination of all the consequences that follow upon each of these strategies; (3) the comparative evaluation of these sets of consequences. . . . The function of knowledge in the decision-making process is to determine which consequences follow upon which of the alternative strategies."

rapidly as possible. Especially, don't try to judge whether the advantage or disadvantage being listed is important or even cogent. Don't even worry about whether the item being listed is really an advantage or whether it might turn out to be a disadvantage. Just list the ideas as they pop into mind. Avoid interruptions, and let the ideas spew forth.

When the analyst runs out of ideas for advantages, he should fold the analysis sheet down the middle and concentrate on the disadvantages. The same technique is followed. Keep listing until the flow of ideas halts. After the first alternative has been completed, take a new sheet for the second alternative, and repeat the procedure which was followed for the first. When the second is finished, start on the third, and keep repeating the process until all of the alternatives have been considered.

While the analyst is in the process of listing advantages and disadvantages, his mind becomes lubricated, and his later lists are longer and better than his earlier lists. Therefore it is good practice, after the last alternative has been completed, to go back to the beginning and add to the previous lists.

If possible, the work should be now laid aside to permit the unconscious mind to work it over. Later, when the analyst returns to the job, the entire procedure should be repeated. At no time during the listing process should the analyst permit himself to think about the *quality* of the items on the lists. The great point to be emphasized is this: Get the ideas down, somehow, somewhere, on the analysis sheets. One cannot estimate the value of an idea unless the idea occurs in the first place. So *don't worry about values until you have generated the ideas.*

chapter 8

EVALUATION OF ADVANTAGES AND DISADVANTAGES

After the advantages and disadvantages of each alternative have been listed, it is time to turn our attention to the task of evaluation. The first step in this process is to try to decipher the lists. Because of the freewheeling approach which was taken toward the original listing, this may be more of a job than most people expect. Statements will be incomplete; abbreviations may be undecipherable; handwriting may be illegible; spelling, punctuation, and grammar may be atrocious. Whatever the case, it is well to examine the lists to be certain that each item conveys a single idea and that the idea is sharply communicative to the analyst. Where multiple ideas are involved, break up items into their component units, and list each separately. If ideas are not clear, determine their intents, cross out the old entries, and enter sharply stated ideas.

The next step in the evaluation process is to scan each of the lists of advantages and disadvantages for duplications. Wherever an item or a substantially similar item appears more than once *on the same list,* cross out all but one.

Next, for each item under advantages for the first alternative, consider whether it is, in fact, an advantage. Very often in the listing an item finds its way to the wrong side of the ledger. Wherever this is found, cross it out, and transfer its position to the list of disadvantages. After completing the examination of advantages for alternative number 1, review the disadvantages to determine whether any of those listed should be transferred to the other side. Follow the same procedure for each of the alternatives under analysis.

The fourth step in evaluation is to consider each advantage for the first alternative and to ask whether that advantage is also an advantage for any or all of the other alternatives. Frequently the analyst will enter an advantage for one alternative, but he will fail to observe, or he will forget, its advantage for other alternatives. This process should be extended to cover all advantages and all disadvantages of all alternatives.

Sometimes in this procedure it happens that an item is an advantage of all of the alternatives, or a disadvantage of all of the alternatives. If this should occur, the analyst might be tempted to cross out the item on all of the lists, on the assumption that the item will have no differential effect and, therefore, no influence on the choice among alternatives. This is generally bad practice for, even though an item may appear as an advantage or disadvantage of all alternatives, it rarely happens that the same item will have equal advantage or disadvantage to all.

The fifth step in analysis is to examine all items on all lists of *advantages* and to consider whether any of them are also *disadvantages* for one or more of the other alternatives. Similarly, consider the disadvantages for each alternative, and determine whether any of them are also advantages for one or more of the other alternatives.

The last in this series of evaluation steps is the examination of all items on all lists of advantages and disadvantages, crossing out all that appear to be frivolous or of such small significance as to have no influence on the solution of the problem, one way or the other. In this connection, remember that if the importance of an item is so slight that its value is less than the error of measurement of other items, it might just as well be eliminated now. Despite this instruction, however, the analyst should eliminate items, on the basis of inconsequentiality, with great caution. A number of related items of small-importance may, in the aggregate, be significant. Also, the more successful the analyst is in breaking down large items into component small items, the less value will be attached to individual parts. We shall return to this point in a subsequent discussion. In the meantime, the more important the analysis and the more carefully it is being done, the less frequently one should eliminate seemingly insignificant items.

This process of eliminating inconsequential items, of course, will greatly reduce the lengths of all of the various lists, and it will greatly simplify subsequent analysis. When students learn this, they tend to push this step forward from its proper rank in sixth place to an earlier position. The reason this must not be done is that we will be adding to our lists of advantages and disadvantages until the entire series of steps is taken. Therefore if we eliminate an item because of its small importance early in the procedure, we might also be eliminating an item of large importance which would be suggested by it.

After completion of this series of steps in evaluation, it is necessary to write down the advantages and disadvantages which are left, in clear and succinct language, on fresh analysis sheets. The old sheets, by this time, will be so marked up and written over as to be nearly unreadable. Since much work remains to be done, it is best to make a fresh start with neat and shortened lists.

The big job of evaluation now lies just ahead. All of the steps in evaluation, up to this point, have been preliminary. The present task is to determine the *relative importance* or relative value of every advantage and disadvantage listed. Such an evaluation is absolutely necessary for, as we stated early in this study, the value of a single disadvantage might outweigh a dozen or more advantages. Hence it is our immediate objective to attach weights, or statements of value, to each advantage and disadvantage. For this purpose, let us examine a typical listing for each alternative. These appear in Exhibits 5, 6, and 7.

Before proceeding, we may profit from a review of the six preliminary steps in evaluation by specific reference to Exhibits 5, 6, and 7. Notice, first of all, that the form of statement of items is uniform. All items begin with a verb. This consistency permits the analyst to take a consistent mental approach, and this minimizes the need for the analyst to reorient his thinking completely as he passes from one item to the next. Notice also that statements are short, unitary, and legible.

Second, the reader should observe there are no duplications of items *within any single list*. Third, he should remark that the item "Gets Hayden back to work on his own job" appears on all three lists of advantages, but apparently Hayden regards the value of the item to be different on different lists. Fourth, under alternative number 1, "Stand pat," closely related items, "Lets apprentices know who's boss" and "Offends apprentices" appear, one as an advantage and the other as a disadvantage.

This kind of eventuality is not infrequent. The items simply

EXHIBIT 5   ANALYSIS SHEET
ALTERNATIVE NUMBER 1: STAND PAT

Advantages	Disadvantages
Pleases Becker	Risks a labor strike
Pleases machinists and toolmakers	Requires hiring replacement for Keller
Gets Hayden back to work on his own job	Delays the rush order
	Offends apprentices
Lets apprentices know who's boss	Fails to develop Becker's leadership
Keeps union in its place	Fails to render simple justice to Keller
Assures no further trouble from Keller	Offends Keller
	Lowers Hayden's authority image

EXHIBIT 6   ANALYSIS SHEET
ALTERNATIVE NUMBER 2: REHIRE KELLER
WITHOUT CONSULTATION WITH ANYONE

Advantages	Disadvantages
Gets Hayden back to work on his own job	Offends Becker
Achieves justice for Keller	Offends machinists and toolmakers
Pleases Curley	Risks repetition of Becker's error
Gets out the rush order	Fails to render simple justice to Becker
Pleases apprentices	Gives union too much prestige
Teaches Becker a valuable lesson	Risks further insubordination from apprentices
Avoids need to rehire for Keller	Risks further trouble from Keller
Pleases Keller	
Confirms Hayden's authority image	

Advantages	Disadvantages
Pleases Becker	Gives union too much prestige
Gets out the rush order	Risks further insubordination by apprentices
Avoids strike	Risks further insubordination by Keller
Pleases Keller	Risks failure of Becker to accomplish this alternative
Pleases apprentices	
Gets Hayden back to work on his own job	
Trains Becker in human relations	
Avoids need to rehire for Keller	
Achieves justice for Becker	
Achieves justice for Keller	

mean that, on the one hand, if Hayden stands pat, the apprentices will be less apt to step out of line in the future, and this, then, will head off future production interruptions. On the other hand, if the decision is to back Becker to the limit, the apprentices will be even more resentful of the company, Becker, and the whole situation than they presently are, and covert sabotage may result.

Finally, the reader should note that every alternative lists the reaction of Becker as either an advantage or a disadvantage. No matter what Hayden does, he must take account of its effect on Becker, for Becker is his right-hand man. Similarly, the effect of each alternative on each of the other individuals and groups is considered. It is for this reason that many similar items appear on different lists.

Before we go directly to the task of quantifying the importance of advantages and disadvantages, we must recognize that the statements made on the diverse lists are personal messages or reminders to Hayden who prepared them. The listed items are so briefly stated they have significance only to the analyst. Hence if the reader is dissatisfied with the lists in Exhibits 5, 6, and 7, this is to be expected, for the writer of the lists is the only one who understands their full meanings.

To illustrate this important point, let us examine the effect of each alternative on Keller. If Hayden stands pat, he lists Keller's reaction as a disadvantage; if he rehires Keller, without consultation, he lists Keller's reaction as both an advantage and a disadvantage; and if he influences Becker to rehire Keller, he lists Keller's reaction as an advantage. Actually, behind the shorthand, Hayden has made the following judgments:

1. If he stands pat, the reaction of Keller is a disadvantage, for Keller will give the company a bad name abroad forever in the future. He will continue to poison the mind of fellow employee Edwards. And he might even take personal revenge by doing physical harm to Hayden, Becker, or the tool company plant itself.

2. If he rehires Keller without consultation with Becker or anyone else, the reaction of Keller is mixed. On the side of advantage stands the gratitude of Keller toward Hayden and the company for his reinstatement at a time of severe economic depression, but on the side of disadvantage stands the feeling of victory Keller will have over Becker. This might lead to further insubordination and new plant disturbances in the future. Someday Hayden may, in fact, be faced with a repetition of this same problem and, sooner or later, he may have to fire either Becker or Keller or both.

3. If he influences Becker to rehire Keller, the reaction of Keller is an advantage. Keller's attitude will be favorable not only toward Hayden and the company but also toward Becker.

Hence the shorthand lists contain comprehensive messages which are fully comprehended only by the fellow who wrote them, and the values represented by the items in the lists can be assigned only by that analyst. Therefore the reader is warned against being too critical of another man's list, for its contents are intended to serve only the private needs of the analyst who made them. In a later chapter we shall return to this point when we consider the question of reporting decision recommendations to others. Obviously the report cannot be a transmittal of analysis sheets, for these will be almost meaningless to anyone but the one who prepared them.

Clearly, on the other hand, critics may argue that if the statement (alternative number 1—advantages) "Offends Keller" conveys all of the ideas claimed in paragraph 1, above, Hayden has violated the rule which demands statements which convey simple ideas only.

Objectors would argue that the item "Offends Keller" should be eliminated under alternative number 1, and the following statements should be substituted in its place:

1. Risks Keller's giving company a bad name
2. Risks Keller's poisoning Edwards' mind and attitude
3. Risks Keller's revenge on Hayden
4. Risks Keller's revenge on Becker
5. Risks Keller's attack on the physical plant

Each of these items, moreover, might be subdivided still further into component disadvantages. All of these contentions are quite correct, and the objections are valid. The only question is that of how far one wishes to go in the matter. In very important decisions the greater the detail, the better, but at some point in the analysis, as always in complex problem solving, one must call a halt and get on with the job of problem solution.

Another point arises in connection with the question of how far one should go in subdividing advantages and disadvantages into component parts. If one subdivides everything into its very simplest terms, each of the elements may become of such minor significance as to be eliminated entirely from subsequent consideration. Hence a kind of compromise between the rule of simplicity and the rule to eliminate frivolity is demanded on technical as well as practical grounds.

In any case, the important point we are making in the present discussion is this: The statements of advantages and disadvantages are and remain personal reminders or messages which convey meaning to the analyst who wrote them, but they convey only general ideas to others.

Turning now directly to the task of placing specific values on the advantages and disadvantages for each alternative, the reader will be impressed with obvious difficulties. What single scale is available to measure such items as "Pleases Becker," "Gets Hayden back to work on his own job," and "Fails to render simple justice to Keller"? These items appear to be like apples, oranges, and grapefruit, and, as everyone learned in fourth grade, we can't add apples, oranges, and grapefruit.

The first item, "Pleases Becker," means something like this: If we stand pat, Becker will be reassured of our support, and he will continue to take the initiative required to get the work out and to get it out right. This, in turn, means operational efficiency and low costs. Hence the first item has meaning to Hayden in terms of dollars and cents.

The second item, "Gets Hayden back to work on his own job," probably means something like this: If we stand pat, no further action on the Keller affair is needed, and Hayden can go back to his job of beating the bushes for the work orders which are the lifeblood of the business. Every hour lost from sales activity means loss of revenue, and this, too, can be measured in terms of dollars and cents. But something else is probably involved here. Hayden hates the shop, and although he can do shop work and shop management when it is required, he much prefers to be out with the customers. This is a personal value of Hayden's. It is the kind of psychic value that cannot be easily measured in terms of dollars and cents.

The third item, "Fails to render simple justice to Keller," means that Hayden is also concerned with a problem of ethics. Regardless of Becker's innocent intent when he looked over Keller's shoulder, there is doubtless some excuse for Keller's irritation. Therefore it is essentially unfair to punish Keller without also punishing Becker. Simple justice demands either forgiveness of Keller or retribution for Becker. Now every man has his principles, and the higher one climbs on the ladder of authority, the more one is concerned with his own power and the awful responsibility which goes with it. So in the present case Hayden is confronted with the need to determine the value of justice, and he revolts at the notion of placing a dollar sign on it.

Hence, in considering the values of the three items just mentioned, we are faced with difficult measurement questions. We have to compare ethical judgment, personal preference, and dollar gain or loss to the business. This is, indeed, a problem of apples, oranges, and grapefruit.

In the sixth grade, the teacher did show us how to accomplish the task. She said, "If you have four apples and two oranges, and if apples are worth 5 cents apiece, and oranges are worth 10 cents apiece, then you have 40 cents' worth of apples and oranges." In other words, dissimilar things can be aggregated whenever a common measure of value among them can be found. In the case of apples and oranges, a common unit of value was available in dollars and cents, but any other common unit of value would have served as well.

Sometimes economists speak of special units to measure the usefulness of various things to human welfare. Ordinary dollars and cents, as understood in the marketplace, are defective for that purpose because the price of an article depends not only on utility but also on scarcity. Hence, for special purposes, some economists have spoken of value in terms of "utils." Similarly, psychologists have spoken of special measurement scales which are related not to market price, but to the satisfaction a person receives from possession. Hence the value of a thing is measured in terms of the pleasure derived from it, and one speaks of its "psychic value." [1]

Now any common scale can be used to add dissimilar things, but as we have just seen, the scale selected should be appropriate to the need of the problem. For business problem solving, it is usual to estimate need in terms of profit and loss, and this is measured in terms of dollars and cents. Whether this is always true may, of course, be argued, but one thing is certain. Whatever scale one uses, *the same scale must be used for all of the items.* Hence we do not insist, in the present problem-solving model, on any particular scale, but experience has definitely demonstrated that the common dollars and cents scale is easiest for most people to apply, mainly because almost everyone is familiar with it and most people find it appropriate for business analysis. In addition, when one is faced with the problem of communicating value information to other people, the dollars and cents scale is easiest to employ.[2]

---

[1] Our discussion of value scales is a highly simplified statement of an extremely complex matter. A very extensive and extremely technical literature on the subject exists, but it is beyond the scope of our present work to do more than indicate its presence. One of the best reviews of this literature, and one which is not frightfully difficult for nonmathematicians, is to be found in Ackoff's excellent book (*op. cit.,* pp. 76–106).

[2] For application of the problem-solving model in the Armed Forces, the dollar-value system is applicable to most situations, especially those involving services and logistics. In some situations, however, especially those concerned with tactical missions of field commanders, other value systems are usually more appropriate. In some cases, alternative courses of action may be evaluated in terms of cost expressed as expected casualties or as expenditures of matériel. In other situations, costs may be compared in terms of time required to accom-

Of course there are objections. How, people ask, can we place a dollar value on things like human life, honor, and justice? [3] The answer is easy. If the analyst either cannot or will not, he is automatically rejecting his own ability to solve complex problems. Perhaps the dollar value of things like justice is high, and perhaps the measurement is crude, but some kind of estimate is essential.

A little practice in difficult valuation problems usually works wonders for beginners. For example, the normal, eighteen-year-old co-ed, when asked to place a value on her own virginity, will usually be horrified and declare that no amount of money could buy her virtue. If co-eds are questioned closely, however, many will admit that marriages of convenience, without romantic love, are perfectly moral. Again, we find young men who declare that human life is beyond dollar value. Still these same men are known to risk not only limb but life itself for the excitement of participation in dangerous sports.[4]

No one claims that valuation in dollar terms is easy. It's like 40-cent porterhouse steak—tough. Unless one feels more confident, however, both in the appropriateness and in the practicability of some other scale, he will sooner or later return to the dollar scale. Hence, in our system of analysis, we proceed on that basis. The job is to put a dollar value on each and every advantage and disadvantage.

Some analysts have tried to simplify evaluation, and at the same

---

plish a mission or time required to regroup or reequip after completion of a mission. In any case, however, whatever unit of value is selected for use in a particular problem analysis, the same unit must be used to measure all advantages and disadvantages. Moreover, the measurements must always be made on cardinal (preferably ratio) scales. The analyst must never forget the inherent difficulties of ordinal measurements which were described in the footnote on page 1. In this connection, Drucker (*op. cit.*, p. 25) writes, "The economic consequences of military decisions are secondary, a limiting factor in these decisions, not a starting point or their rationale. A General Staff, being the specific organ of a military organization, must, by necessity, put security first. To act differently would be a betrayal of its responsibility and dangerous malpractice." We subscribe to this statement.

[3] Churchman, Ackoff, and Arnoff (*op. cit.*, pp. 136–137) discuss the difficulties of using dollar-value scales. They conclude, however, that "Operations research does use monetary scales in almost all of its research."

[4] H. G. Thuesen, *Engineering Economy,* Prentice-Hall, Inc., Englewood Cliffs, N.J., 1957, pp. 535–536. This author reports that the National Safety Council places a value of $25,000 on a human life.

time to get around the dollar-valuation difficulty, by simply *ranking* the advantages and disadvantages in terms of relative importance. This system assumes that if the important items are all favorable, while the unimportant items are all unfavorable, the course of action under investigation is highly attractive. And so it is. Unfortunately the rankings of items will usually get mixed up. Some of the high-ranking items will find places on both sides of the ledger, and some of the low-ranking items will also find places on both sides. Hence one cannot always tell whether a single alternative, on balance, is either generally good or generally bad. Even if this fault never arose, one would still be at a loss to choose the most favorable of a number of attractive alternatives, or the least unfavorable among several unattractive alternatives. In short, the trouble with ranking is the usual difficulty with ordinal scales; that is, rank ordering impedes further analysis, and the problem investigation ends without a solution.

If the reader is now satisfied that cardinal statements of value are required, and if he is convinced that the dollar scale is usually most convenient, we may proceed with the actual determination of values for each advantage and disadvantage.

Experience dictates that the job goes better and faster *if we do not begin at the beginning*. Some items are easy to value, and some are extremely difficult. If we take the easy ones first, we will establish a few landmarks or reference points for the valuation of the medium-hard items. When the medium-hard items are finished, we will have a large number of reference points for the valuation of the very difficult items. This is an extremely important point, and the procedure, if followed, will greatly ease the burden of valuation.

Suppose all of the items, except the very hardest one to measure, have already been valued. To measure the last remaining item, compare it with any other item and ask, "Is this item more significant? " If the answer is yes, look for another, more highly valued, item, and ask the same question. If the answer is still yes, compare it with a still more important item, and ask the question again. If the answer is no, look for an item which is less important than the last but more important than the next to the last, and compare again. Continue this process until, by comparison with already valued and established items, the value of this item can be closely approximated. In following this procedure, it will become obvious that the more items one has already valued, the easier it will be to measure others.[5]

The easy-to-value items are those which lend themselves to dollar-scale measurement. In the Hayden Tool Company case, one of the easy items is "Requires rehiring for Keller." A little investigation (more research) should turn up close estimates of how much it costs to recruit, hire, orient, and train a man to the level of competence of Keller. Depending on available time and money, such an estimate could be very close, or it could be rather rough. In either case, however, in comparison with other items, the replacement cost of Keller is an easy one to determine.

Even the easy ones present some difficulty. The analyst must recall the meaning the item was intended to convey, and all of that meaning must be translated into the estimate of value. For this item, Hayden must consider each of the component costs separately. If he forgets any of them, his estimate will be lower than it should be. When this principle is applied to a more difficult item, say "Offends Keller," Hayden must recall all this phrase was intended to convey, and he must place values on the damage Keller could do by complaining abroad, by poisoning the mind of Edwards, and by taking revenge on Becker, Hayden, and the tool company plant itself.

By proceeding carefully, from the easy ones to the more difficult, and from the more difficult to the very difficult, the student will be agreeably surprised to find that valuation is not as difficult nor as onerous as he expected. Even more important, he will discover that speed in this operation improves with practice. Finally, and most important, the student will find that his confidence in the system and in himself will rapidly increase, and his willingness to act on decisions reached will rise.

A last remark on valuation is in order. The reader should note

---

[5] Professor Eaton (*op. cit.*), while generally agreeing with this procedure for valuation of difficult items, cautions the reader at this point that items already valued may not always serve as adequate reference points. Gaps in values may be so great (i.e., $100, $150, $10,000) among already established items that additional easy-to-value items, even though they do not appear among the advantages and disadvantages in the current analysis, might profitably be evaluated in order to give additional closely related values for comparison.

that many problems of valuation are *simple problems* in which all of the variables are known and cardinally measured, and relationships among the variables are established by mathematical formulas. Whenever this is found, the techniques of complex problem solving should be abandoned in favor of the more elegant mathematical techniques.

chapter 9

THE FACTOR OF UNCERTAINTY

In the previous chapter, we completed the valuation of all advantages and disadvantages of all alternatives. By this time in his study of complex problem solving, the reader will have observed that each of those advantages and disadvantages is a *prediction of the expected consequences of each of the alternatives.* For example, when we list "Pleases machinists and toolmakers" as an advantage of the alternative "Stand pat," what we mean is this: If we stand pat, the machinists and toolmakers will be reassured in their customary behaviors and attitudes toward Hayden, Becker, the apprentices, and each other. In short, there will be no change in shop routines or in personal or group relationships. This no-change effect means no loss of time and no emotional upset within the most important work group in the shop.

In like fashion, every other statement of advantage and disadvantage is a prediction of what will happen as a result of selection of each of the alternative courses of action. When we assign values, however, some students have uneasy feelings. They worry about whether the predicted results of diverse actions would actually occur. There is a chance, for example, that some of the machinists and toolmakers dissented from the report which was made to Hayden by the machinist who had been supervising Keller and who was interviewed by Hayden. There is even a chance that the man lied to Hayden or, at least, that Hayden misunderstood what he said.

In a similar vein, all of the other statements of advantages and disadvantages are predictions of good or bad results which are *expected* from various alternative actions. All of the results, however, are clouded by varying degrees of certainty of occurrence. Maybe they will happen, and maybe they won't.

In the commonly used models for complex problem solving, such as that of the United States Army and the Harvard Business School, the analyst is expected to take account of the "iffiness" of expectations at the time he is evaluating advantages and disadvantages. In view of the complexities of evaluation, however, this practice is not recommended in the present system. It is, we believe, safer, sounder, and faster to evaluate each item on the analysis sheet as though its effect was certain. Then, in a separate inspection, the analyst should estimate the degree of certainty of each prediction. Hence, during evaluation proper, the analyst should assign dollar values to all predictions with the temporary assumption that the result is absolutely certain. Then, after all items are evaluated, the analyst should return and make appropriate, separate estimates of their degrees of certainty, or the confidence the analyst has that the effect or event will occur.

To facilitate this operation, additional columns are needed on the analysis sheets. A typical arrangement is illustrated in Exhibit 8. In the column marked "Certainty value," we enter the dollar's worth, either positive or negative, of the event described by the item of advantage or disadvantage. This dollar value is estimated on the assumption that the event is absolutely certain. In the column marked "Chances of occurrence," we enter our estimate of the chances the event will occur. For example, the listed advantage "Pleases machinists and toolmakers" may or may not be realized. If we believe that the report to Hayden by the machinist supervisor was truthfully given and correctly understood, and if we feel that this opinion is the same as that held by all of the machinists and toolmakers, then we might regard this event to be absolutely certain. In that case, the chances of

EXHIBIT 8   REVISED ANALYSIS SHEET
ALTERNATIVE NUMBER 1: STAND PAT

Advantages

Item	Certainty Value	Chances of Occurrence	Adjusted Value
Pleases Becker			
Pleases machinists and toolmakers			
Gets Hayden back to work on his own job			
Lets apprentices know who's boss			
Keeps union in its place			
Assures no further trouble from Keller			

Disadvantages

Item	Certainty Value	Chances of Occurrence	Adjusted Value
Risks a labor strike			
Requires hiring replacement for Keller			
Delays the rush order			
Offends apprentices			
Fails to develop Becker's leadership			
Fails to render simple justice to Keller			
Offends Keller			
Lowers Hayden's authority image			

occurrence versus nonoccurrence are 100 to 0, and the value for entry in the space "Chances of occurrence" is 1.0.[1] If, on the other hand, we believe half of the toolmakers and machinists are indifferent to the Keller incident, the chances of pleasing them as a group might be estimated at 50-50, with a value for "Chances of occurrence" set at 0.5. If half are pleased and half displeased or if all are indifferent, the value for "Chances of occurrence" might drop to zero.

[1] The values assigned to "Chances of occurrence" can be interpreted as probability factors. They are used as weightings for the computation of adjusted values. If an event is absolutely certain, therefore, the weighting is 1.0, and if the nonoccurrence is certain, its value is 0. For in-between items, the higher the degree of certainty of occurrence, the closer the weight approaches 1.0, and the lower the degree of certainty, the closer the weight approaches 0.

Actually the determination of the chances of the event "Pleases machinists and toolmakers" is much more difficult than the reader might infer from the preceding paragraph. The item itself refers to six different individuals. Moreover, each of them may experience different degrees of pleasure. Hence the true situation might vary from one in which all six experience maximum pleasure to one in which all six experience maximum displeasure. If there are five different levels of pleasure (very pleased, pleased, indifferent, displeased, and very displeased), there are 18,125 permutations of people and states of pleasure. The number of combinations is very much less, but it still comes to 210. In the actual situation, therefore, it would be desirable to make a separate determination of the amount of feeling, positive or negative, each man in the machinist-toolmaker group has toward standing pat. Such a determination might result in an array somewhat as follows:

Very pleased	2
Pleased	1
Indifferent	1
Displeased	1
Very displeased	1
Total	6

Assuming that the negative feelings balance the positive and that indifferent feelings have no effect on the total feeling, the net feeling in the group is:

Very pleased	1
Indifferent	5
Total	6

Hence, in such a case, the chances of gaining maximum group pleasure from the action of standing pat might be estimated at 1 to 6 or 0.17.

In this illustration, the net feeling of the group toward standing pat is positive, so (in Exhibit 8) we have placed the item on the correct side of the ledger, but the feeling is extremely disbursed throughout the group, and the weight which is entered for chances of occurrence is small. The adjusted value of the item, therefore, will be correspondingly small, for adjusted values are the products of certainty values and chances of occurrence. If, by some chance, feelings of displeasure had been found to exceed feelings of pleasure, the item would be changed to read "Displeases machinists and toolmakers," and it would be moved to the disadvantages side of the ledger.

The likelihood of occurrence for all other items of predicted advantage and disadvantage is treated in a similar manner. As we proceed with the operation, however, we may discover other complications. Recalling the discussion on page 78 concerning Keller's reaction, we observed that the item "Offends Keller" is really not a single item but, like the one we have just considered, a multiple one. We assumed that the meaning included all of the following:

1. Keller will give the company a bad name
2. Keller will poison the mind of Edwards
3. Keller will take personal revenge on Hayden
4. Keller will take personal revenge on Becker
5. Keller will sabotage the physical plant

Now it should be observed that even in cases where a single, composite value, under conditions of absolute certainty, may be estimated for the item "Offends Keller," it may not be possible to attach a single estimate of the likelihood of occurrence. Hence, in some cases where the analyst had previously believed the item had been sufficiently subdivided, he may now decide that further breakdown is desirable. In the present illustration, for example, the chances that Keller will give the company a bad name abroad might be close to certain, and a value for "Chances of occurrence" of 1.0 might be assigned. The chances that Keller will sabotage the plant, however, might be judged to be extremely remote, with a "Chances of occurrence" of only 0.001. Therefore, it would simplify the analysis in such cases as this to make a change from the original listing and to subdivide the item further at this time.

From the two examples we have just given, the feelings of pleasure of machinists and toolmakers and the effects of offending Keller, it is apparent that the problem of estimating certainty versus uncertainty will often lead to complicated computations and even to changes in the lists of advantages and disadvantages.[2]

After the chances of occurrence have been estimated for each item, "Adjusted values" are simply calculated as the products of the first two columns on the analysis sheets. Multiply the "Certainty value" by the "Chances of occurrence" value. Thus an event with a certainty value of $1,000 and a chance of occurrence value of 0.5 has an adjusted value of $500. The adjusted value is sometimes referred to as the payoff value of the predicted event, but many statisticians reserve the term payoff to mean what we describe as certainty value.

---

[2] For students who are familiar with statistical decision-making techniques, there is plenty of room for their practice in this area. Such techniques are to be viewed as simple problem-solving methods and, again, mathematical techniques should be applied, in preference to complex problem-solving methods, whenever feasible. Readers who are not familiar with statistical decision-making techniques but who would like to examine these methods are referred to Robert Schlaifer, *Probability and Statistics for Business Decisions,* McGraw-Hill Book Company, New York, 1959.

chapter 10

SELECTING THE
BEST ALTERNATIVE

Instructions for selecting the best alternative are brief and straightforward. In all of the previous steps in complex problem solving, ultimate reliance is placed on the judgment of the analyst. Judgment is used to select the problem; judgment guides the collection of facts; judgment suggests the selection of alternative courses of action; judgment inspires the listing of advantages and disadvantages; judgment determines the values of action predictions; and judgment governs the estimates of likelihood that predictions will materialize.

In the selection of the best alternative, however, no judgment is needed, for selection is purely mechanical. Add the adjusted values and thereby compute the aggregate adjusted value for the advantages of each course of action. Similarly, add the adjusted values for the disadvantages of each alternative. Then, for each course of action, subtract the aggregate value for disadvantages from the aggregate value for advantages. Now select the alternative with the greatest net advantage or the least net disadvantage.

In the decision-making operation, the reader will observe that the aggregate of adjusted values of advantages for a given alternative is an estimate of total contribution to company *profit* which can be expected from selection and implementation of the alternative. Contrariwise, the aggregate of adjusted values of disadvantages is an estimate of total contribution to company *loss* which can be expected. Hence when the aggregate of adjusted values of disadvantages is subtracted from the aggregate of adjusted values of advantages, for any given alternative, the difference, whether plus or minus, is the expected total contribution, from selecting the alternative, to company profit.[1]

For example, if five alternatives are under consideration, a table for selecting the best course of action may be set up in a manner similar to that in Exhibit 9. A comparison of net effects on profit demonstrates that, if all of the work completed in the earlier steps is correct, alternative number 5 is, by far, the one which should be recommended or selected for action. So ends the decision-making process.

EXHIBIT 9   COMPARISON OF ALTERNATIVE COURSES OF ACTION

Alternative Number	Aggregate Advantage	Aggregate Disadvantage	Effect on Profit
1	$20,640	$ 21,780	—$ 1,140
2	6,400	200	6,200
3	47,600	41,900	5,700
4	9,380	206,400	— 197,020
5	88,000	20,790	67,210

[1] This "common-sense" method of aggregation of expected payoffs has the great merits of simplicity of computation and ease in understanding. It is recommended especially for these reasons but, in view of the crudeness of internal measurements in most complex problem solving, it is probably also justified on theoretical grounds. Nevertheless, the reader must be reminded that, in this area of decision making, a vast literature exists. A description of this literature is beyond the scope of the present book, but interested readers are referred especially to the excellent book by Schlaifer, *op. cit.* Another, briefer and simpler, treatment is to be found in Irwin D. J. Bross, *Design for Decision,* The Macmillan Company, New York, 1953.

chapter 11

IMPLEMENTING ACTION DECISIONS

As we indicated at the end of the last chapter, we have completed the decision-making process. At the present stage, however, we have only a *paper* solution, and there still remains the question of putting the decision into practice. This question of implementation is so important that it is difficult to overemphasize it. Many authors confirm this judgment.[1]

Frequently, even usually, the problem analysis itself will be a fair guide to action implementation. It sometimes happens, however, that rather important aspects of action implementation are not obvious from the analysis. Therefore it is always appropriate, before taking action, to consider in detail how the decision is to be put into effect. Sometimes, in this phase of the problem, additional analysis will be required, for there may be choices among various implementing actions. Moreover, it will sometimes happen that additional facts may be required, and additional research may be indicated.

[1] Drucker (*op. cit.*, p. 353), for example, writes, "More important and more difficult is to make effective the course of action decided upon. . . . Nothing is as useless, therefore, as the right answer that disappears in the filing cabinet or the right solution that is quietly sabotaged by the people who have to make it effective." Churchman, Ackoff, and Arnoff (*op. cit.*, pp. 575, 621) state, "This implementation phase of the research can 'make or break' a project. Consequently, it should be as carefully planned and controlled as possible. . . .

For purposes of the present discussion, let's assume Hayden has decided to implement alternative number 3, "Convince Becker to rehire Keller." Before calling Becker in to communicate his decision, Hayden must consider the various possibilities of the situation. First of all, what will happen if Becker can't be convinced? Again, should the decision be communicated to Curley before the first question is answered? Next, how should Keller be informed, and how should the decision be fed to the machinists, toolmakers, and apprentices? Will Becker need instruction on how to handle his end of the action? Just how should Hayden approach Becker? If the action fails, is there a suitable way out? Should Hayden spend more time in the shop, at least for a while, to see that matters work out as expected? What time schedule should be set for rehiring Keller? Should we apologize to Curley, or should we let him know we are doing Keller and the union a favor? Just what should Becker say in his interview with Keller? What should Becker's attitude be? Should Hayden interview Keller? If so, should it be a formal interview in Hayden's office, or should it be a casual affair, like a chance meeting in the shop?

These and a host of other questions will pop into Hayden's mind if, but only if, he stops to think specifically about the question of implementation. If Hayden fails to stop and think here, he runs the risk

---

There is a tendency among researchers to lose patience with a problem once they have solved it on paper. They are anxious to get on to the next problem and leave the 'dirty' work of control and implementation to others. This impatience more than anything else is responsible for the fact that so many paper solutions are either never put into effect or, if put into effect, yield such disappointing results. Not only must the operations researcher realize that control and implementation are important to the success of the project but also that these phases of a project present a real challenge to scientific method. In implementation, we deal with the most difficult subject matter confronted by science, people, and social groups." Ackoff (*op. cit.,* p. 408) writes, "The researcher's role in implementation should be much the same as the architect's in the construction of a building he has designed: that of active supervision." In addition, many writers have pointed out the need for preparing others for changes which are contemplated, in advance of the announcements of change. In a recent article, for example, Jacobo A. Varela ("Why Promotions Cause Trouble, and How to Avoid It," *Personnel,* November–December, 1964, pp. 17–21) indicates the need for careful preparation by conference with the unsuccessful candidates for promotion before the name of the successful candidate is announced.

of ruining his whole solution, for a good decision, badly executed, may be worse than a bad decision, skillfully implemented.

Clues to answers to most of the questions arising in connection with action-taking are contained in the problem solution. Looking back to Exhibit 7, we observe that one of the advantages of the selected course of action is "Pleases Becker." That being so, it is imperative, in placing the decision into effect, not to antagonize Becker, and the best way to avoid doing so is probably to discuss the problem with Becker and try to lead him to propose the action which has already been selected by Hayden. If the idea is Becker's, rather than an order or even an obvious suggestion by Hayden, the chances of offending Becker are minimized. If this cannot be fully accomplished, it is still better to suggest and persuade than to order.

If, because of ineptness or bad luck, Hayden cannot convince Becker to rehire Keller voluntarily, the whole solution to the problem blows up in Hayden's face, and a new analysis will doubtless become necessary. Therefore it would be eminently premature to inform anyone, especially Keller or Curley, of the decision until it is known whether Becker will cooperate.

If Becker is sold on the selected decision, it is probable that he should be briefed on how the action is to be taken. From all reports, Becker is phlegmatic and uncommunicative, and human relations is not his strong suit. It even appears that a mention of human relations, by name, might be offensive to Becker. Therefore Hayden should plan to convince Becker that he, and only he, should rehire Keller. Hayden should also try to lead Becker to anticipate his own problems in accomplishing the task. Becker, however, must not suspect that Hayden considers him to be either unsympathetic or blundering. Therefore Hayden must lead Becker to understand the delicacy of the task. Hayden might, for example, during his interview with Becker, express real concern over whether anyone short of a genius could pull off the stunt. Hayden might remark that he's glad he himself doesn't have to do the job because he would worry about being able to do it successfully. In such a manner, Hayden could command Becker's close attention to the problem of execution of the mission, but at the same time, Hayden must avoid frightening Becker. This is a delicate matter which Hayden undertakes, and he should try, before the interview with Becker, to anticipate as many of the difficulties as possible.

Therefore, in planning the implementation of his selected course of action, Hayden must move cautiously.

In many situations, where the analyst is contemplating the precise manner of executing his decisions, it is helpful for him to rehearse in private what he will say and how he might expect the interviewee to respond. In the classroom, the teacher frequently demonstrates the action by the technique called role playing. In such plays, the decision maker is given another student to assume the role of the interviewee. This is a fine teaching technique in many types of courses, especially human relations, and it is frequently possible to use it, or a variation of it, in actual business situations. In large business organizations especially, it is often possible to get a friend from the next office to lend a hand. If this is impracticable, and if time allows, the analyst's brother or even his wife might serve at home. At the very least, the analyst can sit back and imagine what the interview will be like, and he may be able, from his knowledge of the person to be encountered, to anticipate reactions to various approaches with considerable accuracy.

Returning to our earlier list of questions on how the action is to be initiated, the decision on how to inform Keller is now fairly obvious. After Hayden is certain that Becker concurs in the decision, and after he is satisfied that Becker can do the job effectively, Hayden should inform Curley that Mr. Becker has agreed to meet with Keller, and that he, Hayden, believes Becker is sorry he had to fire Keller; further, that he believes Becker might relent if Keller is repentant. While talking to Curley, Hayden must also inform him that Becker had no criticism of Keller and that, in fact, he was working out a production problem in his own mind and was hardly aware that Keller was present. In short, Hayden must get across the point that Keller was completely mistaken about the whole situation and that Keller was horribly wrong. Hence, in his interview with Curley, Hayden must at once satisfy Curley and give Curley a background which will be communicated to Keller and which will put Keller in the proper receptive attitude for his meeting with Becker. In planning the interview, Hayden must rehearse as far as possible, but he is at a disadvantage because his knowledge of Curley is much less complete than his knowledge of Becker. At the same time, this interview is not really a difficult one, and ordinary good manners combined with as much good humor as may be appropriate should assure its success. Mainly, in this interview, Hayden needs to plan his objectives and the friendly tone he hopes to achieve.

As far as the machinists and toolmakers are concerned, Becker should be shown the need to get the true word to them as soon as possible after he completes his successful interview with Keller. It would be a serious error to have Keller suddenly appear on the shop floor without warning. Such a happenstance could lead only to the wildest and most harmful speculation. Now the question of how to communicate the facts is apparent. No big production is desired. The aim is to play it down. Certainly, Becker should not close down the plant and call a meeting. Instead, he should communicate the information, rather casually, to the machinist who had been supervising Keller at the time of the firing incident. He should express his regret that a fine boy like Keller should have done what he did, and he should speak of his reconsideration of his own action. He should express hope that no such misunderstanding will ever recur. He might even speculate, while talking to the machinist, on why Keller had been so touchy. In any case, the objective of this approach is to get the decision and the reasons for it to the machinists and toolmakers. By telling this one, most concerned, member of the group, in view of the fine relationships existing among these men, Becker and Hayden can be sure that the true word will penetrate the entire group very rapidly.

Regarding the apprentices, it is clear that, since the morale of this group is believed to be the primary problem in the case, very special care must be taken to implement the present action decision in such a way as to achieve the greatest possible benefit. Simply rehiring Keller does not get the most out of the situation, for if the action is misinterpreted more harm than good might result. Nor should this decision be accompanied by any other unrelated actions to improve morale, for they might be similarly misinterpreted. For example, no apology should be made for past hazing, and no promise of better treatment of apprentices in the future should be given. The apprentices, for the time being, should be informed of the situation in a casual manner, probably in a planned chat between the machinist supervisor and Edwards. Edwards is probably the leader of the apprentices, and shortly after the word reaches him, all of the others will know about it. After the full, true facts are communicated, and before Keller comes back to the job, Becker himself might well take occasion to chat with Edwards. In this interview, Becker should reaffirm his liking for Keller and his complete satisfaction not only with Keller but also with all of the apprentices.

In the back of Hayden's mind, during all of this planning for implementation of the selected course of action, there should be constant alertness to the continuing menace of the primary problem, the morale of the apprentices. Hayden should already be thinking ahead to the possibilities of leading the machinists and toolmakers to take the apprentices *into the fun* rather than to make them the *objects* of it.

Throughout this discussion of planning for implementation, we have made constant reference to the implementation cues and clues which have already come to light in the analysis of the problem. We may now, therefore, enunciate the major principles which should be followed in the planning for implementation. These principles are brief and straightforward.

In the implementation of action decisions, one must try to maximize the chances of occurrence of all of the favorable consequences which were forecast in the problem analysis, and one must try to minimize the chances of occurrence of all of the unfavorable consequences. The procedure works like this: Go back to the analysis sheet for the alternative which has been selected for implementation. On that sheet, the problem solver has listed a large number of advantages and disadvantages for that alternative. Each advantage should now be reconsidered, and the analyst should ask, "How can I, in the implementation of this action, assure myself that this advantage will actually be realized?" This is another way of asking, "How can I, in the implementation of this action, increase the probability that this favorable consequence will be achieved?" In our analysis of the Hayden Tool Company case, for example, in Exhibit 7, one of the advantages of the selected alternative is "Pleases Becker." In our implementation plan, we were especially anxious to assure that Becker would actually be pleased. If, in the implementation, we were to forget and to do something which displeased Becker, we might impair the solution to such an extent as to destroy its overall effectiveness. Hence we repeat what we have said before; namely, a good decision, badly implemented, may be worse than a bad decision, expertly implemented.

After examining each of the advantages and planning to maximize the chances that it will be realized, the analyst should examine each of the disadvantages. In these examinations, the analyst should ask, "How can I, in the implementation of this action, avoid completely or at least minimize the effects of these disadvantages?" Hence, in planning for implementation of the action decision, the problem solver tries to squeeze out the last bit of advantage and to eliminate or to mitigate all of the disadvantages. To the extent that one succeeds in these efforts, the overall effectiveness of the decision is increased, and it may be increased to a point where its actual effectiveness is many times its originally predicted effectiveness.

A final principle in implementation has been implicit throughout this discussion. It is this: Any problem solver who loses interest as soon as he has finished the paper work and who turns it over to someone else for implementation will be disappointed in the result. If the decision is implemented at all, it will be badly implemented. Others will not have an equal interest and may actually oppose it. Even those who are interested and approving will lack a full understanding of the complications. Hence it is strongly recommended that problem solvers look at the job of implementation as an integral part of problem solving itself.

In summary, therefore, we list the principles of decision implementation as follows: (1) The problem solver should view the task of implementation as an integral part of the problem-solving process. (2) The best guide to action-decision implementation is the problem analysis. (3) The implementation plan should seek to maximize the chances of occurrence of all of the advantages which were predicted for the selected alternative. (4) The implementation plan should seek to minimize the chances of occurrence of all of the disadvantages which were predicted for the selected alternative. (5) In planning for decision implementation, unless the problem selected for solution is the primary problem in the case, one must constantly bear in mind the effects which the solution to the present problem will have on the primary problem situation, and one must be careful, in the implementation plan, to avoid any action which would be inconsistent with the expected actions which will be required in the primary problem solution.

chapter 12

REPORTING DECISION RECOMMENDATIONS

In many business situations, the problem analyst is a person other than the one who has uncovered the problem, and the analyst is merely the problem-solving agent of a principal. A young executive, for example, might be called in by his superior, who says, "Joe, you've heard about the mess we have in our Atlanta sales office. I want you to drop everything here and go down there to find out what the devil's going on. Leave as soon as you can, and stay as long as you have to, but damn it all, bring back the answers." Or, during a meeting of the finance committee, a number of different proposals are advanced for raising funds for a major expansion of production facilities. Discussion of many proposals has taken place, but before a vote on any of them is taken a senior committee member states his reluctance to decide the issue until a more thorough study is made. He moves that a subcommittee be appointed to look into the problem and to bring a recommendation to the next meeting. The motion carries, and Joe is appointed a committee of one to do the job. Or again, Joe discovers a problem, and he analyzes it. The solution, however, involves actions which lie outside the area of his authority, and he must convince his boss of the need for action at a higher level. Still again, Joe may be a complete outsider, an independent consultant, for example. His business is a constant round of being called in to study problems confronting his clients, and he has no authority to do anything but report his findings and recommendations.

Under all such circumstances, the complex problem-solving task is not finished until the problem is solved, the plan for implementation is detailed, and the report is written. Hence some attention to the writing of the report is essential, for although the report's contents may be obvious to the analyst, the manner in which they should be presented may not be. Therefore the following organization for reporting decision recommendations is suggested:[1]

1. Letter of transmittal
2. Summary of recommendations
3. The report proper
   a. the facts
   b. the problem
   c. the alternatives (sometimes omitted)
   d. the analysis of selected alternatives
   e. the decision
   f. recommendations for implementing the decision
4. Appendixes (frequently omitted)
   a. analysis sheets
   b. evaluation data and computations

A sample letter of transmittal is illustrated in Exhibit 10. This is simply a covering letter from the analyst to the person for whom the report is intended. It should be written in ordinary letter form and should carry the following information:

1. Name and address of the writer
2. Date of submission of the report
3. Name of the person for whom the report is intended
4. Subject of the report
5. Reason for the report's being written

---

[1] There are many good texts in and related to the field of report writing. One of the best in the area of technical writing is Frank Kerekes and Robley Winfrey, *Report Preparation,* Iowa State College Press, Ames, 1951.

EXHIBIT 10   SAMPLE LETTER OF TRANSMITTAL

John J. Jones & Associates
444 Main Street
Hartford, Connecticut

July 15, 1931

Subject: Report on the Keller Dismissal

To: Mr. James G. Hayden
     Hayden Tool Company
     88 Lakeview Road
     Hamden, Connecticut

Dear Mr. Hayden:

In accordance with your request in our conversation on July 12, 1931, I have conducted a study of the dismissal of Paul A. Keller at your plant on July 11, 1931. The report of my findings is enclosed.

Very truly yours,

_____

John J. Jones

1 encl: Report
JJJ/ab

Immediately after the letter of transmittal we place a summary of recommendations. This summary might be limited to recommendations only, but it is neither unusual nor inadmissible to include brief statements of reasons for them. The primary objective is to place the recommended action at the very beginning so that the person who receives the report, if he has absolute confidence in the reporter, can complete the recommended action and get on with other duties. In order to accomplish this, one must tell the reader at the very start what the recommendation is.

If there is any doubt that the reader of the report will act without being persuaded that the recommended action is correct, it is appropriate to cite the major arguments favoring the recommended action. On the other hand, too much argument in the summary defeats the purpose in two ways. First, the summary should be as short as possible. Second, too much argument in favor of the recommended action distorts the picture, for it fails to alert the reader to possible disadvantages. A sample of recommendations is given in Exhibit 11.

EXHIBIT 11   SAMPLE SUMMARY
OF RECOMMENDATIONS

SUMMARY

I. Objectives
    A. To improve the morale of apprentices.
    B. To support Becker's role as plant superintendent.
    C. To instruct Becker in human relations techniques.
    D. To maintain cordial relations with the machinists' union.
    E. To avoid forfeiture of management prerogatives to the union.
    F. To render simple justice to Keller.
II. Primary action recommendation: Persuade Becker to rehire Keller.
III. Implementing action recommendations
    A. Interview Becker, discuss the situation, and review the facts to permit Becker to convince himself, as follows:
        1. Keller's reaction was symptomatic of low morale in the apprentice group.
        2. Keller's reaction was a normal outgrowth of low morale and the circumstances of Becker's study of the work problem.
        3. Keller should be reinstated.
        4. Apprentices should be led to believe Keller's reinstatement is governed solely by:
            a. Becker likes Keller.
            b. Becker feels Keller misunderstood the intent of Becker's study of Keller's work.
            c. Becker has been pleased with Keller's work.
            d. Becker wants to give Keller a break.
        5. Machinists and toolmakers should be informed of the decision before Keller reappears on the floor.
        6. Machinist who was supervising Keller at the time of the discharge should be the agent to inform the other machinists, the toolmakers, and the apprentices of the decision reached.
        7. Communications to the apprentices should be made through Edwards.

8. Communications to the apprentices should be made with studied casualness.
9. Becker should repeat to Edwards the information already communicated by the machinist supervisor.
10. Becker's communication to Edwards should also be thoroughly casual.
11. No promises and no apologies should be made to the apprentices by either Becker or the machinist supervisor.
12. Becker should suggest to the machinist supervisor that hazing of apprentices should stop soon, if not now, and that apprentices should be brought into the fun group.

B. Inform Curley that
1. Keller misunderstood Becker's behavior.
2. Keller was dead wrong.
3. Becker likes Keller and regrets the incident.
4. Becker is eminently satisfied with Keller's work.
5. If Keller approaches Becker and apologizes, Becker would probably take him back.

C. In the Curley interview
1. Set a friendly tone of good humor.
2. Maintain, by implication, management prerogatives.
3. Suggest management's desire for cooperative union-management relations.

In the summary of recommendations, the objectives of action are always given. They prepare the reader for the recommendations and, in general, they are statements of the problems contained in the case. The primary objective should be stated first, and additional objectives should be stated in the order of their importance. The statement of objectives is always followed by a clear, concise statement of the principal recommendation. Almost always, under the heading "Implementing action recommendations," the details of the recommendations are enumerated. In some cases a fourth paragraph, explaining the recommendations, is admissible. In the present illustration, it is believed that explanation is neither necessary nor desirable. The summary of recommendations should be written as briefly but as clearly as possible. In many ways, the summary is the most important part of the report. Care taken in the preparation of the summary will usually pay rich rewards.

In the report proper, a suitable heading is selected for the report title. The title is often the same as the subject in the letter of transmittal. Under the title, the report begins with a statement of the facts. This record includes all facts that the analyst observes and all that are communicated to him by others. A sample statement of facts for the Hayden Tool Company case appears in Exhibit 12. In this record, the student will note that a great deal more information appears than was given in the original statement in Exhibit 1. The additional information is the result of Jones' research of the problem for needed but missing facts. This kind of research is eminently representative of problem-solving activity in the real world, and this illustration should go far to convince readers that, regardless of the positions they may someday occupy in industry, they will always have need for personal competence in business research.

EXHIBIT 12   SAMPLE STATEMENT OF THE FACTS

REPORT ON THE KELLER DISMISSAL

1. The Facts

The Hayden Tool Company is located in Hamden, a suburb of New Haven, Connecticut. Hayden's is a small, family-owned corporation with the majority of stock ownership in the hands of Mr. Hayden, the founder and active manager of the business. The company is engaged in the manufacture of machine tools and dies and of machine parts and subassemblies, all on contract for other manufacturing concerns located in Massachusetts, Rhode Island, Connecticut, and New York. The shop consists of one large building and, except for offices at the front end, it is completely unpartitioned.

The total staff consists of Mr. Hayden, who spends most of his time out of the office as salesman and customer-contact man, Miss Holman, who handles all of the office work, and Mr. Becker, general foreman and shop superintendent. The company employs two die makers, four machinists, and six apprentice machinists.

The national economy, in general, and the machine tool industry, in particular, are in the midst of a severe depression. The outlook is for business conditions to become worse before they become better. Hayden is finding new orders difficult to obtain, and he is doing everything possible to retain the clients he has as well as everything he can to get new customers.

All employees of the company, except Mr. Hayden and Miss Holman, are members of the machinists' union, and Hayden is a former member. Becker is not active in the union, but he pays his dues and carries a card. The union is gaining strength in the community, and employers are having increasing difficulties with union leaders. A number of strikes by machinists have already occurred in the area, but Hayden's, up to now, has had no trouble.

On July 11, 1931, Paul Keller and Jack Edwards, apprentice machinists, had been assigned to a job order under the supervision of one of the machinists. Both men had been with the company for slightly over one year and, up to the time of the present incident, they had been regarded as eminently satisfactory by the general foreman and the machinists. On the day in question, Keller and Edwards were working on a rush order for small machine parts which were to be turned out by two simple operations on the turret lathes. After the machines had been set up, both men had received the necessary instructions for the accomplishment of the task. They had both been impressed with the need for speed, and the work was begun by 7:30 A.M. Wednesday. No difficulties were encountered, and both Keller and Edwards worked without supervision or assistance until shortly after ten o'clock. At this time Mr. Becker, on his way through the shop, stopped behind Keller, looked over his shoulder, frowned, and uttered a somewhat disturbed, "Tsk, tsk." He said nothing, however, and soon passed on to other duties. Some ten minutes later, he returned and repeated his first performance. Then, again, a short time later, Mr. Becker appeared for the third time and repeated his two previous routines.

Keller turned abruptly and, shaking his clenched fist in Mr. Becker's face, cried out above the noise of the running machinery, "I'm warning you, Becker, if you don't stay away from me, I'll punch ya' in the kisser."

Mr. Becker looked startled but said nothing and walked away. He went to the office and instructed Miss Holman to make out a discharge notice for Mr. Keller and to deliver it immediately. These instructions were carried out, and Keller left the shop within thirty minutes.

In the early afternoon, Mr. Curley, president of the local machinists' union, called on Mr. Hayden and protested Keller's discharge. He repeated the facts as told to him by Keller and exactly as they had happened. Hayden had already been notified of Keller's discharge when Curley called. In fact, he was about to call in Becker to get the details when Curley arrived.

After listening to Curley's complaint, Hayden stated that he had just learned of Keller's dismissal, and he would have to have a little time to investigate and consider before he would be able to tell Curley anything. He promised to look into the matter immediately, and he assured Curley he would get in touch with him within a few days.

As soon as Curley left, Hayden called Jones, of John J. Jones & Associates, and, on the telephone, he briefed Jones on the facts. Jones agreed to study the situation, and he stated he would be down to see Hayden the first thing in the morning. Later that afternoon, Hayden spoke with Becker and told him that Jones, a management consultant from Hartford, would be coming the next day to investigate a grievance lodged in Keller's behalf by Curley. His purpose would be to advise Hayden on what he should tell Curley.

On his arrival at the Hayden Tool Company on Thursday morning, Jones chatted with Hayden, and the latter, after introducing Jones to Becker, left for the day. Jones continued the interview with Becker with the following results: Becker appears to be somewhat confused about what actually happened. He states that he has always liked Keller, and he has been completely satisfied with Keller's work. At the time of the incident, Becker was watching Keller's operation to check out an idea, which had been going through his head, to simplify and speed up the work. He had no criticism of Keller's performance and, in fact, he was hardly aware of Keller's presence as an individual person. All Becker was doing was working over an idea and returning to observe the present operation as performed by Keller. He was taken by complete surprise when Keller turned on him, and he can't explain what caused Keller's threat. Becker believes himself to be entirely innocent of provocation. Whatever the explanation of Keller's behavior, however, Becker does not see any other course he could have taken, and if the incident happened again, Becker is certain Keller would have to be discharged. In all of Becker's experience, he had never before seen such gross insubordination, and it would be intolerable to have Keller at work again in the shop. Becker regrets the incident, and he wishes it had not occurred.

At the end of his conversation with Jones, Becker introduced Jones to the machinist who had been supervising Keller at the time of the discharge incident. Becker went about his own duties, and Jones continued to talk with the machinist supervisor. He stated to Jones that, at the time of the incident, he was at the other end of the shop and that he didn't know about it until after Keller had actually left. Soon thereafter Becker did tell him about it, and the machinist supervisor had agreed, and still agrees, that Becker had no alternative to the action he took. The machinist also stated that he, too, liked Keller and that he, also, was completely satisfied with his work. He went on to say that Becker acted properly in discharging Keller without consulting with him, for in critical situations, direct action, without observance of normal channels, is sometimes necessary. Becker promptly reported the action at his earliest convenience.

In speaking about Becker, the machinist said that everyone knew that Becker was the best toolmaker in the metropolitan area and that he was generally liked by everyone. In describing personal relationships in the shop, the machinist pictured Becker as a rather silent, thoughtful man who paid strict attention to business at all times. Becker is described as serious and uncommunicative, but not unfriendly. Becker is still young, in his early forties, and he is always looking for cheaper and quicker ways to do work without sacrificing work quality. Although he seldom takes part in nonbusiness conversations around the shop, Becker is not a slave driver, and he does not interfere with the relative freedom of the men and their occasional, good-humored horse-play. Hayden's is a good place to work. Wages are standard, and working conditions are excellent. All of the machinists and toolmakers are friendly with each other, both on and off the job.

At the conclusion of this conversation with the machinist supervisor, Jones asked to talk with Edwards who was summoned and introduced. The machinist went back to his own work, and Jones continued his investigation with Edwards.

This apprentice had observed the whole incident which led up to Keller's dismissal. He was not in the least reluctant to state that Becker was a stinker, and that if it had been he, instead of Keller, who had been involved, he would have punched Becker in the nose instead of yelling at him. In fact, Edwards boasted, it was he who advised Keller to lodge a complaint with Curley.

Edwards also complained that the apprentices at Hayden's always get the dirty end of the stick. Although they are paid standard wages, it's a lousy place to work, and if jobs were available any place else, Hayden would not have a single apprentice left. The work is monotonous and confining. The men are tied to one place on close production schedules. The rest of the people have great freedom and have more play than work on the job. The machinists and toolmakers often amuse themselves by playing practical jokes on the apprentices. The apprentices would not mind the pay differentials between the apprentices and masters if the latter did any work, but they are all freeloaders who take advantage of the apprentices in terms of both the work performed and the social position enjoyed. The apprentices have been talking among themselves, and they are talking about doing something about the situation. Edwards thinks Hayden ought to be around more to see what goes on in his shop. Becker's no good at all, and the machinists and toolmakers aren't much better.

Before leaving the shop, Jones inspected some of the company's financial, employment, and production records. He noted that wage scales, for all employees, were similar to others in the area for like jobs. The range for apprentices is 25 cents to 50 cents per hour, depending on initial training and length of service. For journeymen machinists and toolmakers, the range is 75 cents to $1.00 per hour, and for masters, the range is $1.25 to $1.50 per hour. The company employs one master and one journeyman toolmaker, and it employs one master and three journeyman machinists. Becker is in a special pay category. He normally receives a salary of $5,000 per year and an annual bonus of 10 percent of net profit. Six months ago Becker took a temporary pay cut of 10 percent. Becker came to the company as plant manager, and he has been personally friendly with Hayden for almost twenty years. He has been employed at Hayden's for six years.

Since the start of the depression, over a year ago, the company has been able to maintain full employment and work schedules. Although profits have almost disappeared, no losses have occurred. The chief reason for the company's continuing viability is its capacity to bid low on work contracts and still make small profits. Hayden is a fine salesman, and Becker is a work-producing, cost-cutting expert. The company's financial resources are, in these trying times, strictly limited. Even small losses over any long period of time would be fatal, and a large loss would put the company into almost immediate and certain bankruptcy.

The personnel files of the master machinist and the master toolmaker disclose that both of them had been with Hayden for some years before Becker came to the company. Becker was employed when the former superintendent died of a heart attack. While Becker was being considered for the job, the two master craftsmen were also being considered. Neither one of them wanted to accept the responsibility of the shop foreman's job, and both had been delighted about Becker's appointment.

Jones left the Hayden Tool Company at noon on Thursday and continued his study of the problem in his own office in Hartford. His first step in that phase of the investigation was to estimate the cost to the company of losing any one or all of its employees. In this computation exercise, it is apparent that, in view of the extensive unemployment in all labor categories, recruitment costs are zero.

The cost of replacing Becker is, nevertheless, huge. Hayden himself would have to spend several days interviewing applicants, and after his man was selected, several more days would be required to orient him to the job. At the present time, a day's work for Hayden just about produces enough orders to keep the factory working. The cost of the loss of a day for Hayden is not easy to compute. Keeping in mind the fact that all work in the shop is of the job-order variety and no production for stock is ever performed, if Hayden loses a day's work, the shop loses a day's production. Since, for short periods, men will be kept on the payroll whether work is available or not, the loss of one day for Hayden will equal the total company payroll, plus daily profit, plus overhead, minus shop housekeeping expenses for work which can be done in slack periods, and minus Hayden's traveling expenses. The daily payroll is $102.60. The plant is valued at $30,000, and interest at 4 percent is about $3.85 per working day. Depreciation runs about double that, at about $7.70. Property tax is about $0.96 per day, and inventory carrying costs are negligible. Daily profit is about $3.20, and Hayden's traveling expenses are also about $3.20 per day. Housekeeping expenses for work which can be done in slack periods are negligible. Therefore the total cost of the loss of one day's work for Hayden is about $115.11. If Becker is replaced, the immediate cost will be about $690.66 (six days' work for Hayden).

Equally serious, if Becker must be replaced, would be the effect on production costs. It is believed the effect would work out in some such fashion as this: Every person in the shop would lose one full day's work in his initial contact with the new foreman. The foreman must get acquainted with each man and the work he does, and the man must be given a chance to get acquainted with the new foreman. While it is not expected that the new foreman would routinely spend one full day with each man on their first contact, it is certain that the men will spend considerable time talking about the new foreman with each other, and the new foreman will spend time thinking over, in private, his impressions of the men and their work. Therefore, it is not unrealistic to estimate that every man in the shop will lose one day's work in, or as a result of, his first contact with a new foreman. In subsequent contacts with the new foreman, each person would, we estimate, lose one-half of the time lost on the previous contact. Hence the time lost for each person would constitute a series *somewhat* as follows: $1 + \frac{1}{2} + \frac{1}{4} + \frac{1}{8} + \frac{1}{16} \ldots$ days. Inasmuch as the sum of such a geometric series is 2, the lost-time cost would be two days' work for each person on the payroll,* except Hayden and the new foreman, plus the cost of lost time for the new foreman. For Miss Holman, the machinists and toolmakers, and the apprentices, the total would come to about $136.00. Lost time for the foreman would constitute a series somewhat as follows: $12 + 6 + 3 \ldots$ days, or a total of 24 at a cost of about $415.20.

Hence, to replace Becker and get the shop running again, the cost would come to about $1,250. But this is not the only cost associated with replacing Becker. The $1,250 cost is relatively certain, but what about the costs if the machinists and toolmakers dislike the new foreman? Under such circumstances, efficiency might drop as much as 25 percent, and cost, therefore, might rise by 25 percent. This would figure out to be an annual cost of about 25 percent of the machinist-toolmaker payroll, or about $3,225 per year. This is approximately three times last year's profit. Hence, if this event occurred and if business conditions remain about the same, the company, next year, instead of enjoying a profit of about $1,000, would suffer a loss of about $2,000. In view of Becker's popularity with this group, the chances of some loss of efficiency are high, and an estimated loss of half of this figure is not unreasonable. Hence the loss from this source of replacing Becker is estimated at about $1,500 per year. The present value of such an annual loss would be about $23,500 (4 percent for twenty-five years).

Nor are these all the costs of replacing Becker. It is conceded that Becker's really important value to Hayden's is his creative ability as a cost cutter. The record indicates that Hayden is able to quote prices on contracts at an average of 10 percent below the competition. This may, then, be taken as a measure of Becker's value to the firm. Now the question is, if Hayden were not able to quote prices at 10 percent below the competition, what would he be able to sell? Very likely Hayden's sales would fall to a level of something like 10 percent of last year's record, or about $4,000. With this sales figure, even despite higher selling prices, huge losses would be incurred. All employees would have to be laid off (Hayden's salary alone is $4,500 per year), and Hayden would be required to do not only the sales job but also the office and shop work as well. In short, without Becker's ability to hold costs down to their present levels, Hayden would be forced out of business. The plant would probably, under present business conditions, be a dead loss of $30,000. In addition, Hayden would lose his salary of $4,500 per year, and he would lose his profit of another $1,000 per year. Finally, he would lose the chance of staying in business to enjoy normal profits (over the full course of a business cycle) of about $5,000 per year, when business conditions improve. Hence Becker's value as a cost cutter is crucial, and all other costs of replacing him are academic. Becker's value as a cost cutter, and the cost of losing him, therefore, is estimated at

---

*A more sophisticated analysis of these losses would attempt to segregate, for each man, his individual contribution to total revenue. If we assume, however, that each man's wage is equal to his marginal revenue product, the simple analysis we have made is correct with respect to shop personnel.

$30,000 for the value of the plant he is saving, plus the $23,500 present value of Hayden's salary differential between what he earns working for himself and what he would earn working for someone else (about $1,500 per year, at 4 percent, for twenty-five years), plus the $78,110 present value of the normal profits of the business (about $5,000 per year, at 4 percent, for twenty-five years). Thus the cost of replacing Becker figures out to something like $130,000.

In contrast with the high cost of losing Becker, the costs involved in losing any other one man are modest. In the case of a master machinist or master toolmaker, a simple loss of services would be computed by the time lost by Becker in hiring the replacement, plus the time lost in orienting the man to his duties, plus the time lost by other members of the work force in getting acquainted. Under present labor conditions, Becker would probably lose not more than a day in the hiring and half a day in the orienting. The man himself would lose another day in getting acquainted with the other people in the shop, and these, in turn, in the aggregate would also lose one day. Therefore, the total cost of replacing a master toolmaker or a master machinist would be approximately $95. Similarly, the cost of replacing a journeyman would be about $93, and the cost of replacing an apprentice would be about $91. The major costs, in all cases, are Becker's time and the times of the other members of the work force. Therefore it is not surprising that replacement costs are about the same for all classes of workmen. Also, with a loose labor market, it is probable that high quality replacements are available, and actual training costs are zero.

After completing computations of replacement costs for each separate employee, Jones turned his attention to the question of costs involved in cases of employee retention under conditions of various degrees of dissatisfaction. Obviously, it might be less costly to replace a man than to retain him while he is in a state of disgruntlement.

In this series of computations, Jones began with Becker. If Becker were to be reprimanded, or if his authority were to be reduced or even questioned, his efficiency might be seriously impaired. If Becker had to worry about whether the boss would or would not approve of every little thing he did, Becker might very easily and quickly become no better at his job than any other master toolmaker who might be hired to replace him. Therefore the cost of displeasing or of even worrying Becker would probably be very high. Hence we estimate the cost of upsetting Becker over the Keller incident is one-half the cost of losing him, or $65,000.

If Keller is rehired over Becker's head, the efficiency of the machinists and toolmakers would probably be reduced. A fine relationship exists between them and Becker, but if Becker's authority were undermined, their efficiency might drop as much as $750 per year. This represents a present value loss of about $12,000. If matters are left as they are, the machinists and toolmakers will side with Becker, and no loss of efficiency is expected from following this course.

The apprentices are low-cost employees, but they do a considerable amount of production work. As much as 20 percent of sales is directly traceable to their activities. Hence, at the present level of efficiency of apprentices, about $8,000 per year is directly attributable to their efforts. Therefore, if efficiency were to drop by 50 percent, the loss would be about $4,000 per year with a present value of more than $60,000. Even a 10 percent decrease in apprentices' efficiency would cost about $800 the first year and as much as $12,000, present value, if the condition persisted for twenty-five years. On the other hand, if something could be done to increase the morale of the apprentices, the value would be the same, but in the opposite direction. Thus it is apparent that the true value of the apprentices is far greater than that indicated by the small cost of replacing them.

The crucial importance of apprentices is fully appreciated by Edwards, and the problem of their morale is fundamental. Present morale is poor, and it threatens to become worse. Nevertheless, it is extremely doubtful that a wholesale firing is a proper answer. The cost of that action would be a one-time cost of less than $600, but it is questionable that the morale of a new crop of apprentices, under existing circumstances, would be any better. A simple rehiring of Keller would probably not improve morale in the apprentice group, but it might keep morale from dropping any lower.

The possibility of a labor strike is extremely remote. A strike could not succeed unless it were supported by the machinists and toolmakers, and they are favorably disposed toward Becker. They agree that Keller was out of line, and since they do most of the supervising of the apprentices, the machinists and toolmakers would frown on any thought of making the Keller dismissal a strike issue. If a strike did occur, it would hurt labor a great deal more than management. Hayden's overhead is small, and his daily strike cost does not exceed the sum of his own, Becker's and Miss Holman's wages, plus overhead. Hence the daily strike cost to Hayden is less than $50. A ten-day strike would be very serious to labor, but it would cost the company less than $500.

Failure to get out the rush order would be more troublesome than costly. The order contract is for $1,600. In an extreme emergency, Hayden could sub-contract it to any number of other shops which would be delighted with the windfall. In such an emergency, Hayden would lose his profit of about 5 percent plus an additional cost of about 10 percent. Hence the cost of failure to turn out the rush order would not exceed $250.

The reader should also notice, in the sample statement of facts, that considerable amounts of data are presented which will be needed in the evaluation process. A computation which is based on facts is itself a fact, and it properly belongs in the statement with other facts. Again, one should remark the use which Jones made of simple problem-solving techniques. Therefore we repeat our previous statement to the effect that simple problem-solving methods will and should be used whenever feasible. Finally, it is clear that, whenever the analyst finds it impracticable to gather additional actual, verifiable facts, assumptions are made as needed to plug the gaps. In the present problem, Jones has no way of determining the amount of time a new foreman would spend or how much of other employee time he would require to get the shop into regular production after his take-over. An estimate, however, is necessary. Therefore Jones *assumed* what he thought was a reasonable guess, and he made his computations on the basis of a theoretical geometric series. Since the assumption will be acted on as though it were a fact, it is properly placed in the section entitled "The Facts." All assumptions, of course, must be clearly labeled as such.

Immediately following the statement of facts, the report must give a statement of the problem. If a good statement of the facts is detailed, the primary problem, the secondary problems, and the urgent problems will be fairly obvious. For the Hayden Tool Company, a sample statement of the problem is given in Exhibit 13.

The problem statement, of course, may be an outline with terse remarks about each of the areas of difficulty. The cursive, literary approach, however, is usually more interesting to read, and although it may be slightly longer than an outline, it is almost always clearer. In any case, the descriptive approach has greater flexibility. Hence if the cursive approach is used, as in the illustration in Exhibit 13, the particular problem chosen for analysis should be particularly stated. This was accomplished in the illustration by the use of italics, and by placing it at the tail end of the problem statement.

EXHIBIT 13   SAMPLE STATEMENT OF THE PROBLEM

REPORT ON THE KELLER DISMISSAL

1. The Facts

. . . .

2. The Problem

The primary problem is the morale of the apprentices. Everyone else in the company is apparently happy and efficient. The apprentices are unhappy and, very likely, inefficient. Improvement of morale in this group would be likely to pay rich dividends.

A large number of secondary problems exist. Although Mr. Becker is doubtless a fine craftsman and a proven production expert, he appears to be unaware of the low morale of the apprentices and of the probable losses in efficiency resulting from it. If Becker could be made more sensitive to human relations problems, his value to the company would be even greater than it presently is.

The solution to the problem of the apprentices' morale should carefully avoid undermining Becker's authority or self-confidence. Any action taken must be with Becker's approval, and preferably on his own initiative.

The union does not appear to be a threat to management authority, but relations with the union should be maintained at as cordial a level as possible, without jeopardizing management prerogatives in any way.

Keller was a victim of his own low morale and of the way in which Becker looked over his shoulder while Keller was at work. Keller could not have known that Becker's attention was on the operation rather than on the operator. Therefore, some excuse exists for Keller's behavior, and if he is to be forgiven, as seems only just, action should not be delayed. This, while minor, is an *urgent* problem.

The action taken with respect to Keller will have repercussions on Becker and on all of the work groups in the shop. Hence the way in which Keller is handled will affect all other problem areas. Therefore the problem presented for immediate solution is: *What should be done about Keller's dismissal?*

The reader may notice that in a few places the problem statement anticipates the problem solution. While this most certainly cannot be done in the analysis, it may be useful to do so in the report. After all, the reader of the report will have read the summary of recommendations before he reads the report, and it will come as no shock to him that the problem statement previews the solution.

The next section of the report is the statement of alternative courses of action. As we suggested in the outline at the beginning of this chapter, this section of the report may sometimes be omitted. It is perfectly possible, in the report, to go directly from the statement of the problem to the analysis. If this is done, the analysis should be written in such a way as to keep the reader of the report informed of what it is that is being analyzed.

If the alternatives are included as a separate section of the report, they will normally be the same as those which the analyst had previously selected for study. A sample statement of alternative courses of action is presented in Exhibit 14.

The essentials of the statement of alternatives are two: First, the actual courses of action which will be analyzed must be enumerated. Second, the reasons for the selections must be explained. In addition, it is sometimes well to state, as in the Jones report to Hayden, why certain obvious alternatives were rejected without detailed analysis.

The statement of reasons for the choices of selected alternatives is so standard as to make this section of the report very easy to write. The reasons for the selection, for analysis, of particular courses of action are about the same in all analyses.

EXHIBIT 14 SAMPLE STATEMENT OF
ALTERNATIVE COURSES OF ACTION

REPORT ON THE KELLER DISMISSAL

1. The Facts

. . . .

2. The Problem

. . . .

3. Alternative Courses of Action

In the present study, the analyst rejected, out of hand, any course of action which would lead to Becker's dismissal or risk of Becker's quitting. Next to Hayden, Becker is the most valuable man in the organization, and any solution of the Keller problem must attempt not only to retain Becker's services but also, if possible, to make him even more valuable.

For analysis purposes, therefore, three alternative courses were considered:

    a. Rehire Keller without consultation with Becker
    b. Stand pat on Keller's dismissal
    c. Persuade Becker to rehire Keller

These alternatives were selected for the following reasons:

The first and second represent the two extremes of the alternative spectrum, and the third represents a middle-course compromise between them. Experience has shown that in complex problem solving, even when extreme alternatives appear ridiculous, it is always safer to explore the entire range of action choices.

An exploration of the extremes of the alternative spectrum will frequently throw special light on actions to avoid, especially in the implementation of the chosen course. In addition, the investigation of extreme actions will often aid the analyst in his efforts to evaluate the expected results of the chosen course.

The third alternative, "Persuade Becker to rehire Keller," was selected for analysis because of a hunch by the analyst that this course might turn out rather well.

The fourth section of the report is the analysis of the selected courses of action. A sample analysis is shown in Exhibit 15. In this analysis, it is usually best to summarize the work which has been done on the analysis sheets, but the analysis sheets themselves *should not* be included in this part of the report. Inclusion of analysis sheets here would tend to confuse rather than to clarify. Instead, the report should state the main points of advantage and disadvantage for each alternative, together with the dollar value of each. In this connection, readers will notice that the lists of advantages and disadvantages which are given in the report are different from and shorter than the lists given in earlier chapters of the book. Also, do not dwell on the difficulties imposed by the factor of uncertainty, but bring this consideration into the discussion when needed. So far as possible, write the analysis part of the report in simple, storybook style.

Almost always the analysis should begin with a description of the expected result of following that course which analysis has found to be least favorable. This is followed by the analysis of the better and better alternatives until the best one is described. By leaving the best for the last, the reader of the report will be progressively pleased as he pursues the analysis.

EXHIBIT 15   SAMPLE ANALYSIS
OF SELECTED ALTERNATIVES

REPORT ON THE KELLER DISMISSAL

1. The Facts
. . . .

2. The Problem
. . . .

3. Alternative Courses of Action
. . . .

4. Analysis of Selected Alternatives
Analysis discloses that Hayden's is presently worse off than it was before the Keller dismissal, and none of the alternative courses of action which we have analyzed will make the situation better than it was before the dismissal incident. Therefore the best we can do is to minimize the damage and plan ahead for future actions to improve conditions.

The least desirable course we have considered would be to *rehire Keller without consultation with Becker*. Among its advantages are the following, listed in the order of their importance:

   a. Maintains friendly relations with the union
   b. Renders simple justice to Keller
   c. Pleases Keller
   d. Avoids need to rehire for Keller

By far, the most important is the first. Although there is little present danger of a labor strike, a bad reputation with the union or an affront to Curley should be avoided. Over the years, on any and all provocations, the union can make trouble. The union *will* make trouble if the company gets a bad reputation or if the union leader is insulted and holds a grudge. These considerations lead us to estimate that the long-range gain from maintaining good labor relations is as much as $10,000. The estimate presupposes that the antagonistic union will repeat the story of Keller's dismissal, with embellishments, long after Keller himself is forgotten. This will reduce the quality of the men Hayden will be able to hire in the future, and it will lower the morale in the shop. At the moment, Curley and the union are disposed to be unfriendly. Rehiring Keller would appease them.

The next two items of advantage for rehiring Keller are much less important. Justice is a weighty consideration, but justice to Keller is neither clear-cut nor unmixed. Keller was wrong, and it cannot be said that the dismissal penalty was completely unwarranted. Nevertheless, the punishment appears too severe for the crime. The question then is, how much would Hayden be willing to pay to right the somewhat minor wrong done to Keller? We believe $2,000 would balance the scale, and this amount, then, is assigned as the value of justice in the present situation.

The next advantage of rehiring Keller relates to the expected loss to the company if Keller is allowed to depart in his present frame of mind. He believes he has been wronged, and he will do everything possible to strike back. By speaking abroad to anyone who will listen to him, Keller will spread poison in his wake. Even when Keller believes he is telling the truth, and nothing but the truth, he will be mistaken, but damage to the firm will result. The amount of damage is difficult to estimate, but over the years Keller might be able to do a significant amount, for he feels strongly, and he would work much harder to discredit the firm than an antagonistic union. Hence damage caused by failure to reinstate Keller might be as great as another $2,000.

The last advantage of rehiring Keller is small, and its value is estimated at less than $100. Hence the value of all of the advantages of this course of action is estimated at about $14,000.

Rehiring Keller without consulting with Becker, however, is loaded with weighty disadvantages. These are listed as follows in the order of their importance:

   a. Offends Becker
   b. Undermines Becker's authority
   c. Risks repetition of Becker's error

    d. Gives union too much power
    e. Fails to render justice to Becker

If Becker is offended, as he certainly would be under this course of action, his value to the firm might be almost lost. We have already established this value to be in the neighborhood of $65,000. The second disadvantage is also great. Loss of Becker's authority over the machinists and toolmakers has been valued at about $12,000, and a further decrease in efficiency of 10 percent in the apprentice group has been valued at about another $12,000. The first two disadvantages, therefore, total about $89,000.

The third disadvantage of rehiring Keller is the failure of this course to take advantage of the present incident to instruct and train Becker in human relations skills. The act of rehiring Keller causes only resentment, not instruction. Therefore, Becker remains prone to similar errors in the future with similarly disastrous results. The cost of a repetition would be another drop in morale of apprentices and might be valued at still another $12,000.

The next disadvantage is also great. Until now, Hayden's has had no trouble with the union. If we now fall over dead at the sight of the first ripple, the union might feel we are ripe for serious attack on the management fortress. Whether such an attack were to succeed or fail, the result would be costly. Avoidance of the fight, especially when it is unnecessary, is judged to be worth another $10,000.

As far as justice to Becker is concerned, we must recognize how much we owe him. To slap his face now, over a serious but honest error in judgment, would be inexcusable, and Hayden should probably be willing to pay as much as $10,000 to avoid it. In other words, it would be a greater injustice to Becker than a justice to Keller to follow this course. Taking all of the disadvantages together, they total $121,000. Hence the *net* disadvantage of rehiring Keller without consultation with Becker is about $107,000.

The second alternative course of action we selected for analysis was to *stand pat* on Keller's dismissal. The major advantages are:

    a. Keeps the union in its place
    b. Lets apprentices know who's boss

The first of these has already been valued in connection with our analysis of the first alternative at about $10,000. The second appears to be about as much of a disadvantage as an advantage—under the present circumstances at Hayden's. Therefore it is given a value of zero. The fact that this course of action might please Becker cannot be counted as an advantage, for there is no evidence that Becker's morale is low or that it might be raised by this action. Hence the total value of all advantages of standing pat is estimated to be about $10,000.

The disadvantages of doing nothing are much more numerous and much more weighty. They are listed as follows:

    a. Offends apprentices
    b. Fails to develop Becker's leadership
    c. Offends the union

d. Offends Keller
e. Fails to render justice to Keller
f. Delays the rush order
g. Requires hiring a replacement for Keller

The first of these is almost certain to result from standing pat, and this action will lead to a further decline in apprentices' morale. This will cause a loss of efficiency which might equal 10 percent. Such a decline has already been valued at about $12,000. Failure to develop Becker's leadership was valued during the analysis of the first alternative at another $12,000. The third disadvantage, "Offends the union," would be very costly—if it were certain to occur. Under conditions of the present case, however, the union would probably not turn its full wrath on Hayden's, for Curley will recognize that Keller stepped far out of line. Therefore the offense to the union will be mitigated, and instead of carrying a value of about $10,000, it deserves about $3,000. The offense to Keller and the failure to render simple justice to him have already been valued at about $2,000 each. The delay to the rush order and the need to hire a replacement for Keller are valued at about $100 each. Hence the total value of all of the disadvantages together is about $31,000, and the net disadvantage of standing pat is about $21,000. Therefore, although this course would place the firm in a worse position than it enjoyed before the Keller dismissal, standing pat is a much better choice than rehiring Keller without the approval of Mr. Becker.

The third alternative course of action selected for analysis was to *persuade Becker to rehire Keller*. The major advantages of this course are given as follows:

a. Trains Becker in human relations
b. Pleases the union without yielding prerogatives
c. Pleases Keller
d. Renders justice to Keller
e. Gets out the rush order
f. Avoids the need to rehire for Keller

The most important of these is the first. If Becker can improve his skill in human relations, the morale of the apprentice group will rise and productivity of the apprentices might rise by as much as 10 percent. This has a value of $12,000. Pleasing the union without yielding management prerogatives would be worth, over the years, another $10,000. Pleasing Keller and rendering simple justice to him are each worth $2,000. Getting out the rush order and avoiding the need to rehire for Keller are each worth $100. Therefore total advantages estimated for persuading Becker to rehire Keller are worth about $26,000.

The disadvantages are few but extremely significant. They are listed as follows:

a. Risks offending Becker.
b. Risks trouble from the apprentices.

If this alternative is chosen, the possibility of upsetting Becker is very serious and somewhat likely. If, as a result of this action, Becker becomes seriously disillusioned, the loss to the company would run to about $65,000. From the total circumstances of the situation, however, complete disillusionment is improbable, but risk is still high, and it must be counted as a serious disadvantage with a value of perhaps $30,000. The other disadvantage is also difficult to estimate. If Keller is rehired, even if it is accomplished by Becker, the apprentices might feel they have won a victory. Such a feeling, however, would lower morale rather than raise it, and no thanks would be given to Becker. Therefore the best estimate of value we can assign is a possible drop of about 5 percent in productivity, or a value of about $6,000. Hence the total disadvantages of persuading Becker to rehire Keller are estimated at about $36,000, and net disadvantage of this course of action is about $10,000.

The decision section of the report is usually short and straightforward. A sample statement of the decision is given in Exhibit 16.

EXHIBIT 16   SAMPLE STATEMENT OF DECISION

REPORT ON THE KELLER DISMISSAL

1. The Facts

. . . .

2. The Problem

. . . .

3. Alternative Courses of Action

. . . .

4. Analysis of Selected Alternatives

. . . .

5. The Decision

A summary of values for advantages and disadvantages for each of the alternatives is given as follows:

Alternatives	Advantages	Disadvantages	Net value
Rehire Keller w/o consultation	$14,000	$121,000	—$107,000
Stand pat	10,000	31,000	— 21,000
Have Becker rehire Keller	26,000	36,000	— 10,000

From the above data it is clear that none of the alternatives is expected to compensate for the damage which has been done by the dismissal incident, but it is also clear that it does make a difference what course we follow now. We recommend choice of the third alternative. *We recommend that Becker be persuaded to rehire Keller.*

Usually we simply summarize the dollar values for advantages and disadvantages for each alternative and recommend that course of action which shows the greatest net advantage or the least net disadvantage.

The last section of the report contains guides for implementing the recommended course of action. A sample statement of recommendations for implementing the decision is shown in Exhibit 17. As we have previously suggested, a good decision can be ruined by poor execution. This is especially noteworthy in the Hayden case. Unless Becker is approached and handled very, very carefully, the decision reached in the analysis could be the worst rather than the best. On the other hand, if the recommended course of action is expertly implemented, the major disadvantages may be considerably mitigated or even completely eliminated. Such a delightful event would be wonderful, for the recommended course would then lead to a considerable positive gain over the predismissal situation.

EXHIBIT 17   SAMPLE STATEMENT OF RECOMMENDATIONS FOR IMPLEMENTING THE DECISION

REPORT ON THE KELLER DISMISSAL

1. The Facts

. . . .

2. The Problem

. . . .

3. Alternative Courses of Action

. . . .

4. Analysis of Selected Alternatives

. . . .

5. The Decision

. . . .

6. Recommendations for Implementing the Decision

The decision to persuade Becker to rehire Keller is clearly the most advantageous of all we have considered. The execution of that decision, however, is as important and almost as difficult as the making of the decision. In the present case, it is evident that the recommended course of action involves great risk of upsetting Becker, and such an issue is to be avoided, if possible, or attenuated, if not. Therefore our first concern in implementing the action is to consider and to plan the interview with Becker with extreme caution.

In planning the interview, we have a great deal in our favor. We know, for example, that Becker has been through a long and difficult apprenticeship training, and he shows evidence of having profited from it. He has also shown great talent for recognizing and solving new problems. Therefore it may be presumed that, if he is given the facts of the present situation, he will follow his habitual patterns of thought, and he will seek to solve the problem. The only question is how to present the facts without giving Becker the impression he is on trial.

We suggest that Becker be called in and told that our report conveys a belief that real trouble is brewing in the apprentice group. He may also be told that we suggest that Becker, a clearly competent, just, and sympathetic man be asked to review the facts of Keller's insubordination in the light of the low morale of the whole apprentice group as well as in the light of Keller's clear misunderstanding of Becker's action when he looked over Keller's shoulder. Tell Becker that we ourselves cannot have the knowledge and understanding of the shop and the personnel which he possesses. Therefore, while we are sure that the problem is low morale in the apprentice group, we defer to Becker on how to improve it.

The expected reaction of Becker is mixed. He is glad to hear our opinion that he is competent, just, and sympathetic, but he is both surprised and hurt to learn our opinion that the morale of the apprentices is low. If he argues that we are wrong on the latter point, it is best for Hayden not to argue back. Instead, Hayden may wonder (aloud) how we happened to arrive at such a conclusion, and he may ask what other explanation could account for Keller's behavior. This is the line to pursue as soon in the interview as possible. Get Becker's agile mind to work on this as a problem for him to solve. If he can be gently led to accept even the possibility that apprentice morale is low, he will begin to grapple with the fundamentals of the problem. When this happens, Hayden needs only to feed suggestions and pose questions, for in the course of the conversation, Becker himself will suggest the correct answers.

The interview with Becker, then, will be an actual reanalysis of the problem, with Hayden and Becker in conference trying to work out an appropriate course of action. For the most part, Hayden should try to ask questions which Becker will answer with proposals leading up to our recommended course of action. When Becker does suggest appropriate action, Hayden should agree with enthusiasm. When Becker's suggestions lead away from our recommended course, Hayden should be hesitant, and he should point out objections or disadvantages.

The interview with Becker should not be rushed, and Hayden must assume the role of assistant problem solver. If Becker begins to see his error in having fired Keller in the first place, Hayden should agree, but he may soften the implied criticism of Becker's action by pointing out the need for discipline and the need to serve notice on the union that we are still running the shop. In short,

Hayden must always keep, in the forefront of his mind, the need to accomplish the rehiring of Keller without impairing Becker's exceptional talents.

The balance of our recommendations for implementing the desired action are contained in the summary at the beginning of this report. With the present comments in mind, the summary of recommendations is self-explanatory and requires no further discussion here. We conclude, then, with a statement to the effect that Hayden must continue his exploration of the problem with Becker until Becker reaches the desired conclusion and the appropriate decision on what to do. The Becker interview must also be continued until Becker has fully planned his own implementing actions. If Hayden can accomplish his interview with Becker in such a manner as to have Becker himself suggest the primary action with respect to Keller and all of the supporting actions, the results should be eminently rewarding to Becker, to Keller, to Curley, to the apprentices, and to the general welfare of the Hayden Tool Company.

In the recommendations for implementation, the analyst should try to anticipate, so far as possible, the things which might go wrong. He should then try to find ways to avoid the pitfalls. In making these anticipations, the analysis itself is the best guide. The analysis shows not only what we expect to happen but also what we might, by skillful manipulation, influence to our advantage in the implementation.

chapter 13

THE CRUCIAL ROLE OF JUDGMENT

During our entire development of the complex problem-solving model, we have constantly had occasion to refer to judgment and to emphasize its crucial role. The problem-solving model doesn't solve anything. The model serves only to organize and to keep track of large quantities of information and to consider a multitude of facts without getting buried under them. As we have pointed out repeatedly, however, complex problems are solved partially by the use of simple problem-solving techniques, but mostly by the application of the analyst's judgment. The problem-solving model in this book is simply an orderly approach which allows maximum usefulness of judgment's application.

The judgment of the problem solver is needed to decide which facts are wanted, which problems to select for analysis, which courses of action to consider, which advantages and disadvantages to investigate, which values to attach to expected payoffs, and which implementing actions to pursue. It is, therefore, only right to admit that the analyst's judgment, finally, is responsible for both the good and the bad solutions. Hence no analyst who gets a bad solution should blame our model. Our only claim is that analysts who use the model will have better success, on the whole, than those who do not use it.

Returning to our discussion of judgment, everyone concedes that judgment is based on experience. The difference between the callow youth and the mature business executive is judgment based on experience. If we could teach experience in the classroom, we would achieve the final objective of business education.

Despite our bows to maturity, however, it must be admitted that it is probably overrated. Both observation and introspection confirm that we do not, indeed, learn as much from experience as we should, can, or believe. The fact is that we tend very strongly to make the same mistakes over and over and over again. At the age of sixty, we are making the same mistakes we made at the age of sixteen. Some understanding of why this is so is helpful to our present purpose.

Let us state our purpose. We propose to develop a system to improve judgment by making it possible to achieve maximum profit from past experience. We propose to devise a plan whereby the reader may improve his judgment as much in the next year as he has improved it in the past ten years. The importance of such a purpose is incontestably significant to the subject of complex problem solving, for it is judgment that does most of the solving. For the student, the plan has major importance. To follow the plan is to achieve the maturity of a man with thirty years' experience in a matter of three or four.

The first question, then, is why is it true that we learn so little from past experience that we continue to repeat our mistakes—sometimes for as long as we live? To answer this question, a small excursion into the field of psychology is needed. The difficulty is one of forgetting our past mistakes. Yet anyone who has witnessed a demonstration of hypnotism will have been impressed by the fact that we rarely forget anything. In the hypnotic trance, we can recall, with amazing detail and vividness, things which occurred forty or fifty years earlier—even things which happened in very early childhood.

We will also have been impressed, very largely, by the fact that this so-called forgetting is associated with emotional traumas which we experienced at the same time, or shortly thereafter. Hence we conclude, with respectable psychoanalytical support, that we don't ordinarily forget anything (we simply can't recall some things) and also that the things we cannot recall are associated with emotional traumas.

Finally, we observe from additional psychoanalytical evidence that one's ego demands a respectable, if not an elevated, self-image. Failure or error, in others, is obvious. In ourselves, it is not often permitted. When error occurs, we find no fault in ourselves. We find other people or things to blame, and we retain our self-images of excellence.

Experimental evidence confirms the findings of hypnosis and psychoanalysis. Numerous experiments, using both animal and human subjects, have demonstrated the phenomena of retroactive inhibition and spontaneous recovery. Retroactive inhibition refers to the repression of memory by interference of simultaneous or later experience, and spontaneous recovery is the sudden reappearance of an apparently forgotten memory. Experimental evidence also demonstrates the devastating effect which emotional disturbance may have on memory.[1]

Taking all of these observations together, it is clear that man's nature requires him to reject his own failures and to "forget" them as soon as possible. The more successfully we serve our natures, therefore, the less chance we have to profit from past mistakes. Hence it is not surprising that we usually fail to benefit from them. Our boastful references to our wide experience will seldom include references to mistakes we have made. Our recalled experience is almost all related to our triumphs. In actuality, therefore, if we have in the past been wrong as often as we have been right, we have lost about half of the value of our experience. If we have been wrong 90 percent of the time, we have lost the use of approximately 90 percent of our experience.[2]

From his perusal of complex problem solving, the reader may be able to judge how often he is likely to be wrong. Perhaps we lose even more than 90 percent of the benefit we might enjoy from experience.

---

[1] An excellent elementary discussion of remembering and forgetting appears in Norman L. Munn, *Introduction to Psychology*, Houghton Mifflin Company, Boston, 1962, pp. 309–336.

[2] Konrad Adenaur ("Quotable Quotes," *Reader's Digest*, March, 1965, p. 78) states, "History is the sum total of the things that could have been avoided."

Whatever the truth of the matter may be, 10 percent benefit from past experience seems like a reasonable working hypothesis.

Now if the reader is shocked by this estimate, that is good. If he rejects it, however, he may be proving the point against himself, for he is rejecting an unpleasant contemplation. In any case, all readers should be able to go along with our next two propositions. First, large quantities of valuable experience are lost because we fail to recognize and to profit from our mistakes. Second, any plan, system, device, or technique which reduces the loss is greatly to be desired.

If the reader can come along with us this far, the rest is easy. All that is necessary is a technique for recognizing, admitting, and profiting from past failures. Such a system is at hand.

After the complex problem-solving process has been completed, all of the papers which have been used in the analysis must be placed in an envelope or file folder. The whole package must then be placed in a tickler file,[3] with a suspense date estimated to the time predicted, by the analysis, when the full results of the implemented action can be known and reviewed.[4]

When the file comes back, astonishing things begin to happen. The first thing is that we have great difficulty in recognizing it. If the blasted thing were not, in part at least, in our own handwriting, we might even swear that we had never seen it before. Next, we observe that a situation was described under a statement of facts, but we remember it only vaguely. Only by forcing ourselves can we believe we

[3] A tickler file is one which is designed to tickle one's memory. It is built this way: Prepare file dividers marked with numbers 1 through 31 (for the days of the current month) and with month designations from January through December. Also prepare year dividers for next year and possibly for the year after next. Then if a paper or file or envelope should be returned at some future date for further study or action, the package will be placed in the tickler file in a position corresponding to the date on which its return is desired. For example, if today is December 21, 1966, and if a paper is to be returned on March 15, 1967, it should be placed in the March file. On the first day of March, all papers in the March file will be removed and inspected. This paper, marked March 15, 1967, will now be placed in the 15 file, and on the 15th, the paper will be removed and returned to the action desk.

[4] In this connection, Drucker (*op. cit.*, p. 9) writes, "The manager can improve his performance . . . through the . . . systematic analysis of his own performance in all areas of his work and job and on all levels of management."

had ever been concerned with such drivel. Third, we note that some kind of action had been urged, and by now we are reluctantly able to admit we had done something like the action recommended. Fourth, we see that the action taken was predicted to produce specifically stated results, and the expected payoffs even have dollar values attached. At last, at this point, we will probably admit the analysis is our own, and the recommended action was taken. This is the point where we must arrive before we can hope to profit from experience.

We are not, however, all the way home. As we arrive at this juncture, we admit the analysis, but we have not admitted that the obvious discrepancies which appear between what was predicted and what resulted is any fault of ours. The temptation to blame something or someone else is very, very strong. If things did not work out as expected, we find a scapegoat. The lengths to which we may go to duck personal blame is sometimes fantastic. Nevertheless, we must resist all temptation. Be men! Admit that we ourselves are the sole objects of blame, for unless this is done all hope of improvement must disappear. Obviously if we were not responsible for the mistakes, we have nothing to learn from them.

On the other hand, acceptance of blame should not be made with too extreme a feeling of resignation. Let us not throw up our hands as one student did. He looked at the discrepancies between predicted and actual payoffs and remarked, "If an evil event has a 50-50 chance of occurrence, the probability is 9 out of 10 it will happen." [5] Such a philosophical acceptance of error reduces the trauma of failure, but it does not put us in a proper frame of mind to resolve to do better next time.

The whole object of reviewing our analysis is to discover the causes of faulty judgment. We must compare what happened with predictions of what would happen, and try to discover the reasons for failure. The fault may have been in an unwise selection of the problem. We may have neglected to uncover pertinent facts. Our measurements of variables or of their interrelationships may have been too gross or entirely mistaken. Perhaps another alternative—one we neglected completely—should have been thought of and analyzed. Or

[5] This is a local joke on the Michigan Technological University campus. No one knows where it originated, but it is credited to Professor Robert L. Papworth, and it is known as "Papworth's Second Law."

possibly some outside event, an unexpected occurrence, entered the picture and changed the whole thing. Perhaps, finally, the mistake was a simple one of procedural error in the mechanical aspects of the analysis itself. Whatever the cause or causes of failure, however, we must turn the full power of our 20-20 hindsight on the review of the case to determine the reasons for discrepancies. We must also look for clues which were presented, at the time of the analysis, but which were neglected.

In the review, we confirm or correct our facts and especially the accuracy of our assumptions. We learn either to rely on or to distrust the business or scientific principles we employed in the analysis. We observe relationships which are now clear but which were formerly obscure. In short, we learn much more in the review than we did in the analysis itself.

To take full advantage of the opportunity presented for personal growth, we must do two things. First, we must regularly perform full-scale analyses of complex problems; and, second, we must, with equal regularity, subject all of our former analyses to careful review.

By following the rules prescribed, a very young man can rapidly become a very wise one. He will broaden his view of the world around him. He will gain a vast store of knowledge about things and people in his environment. He will learn to pay close attention to detail. He will accept responsibility for his own actions. He will bear up under disappointment. He will truly learn, and he will rarely make the same mistake twice. He will be deliberate, without dawdling. He will act vigorously. He will impress his superiors with his youthful maturity. He will climb rapidly to positions of authority. And best of all, he will have great fun and zest for life.

But the path to all these goodies is paved with persistence and hard work, and the road is neither straight nor smooth. If the young man analyzes the problem of recognition by others, he will observe that a man will probably be deserving of honor before it is recognized. The suitable action, in such cases, is patience and an outward image of modesty. Let a man's work speak for itself, and let his many good friends blow his horn for him. Let him be prepared for bad luck, but let him be ready to grasp opportunity when fortune smiles.

chapter 14

THE RESEARCH APPROACH TO PROBLEM SOLVING

Throughout this work on complex problem solving, we have assigned the place of honor to judgment. Honorable mention, however, has been repeatedly awarded to business research. If the reader recalls the technique we recommended for discovery of the problem, and if he has had a little experience with the old-time psychology of James and Titchener, he will recognize that brainstorming and headshrinking are methods of introspective research. Although the word introspection is now eschewed by most respectable psychologists, the art and the science of retrieving, from memory, facts and relationships of past experience can hardly be described by a better word, and introspection is a fundamental research technique.

In the quest for facts, the problem solver at one time or another will use every research method known to science, from field observation to logical deduction. In reviewing alternative courses of action as well as their probable advantages and disadvantages, he will repeat his introspective routines. In his evaluation of payoffs, he will resort to investigations as varied as simple problem solving and inductive inference. In summary, the need for research is apparent at every turn, and the expert problem solver must be an imaginative researcher.

When we speak of the crucial role of judgment, most students listen with interest. When we speak of research, however, many students become wide-eyed and breathless. They seem to be scared half out of their wits. In a technological university like that in which the author happens to teach, business students are even, sometimes, resentful. If they wanted to do research, they complain, they would—perish the thought—have studied physics. What they seem to want is simple directions on how to make a million dollars without half trying.

In deference to these students, we should, perhaps, speak of research in terms of playing a game, but the word "game" is also taboo, for game suggests game theory and that is believed to be mathematics, or if it isn't that it's something worse.

So let's forget about games and math and research. Let's talk about Perry Mason or Mickey Spillane. The job of investigation required for problem solving is proper work for a private eye, and diligent imitation of Sherlock Holmes will accomplish the mission without any research. What we shall do is talk about detective methods for use in uncovering clues to not only "who done it" but also to "what he's gonna do next."

Actually, of course, the last two paragraphs are not meant literally for students who have read this far in this book. They have already had a considerable introduction to the need for and the usefulness of research. They have also, doubtless, a proper understanding of both research objectives and its general techniques. Let us, therefore, review the objectives and then explore research methods in slightly more formal but still highly abbreviated detail.

The objectives of research are: (1) identification of facts, (2) measurement of facts, (3) classification of facts, and (4) clarification of interrelationships between and among facts. The purposes, therefore, are to discover facts, in all of their ramifications, so that we may predict in any given situation what will happen next, or next after that. The aim of prediction is sufficient understanding to enable us to change its course by intervention, if we are dissatisfied with the march of events. Hence the object of research is understanding with the purpose of controlling the environment in which we live. With this objective in mind, let us look at some of the more common, useful, or promising ways in which problem-solving research is accomplished.

FIELD OBSERVATION

This is the primary and most fundamental research method of all. When the first man on earth looked at the world around him and took note of his physical environment, he was engaged in field observation research. Today all of us, whether we realize it or not, do this kind of research as a daily, accepted way of life. We get up in the morning and take note of the minutes we have at our disposal before we must leave for work. We look out the window at the sky, to confirm or reject our wardrobe selections of the night before. The hole in our sock raises questions about whether we really can put up with our wife for even one more day. The breakfast we eat reminds us that the old girl isn't so bad after all—if only she'd brush her hair in the morning. The car's hesitancy in starting tells us to take it around to the garage before the clunker quits altogether. And so it goes, moment by moment, hour by hour, and day by day. If the student can learn that he is already a research expert of considerable stature, even before he enters college, he will not, we hope, be so frightened every time the word research is mentioned.

The difference between everyday observation and professional field observation is not very great. As in life itself, there are a few dos and a few don'ts. Both are important. The primary "don't" of field observation research is this. When making the observation, do not record the meaning or the consequence of the observation. Record the observation itself. If one concentrates, during the fact gathering, on the interpretation of facts, he will encounter great difficulties, and he will commit gross errors. For example, if your boss scowls at you as you give him your merry, "Good morning," take note that he scowled and that you said, "Good morning." Take note too of any other factual circumstances of the incident such as the observation that he was, unexpectedly, walking on crutches or that he was in the act of tearing up the morning newspaper. Do not, however, record a nonfact such as your interpretation of the scowl as meaning that your days in his employment are numbered and rapidly running out.

The interpretation of facts is not observation. This is another form of research, and it should not be undertaken until after the observation phase is completed. If we record meaning rather than fact, we are jumping to conclusions on the basis of extremely limited data. If we destroy the observation by not recording it, we will have lost the datum.

The principal "do" of observational research is to try to perfect the observations of the observer. First, determine what it is that one wishes to observe. Second, prepare a systematic observation schedule. Third, determine, in advance, how observations will be recorded, especially in terms of their measurements. For example, in observing a machine operation, we might wish to count the number of pieces of work completed per hour, whether a particular event or condition was present, or how many pounds of waste were created. Fourth, prepare to describe the sequences of chain occurrences. Particularly, if the researcher plans to take his data to a statistician for analysis, it is frequently necessary to preserve the order in which data were generated. Since researchers do not always realize at the start of a project that a statistician will be required, data-order preservation is a good general rule to follow. Fifth, plan to record anything unexpected that may happen. And, finally, keep a persistent eye on the research objective.

Among the many aids to field observation research, two are especially useful. The first is the time-sampling technique, and the other is the standard procedure for training observers. In the time-sampling technique, we may wish to count the number of times an event occurs, but the length of time required, for reliable estimation, may extend over long periods of time. Therefore, instead of standing by and counting over, say, a one-year period, we make about 1,000 instantaneous observations, randomly distributed over a one-year period.[1] If the event was happening at the time of an observation, it counts as 1, and every time it is observed, another 1 is added. If, at the end of the year, it is found that the event was observed 230 times, we may conclude that the event is present in the situation *about* 23 percent of the time.

---

[1] The word "random" does not mean haphazard, but rather has a technical meaning in this use. In a random selection, observation periods are chosen on a pure chance basis in such a manner that every time has an equal chance with every other time of being selected. For random selection, we normally refer to prepared tables of random numbers (which can be found in almost all statistics texts), or we use such methods as "fish-bowl" drawings.

The training of observers is also a valuable route to excellence in field observation research. The trained observer, first of all, knows what he's looking for. In addition, however, he is expert in making the particular measurements required, whether they are measurements of quantity or quality. Therefore, before the actual observation is begun, the observer should pretest the observational procedure. For example, few people can judge distances in the field with any good degree of accuracy. Yet, as any field artillery officer will argue, a little practice will improve estimates quickly and noticeably. Moreover, training will, in addition to improving the measurements themselves, provide data for estimation of the degree of accuracy with which the measurements are made.

The student may try an experiment to test these statements. Let him draw a large number of lines of various lengths, one each to a sheet of paper. Let him estimate, in millimeters, the length of the first line and then measure it with a ruler. Let him proceed to estimate the next line, and the next and the next, until he has estimated about fifty, each time checking his estimate against ruler measurement. If he then plots his errors on a chart, he will discover his errors grow smaller and smaller with practice until he reaches an accuracy plateau beyond which little or no improvement is made. When the plateau is reached, the observer is ready to observe in the field, and he is also able to state to his reviewers the size of the standard error of his measurements.[2] In other words, the observer is able not only to state his observations but also the degree of confidence which should be placed in them.

In some observational research situations, it is possible and wise, while one is set up in the field, to make observations in groups of three. Then when data are being reviewed in the office, obvious errors of observation can be detected and eliminated. For example, if it is regularly apparent that observations which are made within a short interval of time are closely similar, and if it is clear that one of a group of three is widely divergent from the other two, one may as-

---

[2] The term "standard error" has specific statistical meaning. Readers who desire clarification may refer to any good statistics text such as Robert Ferber, *Statistical Techniques in Market Research*, McGraw-Hill Book Company, New York, 1949.

sume that the divergent observation was erroneously made or recorded, and it should be thrown out. This trick is not only a time-saver but also, sometimes, a project-saver, for it is seldom possible, in observational research studies to duplicate the original situation at a later date, even if one is willing to pay for the cost and sacrifice the time.[3]

Much, much more could be written about field observation research, but we do not have space to do it here.[4] Our purpose is simply to indicate its availability, its usefulness, and its general procedure. There is nothing about the procedure to frighten the novice, for he uses the method, unconsciously, all the time. Finally, of all the research methods available, field observation is probably the most useful and the most commonly employed in complex problem solving.

INTROSPECTION

Next to field observation research, the complex problem solver will rely most heavily on introspective research. Since, on a number of occasions in this book, we have already referred to this research method, we will pass over it very quickly here. Primarily, we wish to repeat that introspection is the method by which we retrieve from memory all of the facts of our past experience. It is, as the reader will observe, immediately related to judgment, and it occupies a position of first rank among research techniques.[5]

[3] This paragraph was contributed by Remington (*op. cit.*).

[4] An excellent discussion of field observation methods, particularly as they apply in anthropology and social psychology, is contained in Daniel Katz, "Field Studies," chapter 2 in Leon Festinger and Daniel Katz (eds.), *Research Methods in the Behavioral Sciences,* The Dryden Press, Inc., New York, 1953.

[5] Harold Koontz (*op. cit.*) gives a strong defense of introspective research techniques. He writes as follows: "In looking at management as an intellectually based art, the earliest meaningful writing came from such experienced practitioners as Fayal, Mooney, Alvin Brown, Sheldon, Barnard, and Urwick. Certainly not the most academic worshipper of empirical research can overlook the empiricism involved in distilling fundamentals from decades of experience by such discerning practitioners as these. Admittedly done without questionnaires, controlled interviews, or mathematics, observations by such men can hardly be accurately regarded as *a priori* or armchair."

The methods we have referred to as brainstorming and head-shrinking are introspective. Our mental trial-and-error processes are introspective. Our internalized role-playing sessions—when we try to imagine how people or things will react to our treatments—are introspective. In short, all of our skills and all of our knowledge, whether organized or subconscious, are retrieved through introspection. Hence no one should decry introspection. Of course, when time and means are available, we use other, more objective techniques, but in many complex problem-solving situations we should be glad we have so much at our disposal for instant use.

The primary objection to the introspective method is the danger of retrieving half-truths or downright falsehoods. What we know may have, in the first place, been distorted in its original perception. This comes from our propensity to perceive what we expect to see rather than what might actually be there. In the second place, there is danger that the reproduced version will be distorted by the unconscious motives of the researcher. Hence, rely on less subjective data whenever they are available, but in the absence of more objective facts, use whatever is at hand—but *use it with full appreciation of the inherent dangers.*

In connection with the introspective method of research, the reader will frequently have occasion to apply the knowledge he has obtained in his reading and in his formal course instruction in the various fields of business administration. Business problems are set in real-world environments, and one of the objectives of instruction in such courses as business law, economics, personnel management, labor relations, industrial management, marketing, and business finance is to give the student a knowledge of the facts in the real world of business. In addition, the diverse functional fields teach not only the institutional facts but also the experiences of men who have attempted to manipulate the facts of the real world for their own benefit or for the benefit of their firms, organizations, or the common welfare; that is, the functional disciplines have developed principles which are useful hypotheses for research and which are "best assumptions" for the solution of urgent problems when time for additional research is not available.

CONSULTATION WITH EXPERTS

Another common method of research in complex problem solving is the act of consulting with experts. When we refer to a man as an expert, however, we do not necessarily define him as a person who is at least 100 miles away from home. He may be, and frequently is, the man next door. One of the most commonly consulted experts in business is a person's own secretary. Therefore, in our definition, an expert is a person who possesses special skills or knowledge. He may be one of the Indians who does the work rather than the chief who is responsible for it.

In the business world, one of the sure marks of a proficient complex problem solver is the range of the man's contacts. In a large organization, he persistently tries to extend his acquaintanceships into every nook and cranny. He attempts to be on speaking terms with important executives, but he works equally hard to find at least one good friend, at the working level, in every department.

In his extraorganizational life, he labors to form acquaintances with other people in his own profession, but he persistently seeks others who are as different as possible from him in background, training, and outlook.[6] In addition, he takes special pains to establish and maintain rapport with as many centers of information as possible. When a man moves into a new community, he should call on such people as a physician, an attorney, the chief of police, the local librarian, the secretary of the chamber of commerce, a clergyman, a master craftsman in one or more of the principal trades, a labor leader, a school principal, the postmaster, a couple of politicians, and each of his close residential neighbors.

With a list of acquaintances such as these, an expert on virtually every subject that can arise is as close as the telephone. A few words of advice from a proper expert can save hours, days, or even years of digging out information by one's own efforts. For many complex problems, time is the thing we have the least of. Therefore, the wise problem solver will line up his panel of experts, and he will nurture it

[6] Churchman, Ackoff, and Arnoff (*op. cit.,* p. 628) emphasize that problem-solving teams should be interdisciplinary; that is, teams should be made up of individuals who are as dissimilar as possible in training and background.

diligently, well in advance of its use. Some of the experts may never be used, but we find from experience that this has never happened to us.

When a problem arises, consultation with an expert is like extending the range of oneself. If we have learned to exploit our own introspections, let us not neglect to utilize the introspections of others. Most short questions can be answered by experts over the telephone in a couple of seconds. For this kind of service even one's lawyer or physician will rarely charge. But if one expects to keep his experts willing, he should always offer to pay. Most offers to pay will be declined, but the gesture will be appreciated. If pay is refused, find some other way to show appreciation. One should insist on paying for long and complicated consultations.

Consultations should also be carefully planned. Even before calling for an appointment, one should know exactly what kind of information is needed, how the expert is to be approached, and how he is to be rewarded. Planning assures choice of the correct expert. It also saves his time and the time of the consultee. Most important, when the consultation is over the researcher will have the facts he went for.

In planning the interview, the first step is to outline the purpose and to list the facts which are needed. Unless one knows his expert fairly well, he should do a preapproach analysis to determine when and where the expert should be contacted, how he should be approached, what is needed to arouse his interest, and what is required to motivate his cooperation.[7] It is almost always best to make an appointment to permit the expert time to prepare and to assure a sufficient amount of time for the interview itself. If the expert has a secretary, it is best to make the appointment in person so that the researcher can get acquainted with her and so that he can inspect the layout. If the information which is sought is confidential or if it requires extensive preparation, the girl herself should be made an object of alliance. She may be the one who will do most, if not all, of the work, and she should be prepared. She may also be the one to decide whether the researcher can even get an appointment with the boss. In

[7] Charles F. Connell and Robert L. Kahn ("The Collection of Data by Interviews," chapter 8 in Festinger and Katz, *op. cit.*) have a first-rate discussion of planning the interview and motivating the respondent.

such cases, it is quite often best to give the secretary a full explanation of what the researcher will be discussing with the expert. If the researcher sells himself and his project to the secretary, she will be more likely to make the appointment and, in addition, she will go far to convince the expert he should cooperate. Moreover, she will prepare, or have prepared, the data required, and when the interviewer comes to keep his appointment, the interview will go smoothly, and the researcher will not have to come back for information at a later date. If the researcher neglects or antagonizes the secretary, she will have neither the opportunity nor the desire to offer her own cooperation, and if the work needed is substantial, the expert might hesitate to give her the unusual work load, and he might refuse the information to the researcher.

In conducting the information interview, the researcher always keeps in mind the need to motivate the subject. When the interviewee is a paid consultant, the fee itself is almost enough, but even in such cases, better results will follow from little attentions paid to the man's personal needs. Usually the best method of getting enthusiastic cooperation is by appealing to the person's desire to impress the interviewer with his knowledge, skill, and willingness to be of service. Therefore the interviewer should assume a role of modesty, and he should express appreciation for the consultant as a person by being properly impressed by his suggestions. Normally, this role is not difficult to assume, for it will not be faked. By now the researcher knows how difficult it is to achieve real skill, knowledge, and judgment.[8]

LITERARY REVIEW

This research method is no harder than those which we have already described, but it usually takes somewhat longer. Any graduate

[8] There is, of course, an extensive literature on the subject of interviewing, but one important sector of it is frequently overlooked by research people; namely, the literature on salesmanship. Although books on salesmanship are specifically oriented toward the "influence interview" rather than the "information interview," many of the techniques which are used are similar. In particular, the literature on salesmanship is very strong on the subjects of the preapproach and motivating the interviewee. One of the many good books on salesmanship is Frederic A. Russell and Frank H. Beach, *Salesmanship*, McGraw-Hill Book Company, New York, 1959.

of a good high school and any college graduate should have no difficulty, except the kind we all suffer—spelling, punctuation, and grammar—whenever we take up our pens to write.

It is true, however, that most library orientation courses are taught either by librarians or by teachers of English. Therefore business and engineering research students usually require special instruction on how to find the substantive materials they seek in the library. Hence the following remarks are intended as special suggestions for library research in business and engineering.

Before discussing technique, let us explore the types of information we shall be seeking. At the outset, we observe that the library is seldom useful for help in solving urgent problems. This does not mean that the librarian or his research assistant cannot be consulted as experts. It simply means that we rarely have time to do true library research when problems require solution within a few hours or days. Second, the library will never yield a complete and direct solution to any complex problem. All real, complex problems are unique, and although similarities among problems are frequent and obvious, the details will always deviate, and unique solutions will be required.

On the other hand, when sufficient time is available, and when the problem is sufficiently important, great assistance can be found in the store of facts which are warehoused in the library. It contains the recorded experience of our culture since the dawn of history, and there is hardly a subject on which the library is silent. The man who has learned to use the library has appropriated the experience of millions who have gone before him.

The problem-solving researcher uses the library in two ways. First, he uses it for quick reference to data he knows exist, and he knows exactly where to find them. A figure, for example, for current bank deposits in his area is known to be available in the latest issue of the *Federal Reserve Bulletin*. It is easy to get this fact. The researcher sends his secretary to the library, or he telephones the research librarian. Similarly, if he needs the name and address of a particular corporation executive, he calls the library and asks to have the information read over the phone out of *Standard and Poor's*. If the research librarian is a personal friend, the request will be promptly granted.

The second use of the library is much more extensive. The objective is to review all of the background information available in a particular area. For example, suppose the problem is concerned with site selection for a new plant. It would be miraculous, indeed, if the library had a book that would solve the problem. Nevertheless, the library has a huge store of literature on such subjects as (1) factors to be considered in manufacturing plant site location, (2) geographic distribution of raw materials and of population, (3) demographic characteristics of local populations, (4) weather and climate, (5) local laws—especially tax categories and tax rates, (6) local labor organization and labor skills, and so on through a number of other subjects which will be suggested as the library research progresses.

The literary review will be used to give the researcher a general understanding of the full scope of his problem. It will suggest considerations which will have to be taken into account but which might not otherwise have occurred to the researcher. It will alert the problem solver to traps and pitfalls which have spelled disaster to others. In short, a good review of the literature will assist the problem solver in his understanding of what the problem is, what facts are needed, what alternatives are available, and what values should be attached to diverse advantages and disadvantages of competing courses of action.

Before going to the library, the researcher should do a sufficient analysis of the problem to know, in considerable detail, what kind of information he will be seeking. Unless this is done, the researcher will lose much time, and he will probably collect many useless data but neglect other greatly needed information. When he arrives at the library, he should approach the subject of research by consulting the broadest reference first. He should then work progressively toward the minutiae. For example, suppose the subject is manufacturing plant location. The researcher should go first to the most general kind of reference and work from that toward the more detailed and specific. Start with a dictionary to be sure of a clear definition of the subject and of the meanings of the words contained in the statement of the subject. Go next to a good encyclopedia to get an immediate, brief overview of the entire field. Then go to a textbook, or several textbooks, and find the general treatments which are given by writers in the field of management. Finally, but still in the general investigation stage, look for specialized books which, nevertheless, give a comprehensive treatment of the subject. This part of the library research can be accomplished rather quickly. After it has been completed, the researcher should have an excellent understanding, at the very least, of the dimensions of the problem area. For some problem-solving situations, especially when a small amount of time is available for library research, this may be as far as the researcher can go. But even this much, rapidly accomplished, may save him from serious error.

In doing library research, students seem always to have great difficulty in taking notes. Some take no notes at all; others spend days just writing down everything their references contain. Both approaches are bad. We suggest the following: Take no notes during the reading of library references. Read rapidly. When a particular piece of material has been consumed, think about it. If no contribution to understanding has been made, forget it, and go on to the next piece. If the reference has something useful, summarize, from memory, the portion which impressed the reader. This is done, for each reference, on a separate 5 x 8 card. It is done rapidly, briefly, and always after the reading has been completed. At the tops of the cards, enter the reference data exactly as they would later appear in the bibliography or footnotes of a written article or report which might be written. If some particular statement in the reference was especially impressive, or if numerical data are involved, the note-taker may now return to the text, find the material, quote it, and list its specific location in the book or article. The important point in this note-taking system is this. Get down on paper what is needed, but don't make a big production of doing it.[9]

If time is still available after the preliminary library research is

---

[9] Many different note-taking systems have been tried and compared by the author, and the one described in the text works best for him. Many students have also used it, and they have uniformly reported excellent results. Nevertheless, readers should be informed that writers do not agree among themselves, and there seem to be almost as many systems as there are writers. Kegel and Stevens (Charles H. Kegel and Martin Stevens, *Communication,* Wadsworth Publishing Co., Inc., San Francisco, 1962, pp. 261–280), for example, recommend a system which is not only different from ours but in sharp contrast to it. Our only claim for ours is that it has been tried, on an experimental basis, and it has been compared with other systems. The trials, so far, have been made by only a few individuals, however, and it may turn out that note-taking techniques must be custom-built for each researcher. In any case, this seems to be an area where additional research is very much needed.

finished, the opportunity for extension of the research is readily at hand. In the preliminary investigation, the researcher has made a number of specific discoveries: (1) He has found, or he will know where to find, a number of references which have been cited in the sources he has already examined. These may now be followed up, and in that process, additional references will be found. By a kind of endless chain operation, sooner or later, virtually all of the pertinent literature can be uncovered. The only big gap which will appear will be in articles and books published since the date of the latest reference originally consulted. (2) The references which have been examined will frequently show that a relatively few previous researchers have made most of the contributions to the literature. The names of these men should be carefully noted, and their most recent works should be sought in the authors' names catalogue of the library. If time permits, the researcher may even write notes to one or more of these men, asking them, as recognized experts in the field, whether they have done more recent research which might not be in the local library, or which might have been missed, or which may not yet even be published. These experts might also be asked whether they know of any other important researchers who have recently entered the field and whether the experts have any knowledge of their works. By following these leads, new and important publications might be discovered. (3) The references which have been examined will also suggest additional subject headings under which information relating to the problem might be classified. By following these new subject classifications, additional recently published material is often discovered.

A final suggestion for library research is appropriate. Most libraries possess indexes of literature such as *Reader's Guide to Periodical Literature,* and such indexes are invaluable. Business and engineering literature researchers will find the following to be especially useful: *The Journal of Economic Abstracts, Applied Arts Index, Business Index, Engineering Index, Industrial Arts Index, Public Affairs Information Service Bulletin,* and *The New York Times Index.*

The note-taking procedure recommended for the more thorough kind of library research is not much different from that which is used in the rapid library research technique. The primary difference is this. When very extensive note-taking is contemplated, it is good practice to head each card with a tab to identify the subject area. When tabs are used, it is best to use separate cards for each subject area—even when the reference source is the same. This practice will permit later sorting of the cards for convenience in problem solving, report writing, and card filing. Nevertheless, even when extensive library research is contemplated, one should content himself with brief notes. If need arises, when the research report is being written, one can always go back for additional notes. For the time being, however, don't let the research bog down in note-taking. Do not, on the other hand, abandon note-taking. Don't avoid the devil by backing up into the deep blue sea.

SECONDARY DATA ANALYSIS

The kind of data we have in mind in the present section may often be found in libraries, but it is frequently also found elsewhere. Moreover, in contrast to the materials we considered under the heading of literary review, the data we contemplate in this discussion are almost always quantitative.[10]

The most generally consulted secondary data are produced within the business organization by data-collecting departments such as the accounting department, the production department, the research department, the sales department, or the personnel department. If the available data, filed everywhere in large organizations, were all brought together in one place, they would produce a fantastic heap. Usually these data were collected for specific purposes for which they have already been used. However, the same data almost always contain information which will also benefit subsequent prob-

[10] There are a number of good discussions of secondary data analysis. Luck, Wales, and Taylor (David J. Luck, Hugh G. Wales, and Donald A. Taylor, *Marketing Research,* 2d ed., Prentice-Hall, Inc., Englewood Cliffs, N.J., 1961, pp. 95–116) have an excellent discussion of sources and uses of secondary data, especially as applied to the field of marketing. Angell and Freedman (Robert C. Angell and Ronald Freedman, "The Use of Documents, Records, Census Materials, and Indices," chapter 7 in Festinger and Katz, *op. cit.*) have a first-rate discussion of the uses of secondary data. Coman (E. T. Coman, *Sources of Business Information,* Prentice-Hall, Inc., Englewood Cliffs, N.J., 1949) furnishes an excellent listing of specialized sources of business information.

lem-solving efforts. In other words, the same data, analyzed from a point of view which is different from that originally intended, may frequently yield important new information. Analyses performed on such data are called secondary data analyses because the data were collected by someone other than the present researcher. A knowledge of the kinds of secondary data which might be available within the organization will greatly assist the problem solver, for it is not at all unusual for researchers to spend large sums of money and great amounts of time in gathering data already available elsewhere in the firm. The way for the problem solver to learn about the existence of such data is to study the whole operation of the company, not merely the little segment of it in which the researcher happens to work. Both the study of overall company operations and the intelligence of secondary data files are greatly facilitated by the researcher's efforts to extend his personal contacts throughout the organization.[11]

The second main source of secondary data is that generated outside the firm. The police department, the fire department, the local power company, the chamber of commerce, the welfare department, the city clerk's office, the building permit office, the office of the superintendent of schools, the state tax collection agency, the motor vehicle department, and hundreds of other public and private agencies have on hand huge quantities of data which may be available for study. Again, the wider the range of one's personal contacts, the greater the likelihood he will know of the existence of secondary data, and the better the chances will be that he will be permitted to use them.

A third source of important secondary data is the government documents section of the library.[12] Most large public libraries and all land-grant college libraries are depositories of government publications. Here the researcher will find all of the regular and most of the special publications of all of the departments and bureaus of the Federal government. The data are voluminous. Some of the publica-

---

[11] Jack Russell ("A System of Sales Analysis Using Internal Company Records," *Journal of Marketing,* April, 1950, p. 676) lists sources of data which can be found within most business organizations.

[12] A description of the statistical series of the Federal government is contained in P. M. Hauser and W. R. Leonard, *Government Statistics for Business Use,* John Wiley & Sons, Inc., New York, 1946.

tions are straight articles on subjects of government interest, but a great many contain page after page of business, economic, industrial, and social statistics which are regularly collected by agencies such as the Bureau of the Census, the Department of Agriculture, the Department of Labor, and scores of others. For the most part, the data are published in raw form, and the citizen-interpreter is required to do his own analyses. The importance of the secondary data collected by the government is the saving of the tremendous cost which would be incurred by any private person or firm in duplicating them. All people who are engaged in problem solving in the areas of business and industry must become acquainted with the government publications depositories in their areas, for to neglect these sources of data is to overlook one of the greatest boons to modern business management.[13]

The first problem in doing secondary data analysis research is that of knowing of the existence of the data. All researchers should be generally familiar with the three principal sources we have described. It is not possible, however, for any one person to be fully aware of the existence of all available secondary data. The best substitute for this unavoidable ignorance is acquaintance and friendly relations with the people who are custodians of the data. Assuming such acquaintance and friendly relations, the researcher who doesn't know but who suspects certain data might be available consults the custodian most likely to have it. The researcher simply asks whether any data of the kind he needs are available. If they are, he gets permission to use them.

The researcher who follows the recommended procedures may very often get the information he needs by direct reference. Frequently, however, it will be necessary to analyze the data contained in a study or a number of different studies from his special, present point of view. These analyses may be relatively straightforward, or they may be extremely complicated. In straightforward analyses, the raw data may be simply converted into percents or index numbers, or the numerical data may be plotted on a chart. Perhaps simple visual

---

[13] In addition to regularly published data, the U.S. Department of Commerce makes available to private researchers, on a cost basis, some unpublished data which can be extracted from its records. Data can often be provided on computor-compatible tapes or cards which make reading out of books or from tables unnecessary. (Remington, op. cit.)

comparisons of the data in one series will be made with the data in another. Or the changes within a single series may be plotted over some time interval. In more complicated analyses, the researcher will wish to apply more sophisticated tools of statistical analysis. He may do studies involving correlation, variance analysis, factor analysis, or estimates of reliability and validity of predictions.

Whether the analysis is simple or complicated, the most important key to successful use of secondary data analysis is the knowledge of data existence. Therefore, whenever a researcher is about to propose, either to himself or to anyone else, the collection of any large amount of primary data, he is advised to think twice, or more times, about whether the data might already be available, and, if so, who is most likely to have them. Speed and economy both dictate against going off half-cocked on primary data collection.

HISTORICAL RESEARCH

A definition of historical research is extremely difficult. When one tries to differentiate the historical method from all other research techniques, huge areas of overlap appear, and discrimination becomes impossible. For example, the research of a particular sequence of past events from library sources might properly be called literary review. If the sources lie outside the library, for instance, in newspaper files, diaries, government records, personal letters, bills of sale, or other commercial instruments, the methodological procedures are different from those employed in library research. These, then, might be called historical methods. If the method is to question people who were participants in the action, the method might be designated survey research or motivation research—about which more later. If the method is to record one's own observations, the technique may be called field observation. If the aim is to reanalyze or reinterpret the data which others have collected, the method might be theoretical—about which, also, more later. Hence, in our present classification of research methods, historical research is regarded more as a distinct research approach than as a separate research method. In our discussion, therefore, historical research will imply the gathering together of bits or chunks of either primary or secondary data, either quantitative or qualitative, which have never been collected in any organized way or published as a collection before. Moreover, the historical research classification probably *requires* the use of two or more different methods or types of source data. For example, if only interviews with participants in events are used, the method would be classified as survey or motivation research, and not historical research. Therefore the greater the variety of sources or of investigation procedures, the more strongly the approach qualifies as historical. Finally, although historical research is normally a study of events in the past and frequently a review of events through a considerable period of time, we do not require the placement of a time period or time interval. Hence we recognize research of current events, if the other defining characteristics are present, as historical.

Thus the historical research approach is a broadly based investigation of either past or present events. It seeks either primary or secondary data, and usually both. It utilizes any available sources of information, from the library to the personal interview. It is painstaking and exhaustive. Its aim is to collect data from widely disbursed, hard to find, and difficult to utilize sources, and to make these data available for analysis or interpretation by the fact finder himself or by others.

The general purposes of historical research are two: The first is to develop understanding and appreciation of why the world, as we view it today, is as it is, rather than some other way. An understanding of how society became what it is makes us more secure in our daily occupations. We know not only where we are but also why. We complain less about apparent incongruities and less about the actions of others, particularly our social, business, and political leaders. We begin to understand that most of their actions are forced on them by the sweep of events which have their roots in the past. We are also warned against trying too desperately to reshape the world in conformity with an ideal which would, in view of the past, be impossible to attain.

The second purpose of historical research is to learn from the past what may be inevitable in the future. Such an understanding allows us, as individuals and as business executives, not only to be effective in the present but also to remain effective as present events condition the future. Finally, an understanding of the past tells us both what is likely to occur in the future and what might be possible in terms of our personal efforts. The business problem solver can learn much from the political problem solver who proclaims, "Politics is the art of accomplishing the possible."

From all of these remarks about historical research, it is apparent that the approach is unsuitable for use in most current problem-solving situations. Nevertheless, an understanding of the approach and its *constant* use are eminently important to the growth of the problem solver himself. He should always be interested in the historical researches of others, and he should, in the areas of his primary interests, be doing considerably more than dabbling himself. While the historical approach is usually unsuitable for solving current problems, its use for building background knowledge that will be valuable for solving future problems is incontestable. Finally, history is a vast reservoir of ideas which are useful hypotheses for other kinds of research. In addition, historical research conclusions may be the "best assumptions" to use in solving immediate problems when time or money for other kinds of research is unavailable.

CASE STUDY

The case study approach is very similar to the historical. The major difference is that historical research concerns itself with a broader subject matter. In case study research, the investigator usually concerns himself with events in the life of a single person or of a single firm. More often, in case study, the researcher investigates the details of a single event or a closely related group of events in the life of a single person or firm. In all other aspects, case study is like historical research. Most especially, the case study investigator utilizes all available source data.

While historical research is rarely used for solving immediate complex problems, case study methods are frequently utilized. When the analyst encounters a problem, he will often know that a similar problem has been recently faced by some other person or firm. In such an event, the analyst would be greatly assisted if he knew how the other person or company analyzed the situation and what decision was made. He would, moreover, be mightily interested to know how the action taken worked out.

Successful use of the case method, for complex problem solving, depends on two primary factors. First, the analyst must know who has faced and acted on a problem similar to the one now confronting him. Second, he must establish contact with the person who can give him the facts.

In many ways, the case study approach is like the method of consultation with experts. Because his range of personal acquaintances is broad, the analyst knows who to contact. The analyst also knows how to make the necessary contacts because he has studied the techniques of the preapproach and the procedures for motivating his subjects. In some instances, the person who analyzed the original problem will have a full set of notes on the problem-solving process. He may even have a full package in his tickler file. If this most fortunate state of affairs should exist, the case study will, for the most part, be ready-made, and the benefits will be immediately available to the present analyst.

More likely, the analyst will find that the decision was reached by the other person or firm either in an executive session or by a single executive after he had interviewed a number of other people, in and out of his own organization. If a single executive was responsible for the decision, he may have notes of his own, or he may have memoranda which he received from others. In such a case, the study may be reasonably well accomplished by the following steps: (1) Interview the executive who made the decision to discover what the decision was, what alternatives were considered, and what major results were predicted. (2) Ask to inspect any notes the decision maker may have, whether they are his own or whether they were prepared by someone else. (3) Ask for background information on how the problem arose and why it came to be recognized as a problem. (4) Interview any and all other people who advised the decision maker during the problem-solving analysis. (5) Gather facts and figures, whenever convenient and possible, from whatever sources are available. (6) Interview all people who are in a position to know and judge the results of the actions taken. (7) Interview all people who may have information on the explicit steps which were taken to implement the decision. (8) Write up the problem, as closely as possible, in the report form recommended in Chapter 12, and make this report a major portion of the statement of facts in the problem being analyzed by the present problem solver.

If the case study firm reached its decision in an executive conference, the chances of availability of memoranda concerning the problem and its solution are somewhat less. If a good set of minutes of that conference is available, however, there will be a discussion of the problem itself, a review of the facts, a consideration of alternative courses of action, a weighing of advantages and disadvantages, and a resolution of the decision. If the problem had been studied by a subcommittee prior to the conference, there might be, somewhere, a written subcommittee report, or at least some notes from which the subcommittee chairman made his report.

All too often, however, in business even today, both major and minor decisions are made horseback style. Very little formal analysis may have been accomplished, and action may have been taken on a "by-guess-and-by-gosh" basis. In such cases, the analyst will, nevertheless, learn a great deal from simply knowing what action was taken and what the results of the action were. The person who made the decision may also be willing to state what he would do if he had a chance to do the whole thing again.

In any event, the case study approach to research for solving current problems holds great promise for those who learn how to exploit it. Unfortunately, it is probably not being used to its fullest advantage in the business world today.[14]

SURVEY RESEARCH

Survey research involves the collection of masses of data. Strictly speaking, it does not imply the analysis of the data after they are collected, but it does require the classification and tabulation of the data into a form which is suitable for analysis. A major require-

[14] The remarks in this section on case study research are geared to the solution of current problems. Case study research, however, has much broader implications, especially in areas of basic research, and we do not mean to imply that the approach cannot be used unless someone else has already studied a similar problem. Obviously, the man who studied the original problem did a case study. Moreover, the reader should observe that the problem-solving model presented in this book is a case study approach. In their study of operations research, Churchman, Ackoff, and Arnoff (*op. cit.*, p. 592) note that case study approaches are especially useful for uncovering "dynamic interactions" which are difficult to write into mathematical problem-solving models.

ment is that the data collected be objective. Most commonly, survey research data are frequency-of-occurrence of categories or classes of variables being surveyed. For example, the decennial census of population of the United States is a survey. Interviewers attempt to count every individual who resides in the country and to record, for each of them, a very large number of individual characteristics such as age, sex, education, national origin, race, and so on. All of the data are simple counts as, for example, the number of males and the number of females. It is for this reason that many people refer to the census as the decennial enumeration.

The survey is, perhaps, the most commonly used, *formal* research method today. Everyone is so familar with it that our description will be brief. What is more urgently needed is a warning that most of the currently produced survey research is badly performed and is, therefore, either unreliable or invalid, or both. Hence the major portion of the small amount of space we have available for the treatment of survey research in this book will be devoted to discussions of the pitfalls of the method.

The steps in survey research may be outlined as follows:

1. Determine the research objective. The objective dictates not only the method of research but also the details of its execution. In the survey research approach, usually at the very beginning, one should prepare mock-up tables of the data he expects to collect. (A mock-up is a dummy showing the title of the table and the descriptive stubs or column headings within the table. The mock-up shows everything which will be contained within the final table except the numerical data themselves.) A major purpose of the mock-up is to assure that the entire research effort will remain constantly oriented toward accomplishment of the final objective. In addition, the mock-up tables go far to suggest the kind of analysis which will be performed. Prospective analyses, in turn, guide the research plan toward the collection of data in a form which can be subjected to appropriate statistical treatment.

2. Review the objective to assure that survey research is the best method to apply. At least half of the survey research studies which are made could be accomplished better by some other method. This is probably due to lack of knowledge, on the part of researchers, of other available techniques, and lack of appreciation of the difficul-

ties of the survey method. For some reason which is difficult to fathom, everyone feels he is competent to do survey research, but very few people regard themselves as competent to do other types, such as experimental research. Yet the latter are usually easier than the former. In any case, before proceeding with survey research, review the research objective and consider the possibility of using each of the other research techniques.

3. Delineate the universe or the population to be surveyed. Failure to accomplish this will almost always result in bad sampling or bad census-taking and, in consequence, it will lead to error in the drawing of conclusions beyond those justified by the data. For example, if one wants to draw conclusions which apply to all college graduates, the universe to be explored is not just those who work in New York City or just those who have graduated from Columbia University. The population is all college graduates, wherever they live or work and whatever their status.

4. If a sample survey (a survey based on a study of a part of the total universe) is to be executed, determine whether the sample will be a simple random sample or whether it will be a stratified sample, a quota sample, an area sample, or some other kind of sample.[15] In general, a *simple random sample* is the safest kind for the novice to use, but it has two major disadvantages. First, it usually requires a larger sample than would be necessary with some other sampling procedures. Second, it usually requires a complete list of all individuals in the population. The *stratified random sample* usually saves on the sample size, but it requires a little extra presurvey planning and a little extra postsurvey analysis. It also requires a complete list of all individuals in the population. Usually, however, the disadvantages are more than made up for by the sample size reduction. Broadly speaking, a stratified sample divides the heterogeneous universe into rela-

---

[15] The theory and practice of sampling are highly technical subjects, and unless the researcher has had considerable training in statistics, he should always check his sampling procedure with a qualified statistician before he executes his research. A statistician can be extremely helpful before the data are collected, but unless correct procedures have been followed in data collecting, the best statistician is usually helpless after the data are in. There are many excellent books on sampling. The author is especially fond of Ferber (*op. cit.*). For a short discussion, see Leslie Kish, "Selection of the Sample," chapter 5 in Festinger and Katz, *op. cit.*

tively homogeneous subuniverses, and each of the subpopulations is separately, randomly sampled. In drawing a stratified sample of households for a given geographic location, for example, if we draw a simple random sample, and if we plan to interview every individual living at the sample addresses, we would run the risk of selecting a large multiple dwelling (a college dormitory, for instance). If this happened, our sample would probably be dominated by college students. On the other hand, of course, if we did not happen to draw the dormitory, the sample would probably not have enough students. Therefore, instead of drawing a simple random sample, one should use a stratified sample in which the large multiple dwellings are listed and sampled separately.[16] After the data are collected, the two subsamples are combined, in proper proportions, and analyzed. The *quota sample* has the advantage of not requiring a list of individuals in the universe. With this system, the interviewer is instructed to locate and interview a given number of people in each of several categories. For example, the interviewer might be told to interview some given number of Negroes, Italians, Irish, and so on. In addition, he might be told to have, in each of the previous categories, so many in each of five different family income groups. Finally, he might be instructed to have, in each of the two previous classes, half male and half female. If this sounds complicated, it is. Moreover, our illustration is not complicated enough to be a realistic statement of some quota sample instructions to interviewers. In addition, the difficulties with quota samples transcend the practical problems of interviewers. The greatest criticism of the quota sample is its purposive rather than its random procedure. Inasmuch as interviewers have enough trouble filling their quotas without worrying about random selection of their subjects, the individuals finally included in the survey will probably represent those who are easiest to find. The hard-to-find individuals, therefore, do not have an equal chance of being selected, and if these are uniformly different from others (as they usually are), a bias error will be introduced, and no amount of refined statistical analysis will ever discover it, to say nothing of eliminating it. Therefore, for survey

---

[16] A carefully executed, stratified sample is illustrated in the author's St. Paul labor market survey. (Kenneth E. Schnelle, *Manpower Resources in a Tight Labor Market,* Minnesota State Employment and Security Division, St. Paul, 1952.)

research purposes, we do not recommend quota sampling. *Area samples* are quite another matter. Area sampling is often the best technique to employ to overcome a common practical difficulty; namely, the absence of a list of individuals in the universe. In a rural area, or in a small city, for example, a directory of residential addresses will usually not be available. Tax rolls give lists of taxable property, but local practices are not uniform, and properties may be grouped together. Telephone lists omit residents who have no phones or unlisted numbers. Power company lists cannot be used for rural areas where many residents have no electricity or where many provide their own. Even in cities where a directory is available, the list may be so out of date as to require a major project to revise it. Hence, in all such cases, area sampling may be used. In one study, an area sample was used for a large, sparsely settled, rural location.[17] A map of the area was obtained, and a 1-square-mile grid was overlaid. (For rural areas, the 1-square-mile grid is best because the grid can be placed to coincide with county roads.) A random sample of these squares was drawn by the "fish-bowl" technique, and interviewers were sent to interview *all* residents within the squares which had been drawn for the sample. For special purposes and under special circumstances, *special sampling methods* are often used. In any event, however, the sampling problem is one of the most difficult in the survey procedure, and it deserves extremely careful consideration. When the researcher is in doubt, it also deserves checking by a qualified statistician. Even fully qualified survey researchers make a practice of having other qualified colleagues check their proposed procedures.

5. If a sample survey is contemplated, determine the sample size. This is another difficult problem and, again, a qualified statistician can be very helpful. Even the procedures for estimating sample size are different for different purposes. In many survey research studies, however, the primary objective is to estimate a statistic with some predetermined level of precision and confidence.[18] In such cases, the

---

[17] Daniel J. Meddleton, Philip S. McVittie, and Alan R. Patterson, *A Survey of Chronic Illness in the Copper Country*, Department of Business and Engineering Administration, Michigan Technological University, Houghton, 1964 (unpublished, but available in Xerox at cost).

[18] A statistic is an estimate of a parameter, and a parameter is the true value of a characteristic of the universe. For example, if we measure body

sample size depends on three things: (*a*) the variability, in the population, of the major statistic to be determined, (*b*) the degree of precision we desire in the statistic (the difference between the statistic and the parameter), and (*c*) the degree of confidence we demand in the precision of the statistic. The greater the variability of the characteristic in the population, the greater the degree of desired precision, and the higher the required level of confidence, *ceteris paribus,* the larger the sample must be. With respect to population variability, it is obvious that if individuals were all alike a sample of one is all we would need. If, however, as we usually find, the population is heterogeneous, a larger sample will be required. Similarly, if only a rough estimate of the parameter is needed, or if we do not have to bet high stakes on the degree of precision, the sample may be quite small, but if the conditions of precision and/or confidence are reversed, the sample must be quite large.[19] If the variability within the population is not known from previous research, it may be estimated from data which will become available from the pilot study which will be executed to pretest the survey schedule. This will be discussed presently.

6. Prepare the survey schedule. In the preparation, be sure to

---

weight of all members of a college class, if we add the weights, and if we divide the total by the number of students in the class, we will have a true measure of average body weight, and this will be a parameter of the population. If, however, we draw a sample of 100 students, measure their body weights, add, and divide by 100, we will have a statistic which is an estimate of the true average weight.

[19] John Neter and William Wasserman (*Fundamental Statistics*, Allyn and Bacon, Inc., Boston, 1961, p. 400) suggest use of the following formula for determining sample size for the achievement of some predetermined level of precision and confidence of a population mean:

$$n = (z\sigma/P)^2$$

where $n =$ the sample size we are trying to determine,
   $z =$ the number of standard errors, in a probability distribution, corresponding to the desired level of confidence one requires in the precision of the survey statistic,
   $\sigma =$ the standard deviation of the characteristic in the population, and
   $P =$ the maximum difference which can be tolerated between the survey statistic and the parameter in the population.

include provisions for obtaining all of the information which will be needed in the proposed analysis, and at the same time, strongly resist the temptation to gather additional information which will not be required. The best method to follow, in meeting these needs, is to check the survey schedule backward from the mock-ups to be certain that all of the data demanded by the tabulations will be gathered by the survey. If this step is omitted, and if some of the required data are not collected in the survey, the value of the project may be greatly diminished, for it may be impossible to go back to the field for the additional information. The survey schedule should also be checked forward to the mock-up tables to be sure that no information is collected which will not be used. As a general rule, one should remember that the shorter the survey schedule, the better, and all unnecessary questions should be eliminated. In the actual preparation of questions, use simple language, and ask one question at a time. Make questions clear, concise, and unambiguous. Use common words, but use them precisely, and word questions in such a way that one and only one meaning can be inferred. Whenever possible, avoid open-end questions, for these will be difficult to code and to tabulate in the analysis stage of the research. Finally, avoid the "check-mark" system of recording answers, especially when interviewers are used, for it is very easy to check the wrong box, but it is difficult to write yes, when the answer is no.

7. Pretest the survey schedule, on a real sample, in a pilot study. The object is to be sure that the survey schedule items are understood by respondents. This step is often the most crucial of all, for if questions are not understood, or if they are incorrectly recorded, the whole survey goes down the drain. Normally, the research project director does the pretesting, for he alone, in the early stages of the research, knows what he is trying to accomplish. This step is never omitted for, in spite of all the experience one may possess in making up survey schedules, we have never heard of a case in which no changes were made in the schedule during the pretest.

8. Prepare the plan for tabulating the survey data. This involves the plan for translating entries on the survey forms into numbers in the final tables which were originally prepared in mock-up form. In most cases, the plan involves a coding of survey schedule data to per-

mit card-punching for tabulation and analysis by mass data processing equipment.[20]

9. Train the interviewers. This normally requires several hours of classroom instruction, a number of role-playing sessions in which interviewers try their skills on each other, and a few hours in the field with a final question-and-answer period in the classroom. The object is to assure understanding on the part of the interviewers and to anticipate difficulties which might arise. The author always requires interviewers to pass a written test before he turns them loose.

10. Determine, in advance of the data collection, the percent of nonrespondents which will be tolerated. Most amateur researchers are satisfied with low percents of response, or they substitute newly selected individuals to replace some of those selected in the original sample. These are both bad practices. Most professional researchers, under most circumstances, require close to 100 percent returns from originally selected sample members before they will dare to analyze or draw conclusions.[21]

11. Conduct the survey. During this phase of the operation, special attention must be given to the problem of survey members who cannot be found or who refuse to cooperate. Often the project director himself must do the call-backs. In any case, we cannot place too much emphasis on the need for getting as high a rate of response as possible. In the author's St. Paul study, 1,056 households were selected in the original sample. Of these, 80 percent were contacted during regular business hours. Call-back experience was better on weekends than nights. At the conclusion of the survey, *all* of the not-at-homes had been found, and only 11 (1.04 percent) refusals were encountered. One substitution, for a lost survey schedule, and two substitutions, for addresses which could not be located, were made.

[20] All researchers today should be familiar with mass data processing equipment. An excellent, nontechnical discussion is available in Elias N. Awad, *Business Data Processing,* Prentice-Hall, Inc., Englewood Cliffs, N.J., 1965.

[21] A. L. Finkner (Methods of Sampling for Estimating Commercial Peach Production in North Carolina," *North Carolina Agricultural Station Technical Bulletin 91,* Raleigh, 1950) describes a perfectly delightful illustration of the shocking results which can follow from a researcher's failure to insist on a very high percent of response from originally selected survey members.

In sum, 98.67 percent of the originally selected survey members were contacted and interviewed.

12. Edit the schedules to assure clarity and completeness. If interviewers are used, the editing should be done as the schedules come in, for errors must be corrected before the interviewers are discharged.

13. Code the survey schedules and punch the cards. Girls are best for coding. They are more patient and more careful. In card-punching, it is best to have two decks prepared by two different key-punch operators. This is quicker than visual checking. After the two decks are punched, they may be machine-inspected, and nonidentical pairs will be rejected. These will then be visually inspected and corrected. In all machine processing, it is good practice to prepare two decks of cards before they are put into the machines, for cards frequently become worn during the machine processing. When this happens, the deck is machine-duplicated at low cost, and the old deck is discarded. One good deck is usually kept, for insurance purposes, in a separate building.

14. Prepare instructions to machine operators for tabulating the data. If required, prepare instructions for computor operators to analyze the data.

15. This ends the list of steps for the accomplishment of survey research.[22]

Survey research has broad application to complex problem solving, especially when important decisions are being made and when enough time is available for application of the method. In large organizations, employee attitude, interest, and performance surveys are useful and common. Many forms of market and marketing research depend on consumer, marketing channel, transportation, and communications media surveys. Public opinion, supplier, and competitor surveys are valuable. There seems to be no end to the applications of survey methods to business and industrial fact-finding. Hence the researcher who knows or who is willing to learn the survey technique

[22] A top-notch discussion of survey research, in nontechnical language, is to be found in A. Angus Campbell and George Katona, "The Survey Sample: A Technique for Social Science Research," chapter 1 in Festinger and Katz, op. cit.

has a most valuable fact-finding method at his disposal, and he will use it frequently and to great advantage. For people who do not have sufficient training to use the survey research method, there are many good survey research consultants and survey research firms which, for a fee, will do creditable and professional jobs. When they are needed, they will almost always pay their way in terms of the value of the services rendered. Some caution, however, is needed for, unfortunately, some of the self-styled experts are not professionally qualified.

MOTIVATION RESEARCH

As the name implies, motivation research is concerned with the investigation of people's inner drives. Motivation researchers are dissatisfied with attitude, interest, and preference surveys. They argue that survey responses are too superficial. On the one hand, the motivation researcher argues, people usually respond with the first thing that comes into their minds. On the other hand, they often do not know their own true feelings, and, therefore, it is quite impossible to communicate them to others. Finally, people may be both intelligent and deliberate but prefer not to state their actual feelings.

Motivation researchers, therefore, tend to ridicule survey researchers by arguing in some such fashion as this. It doesn't make any difference how many thousands of wrong answers one compiles. The results will still be wrong. Large-scale sampling, as we have already noted, does not eliminate bias error. What is needed, say motivation researchers, is not bigger samples, superficially surveyed, but intensively studied, and if necessary, smaller samples. Of course, motivation researchers like samples as large as they or the people who are paying them can afford, but the cost of a single motivation research interview may run to forty or fifty times the cost of a survey research interview.

The aim of the motivation research interview is to discover the fundamental, the basic, the underlying, and the real mainsprings of people's emotions and behaviors. It is not sufficient to ask people, for example, whether they like their jobs. Such a question, asked in a survey research interview, yields an answer, but there is considerable doubt concerning the meaning of the answer. If we are asked, for instance, how we like our work, our answer depends on whether we had a good night's sleep last night, the present state of our digestion, the speed with which we wrote the last section of our book, the temperature of the room in which we are working, and probably a thousand other things which may be closely or remotely related to our job. Then again, we may know very well how we like our job, for we may have recently reviewed it in connection with our consideration of another offer we have received for our services. But perhaps, even though we know we enjoy our work and are well satisfied with our employer, we may not wish to appear smug toward the interviewer who may obviously hate his work. Or we may suspect the interviewer is a spy, and we'd hate to give our boss the idea we're so well satisfied that nothing could make us leave. In short, when a subject is asked to give a simple answer to a complicated and difficult question, he may respond clearly enough, but the meaning of the response may be completely obscure. The truth may be the exact opposite of the response. Under any such circumstances, the survey result is useless, and it might be dangerous.

The motivation researcher would approach the question in an entirely different way. He might start by saying he wants to talk to the subject about his work. He might continue by asking the man exactly what is involved in it. How does he do it? What are the problems? And, pursuing this line, the interviewer asks fewer and fewer questions. He leads the subject to do most of the talking. He tries, by gentle nudging, to keep the subject close to the discussion of his work, but he permits considerable latitude and digression. The researcher becomes an interested and appreciative listener. His job is to keep the subject talking.

It is a characteristic of human nature, at least in our culture, that if people are permitted to talk about themselves, they will do so interminably. If the subject gets wound up, and if the listener is enthusiastic, it is simply astonishing what people will say about themselves, their hopes, and their despairs. People, talking about themselves in a permissive atmosphere with an obviously approving listener, fall into almost hypnotic states, and they will tell things that they have not even been fully aware of. A little push here and a gentle nudge there, to keep the reverie somewhat on the matter of job satisfaction, will uncover the deepest feelings the subject has about the job and all of the things associated with it.

The motivation research interview is a depth interview. It takes time, and it takes a skilled interviewer. For ordinary motivation research, a sensitive person can train himself to do a competent job. The keys to success are, first, to make the subject do most of the talking and, second, to note what the respondent says rather than what he may mean. The meaning should be left until after the interview data, in their entirety, are available for coordinate judgment.[23]

Professional motivation research is not very different, in procedure, from that which we have described. The interviewer, however, is a trained clinical psychologist, not just a trained psychologist. The professional is more expert at listening and more skilled in guiding the interview into desired channels. The professional, moreover, can risk making interpretations of what is said during the interview, and he can take immediate advantage of his interpretations in his further guidings and probings. The professional will dig deeper, and his judgments will be very, very much more valid.

The professional has two primary advantages over the skilled amateur. The first is his objectivity. The amateur interprets what he hears through his own frames of reference; that is, the personality, the likes, the dislikes, the hopes, and the fears of the amateur get between him and his subject. His own personality conditions and distorts what he hears. The professional has, in his training, been cleansed of his subconscious distorters, and his fidelity of perception is very high. Second, the professional has far more extensive and intensive experience in personality diagnosis, and his estimates of personality characteristics in others, both normal and abnormal, are truer and clearer.

It would be improper to suggest that an amateur can ever achieve results, in true motivation research, comparable with those which reflect simple professional competence in an expert. Nevertheless, a skilled layman, with care and persistence, can, when the research situation demands, avoid the foolishness of survey methods by

[23] Luck, Wales, and Taylor (*op. cit.,* pp. 393–408) have a good discussion of motivation research and an excellent appraisal of its objectives and techniques. A good illustration of motivation research technique is found in Orvis F. Collins and David G. Moore, with Darab Unwalla, "The Enterprising Man and the Business Executive," *Business Topics,* Winter, 1964, Michigan State University, East Lansing, pp. 19–34.

utilizing careful interview techniques.[24] When problems assume great importance or where deep personality probing is indicated, the expert's fee will prove to be a bargain.

EXPERIMENTAL RESEARCH

In its essentials, the experimental method is difficult neither to understand nor to use.[25] It requires, first of all, a simple idea on the part of the researcher that some particular event is, or may be, the cause of some other event. The experiment is a physical test to determine whether the idea is true. For example, let's assume, in an ancient experiment, a caveman conceived the idea that the cause of kittens is some kind of relationship between a male cat and a female cat. He might, then, have taken a pair and penned them separately and another pair and penned them together. He would, in due course, have noted that the female penned with the male had kittens, while the female penned separately did not. This would qualify as a simple but true experiment.

Essentially, therefore, the simple experimental method requires comparison of two situations, identical in all respects, save one. The one difference is the suspected cause of the event under investigation. Therefore, when we talk about the simple experimental method, we refer to the comparison of the experimental with the control situation. If everything is the same in both, except for the variable suspected to be the cause of the event under study, and if the event occurs in the experimental condition but not in the control condition, we have presumptive evidence that the experimental treatment is the cause of the effect. In the case of our illustration, the male cat is the cause of kittens in the female.

The single experiment, however, is only meager evidence. It is possible that the female penned with the male will not become preg-

[24] Stagner (*op. cit.*) began his study of top-level managerial disagreements with a survey research plan, but soon after he got into the investigation, he changed it to a motivation research procedure because the former proved to be unsuitable and foolish.

[25] Cf. Leon Festinger, "Laboratory Experiments," chapter 4 in Festinger and Katz, *op. cit.* This is a fine discussion of practical and social problems encountered in the actual performance of social science experiments.

nant. In that case, neither female will produce kittens. If the caveman repeated the experiment 100 times, however, and if he were always careful to keep all conditions, except association with males, exactly the same for both the experimental and the control females, he would discover that none of the separately penned females had kittens, but a large number of the pair-penned females did. He would then properly conclude that males are *probably* a necessary but not a sufficient condition for female pregnancy. We say "probably" because one can *never* be sure.

Scientific certainty that a fact is true, in the real world, is an *impossiblity*. In the kitten experiment, we can never be sure that the male is an absolutely necessary condition until we have examined all female cats—past, present, and future. Hence we can have only a reasonably firm hypothesis, but we will operate on the assumption of its truth until it is disproved. But a *single* instance of a female pregnancy without the association of a male would demolish the hypothesis, and an alternative would have to be devised immediately.

The essentials of the experimental method, then, are these. The experimenter must start with a hypothesis of causal relationship between or among variables. Then, the experimenter must devise a situation which can be controlled absolutely. Third, a *series* of trials must be performed in which the presumed causal factor is introduced, and the presumed consequence is observed or not observed. A companion *series* of trials must also be performed. The companion series must be identical with the first series in all respects, except the presumed causal factor is not introduced, and the presumed consequence is observed or not observed. If the presumed consequence is always observed in the experimental series and never observed in the control series, the experimental factor is *presumed* to be a necessary *and* a sufficient cause.

Most experimental designs are of the simple variety. In business problem solving, for example, the experimenter might have an experimental group of housewives, for some specified period of time, page through a magazine which contains an ad for widgets. The control group would page through an identical magazine, except the ad for widgets would have been removed. A week later, all of the women would be interviewed to determine how many during the past week had purchased widgets. If our hypothesis was that widget magazine advertising leads to increased purchasing of widgets by housewives, we would expect the experimental group to buy more widgets than the control group.

Actually the so-called simple experiment is complicated, as it almost always is in business research, by the fact that we failed to control, rigidly, all of the nonexperimental variables. The ages of the women were different, their backgrounds, family relationships, family incomes, places of residence, and a host of other possibly influential factors, were different. Hence the observed purchasing differences might have been caused by a factor or factors other than the magazine-reading treatment. Thus in business experimentation, where strict controls are not often feasible, some other procedure must be substituted. The substitute procedure most frequently used is that of randomizing factors which cannot be either matched or controlled. In the matching procedure, we try to find pairs of women who are as closely alike in all particulars as possible, and we place one of each pair in the experimental group and one in the control group. For very careful matching, we try to find identical twins who were raised together and who, since their separation by marriage, have lived in substantially similar economic and social circumstances. To rule out the influence of factors which can be neither controlled nor matched, we randomize by using very large samples of women in both the experimental and control groups. The matching procedure significantly reduces the need for large samples.

Although, as we have said, most business experiments are of the simple variety, researchers are more and more frequently using complex experimental designs.[26] Most of these are varieties of the so-called factorial design. In these methods, two or more factors are varied, simultaneously and systematically. These experiments require very careful preplanning, often by research experts, to assure successful analysis of results. Use of these methods, however, frequently yields extremely valuable results with a minimum of experimental cost. The formerly expensive, numerical computations which are required are now much more economical because of advances in both the hardware and the software in the electronic computer field.[27] It

[26] Cf. Ackoff (*op. cit.*, pp. 311–341). This is an excellent discussion of modern, complex experimental designs.

[27] Hardware refers to the computer and its auxiliary machinery. Software refers to the files of prepared programs which are available for use in the solution of standard computational problems.

is not necessary for the researcher to own a computor, for in most locations public computation centers charge reasonable user rates. The only significant cost in using complex experimental methods is that involved in retaining the services of the expert who plans and directs the study. Even that cost, however, is usually a minor consideration, for results will more than justify the expense.

In connection with a discussion of experimental research, one should recognize a growing literature and interest in *simulation* and *game playing*. Simulation is not new. Until recently the term simulation referred to a type of approach which we would describe as controlled observation. In a typical simulation procedure, the physical object being studied, or a model of it, is subjected to a series of particular conditions, and without (necessarily) any hypothesis regarding the outcome, the researcher observes what happens. For example, a model airplane is placed in a wind tunnel, and the force of air is increased until the model breaks up. From many such observations, with many different model designs, the principles of aerodynamics are worked out. In a similar vein, the more recent explorations of the effects of atomic bombing on houses and people, which have been conducted by the United States, are true simulations. Some people call this kind of research experimental. If hypotheses are established, and if experimental and control conditions are imposed, we agree. If, however, no hypotheses and no comparisons between experimental and control conditions are made, we would classify the method as observational research. At best, it might be referred to as exploratory experimentation.

In most early simulations, full-scale, actual models were used in the research. Gradually researchers came to use miniature duplicates of the real objects. The reason for miniaturization is partly the cost saving in the production of research objects, but it is mostly the cost saving in the production of the research environment. In the wind tunnel, for example, the cost of a miniature plane is far less than the cost of the full-scale model but, more important, the cost of a miniature wind tunnel is tremendously less than the cost of a controllable, full-scale environment.

In addition to miniaturization, simulation researchers gradually developed the analogue technique. Instead of producing actual, full-scale or miniature models of the objects under study, modern researchers frequently use objects which represent or are analogous to the object under study but which may not look at all like the real object. Analogue models reproduce the *essential* characteristics of the object under study, and they eliminate everything else. A curved object, for example, might be substituted for the actual or miniature aircraft wing. It would be used in the wind tunnel in place of the actual or miniature model. It is much cheaper to build, and it concentrates observation on the essence of the object being studied without distraction by the side effects which might be produced by nonessential parts of the object itself.

From the development of physical analogues it is but a short step to the development of mathematical or theoretical analogues. This is the current rage. Instead of building scale models and physical environments (usually at great expense), the mathematical analogue abstracts the essential characteristics of the object being studied and represents them in mathematical form. The essential characteristics of the environment are also abstracted and represented by mathematical equations. Then the analogues of the model and the environment are brought together, and as changes in the environment are introduced (mathematically), changes in the model (mathematical) are noted.[28]

Analogue simulations have both tremendous advantages and tremendous disadvantages. On the side of advantages stand the speed with which analogues can be built and the low cost of their construction. Also, the changes in the environment which the researcher desires to study can be introduced and analyzed, both quickly and cheaply. Finally, errors of observation and recording are eliminated, and no uncontrolled, outside disturbances can be introduced. These are mighty advantages. Consider, for example, the tremendous cost which would be involved in building a physical model which is composed of a factory, with all of its plant and equipment and all of its personnel, and an environment which is composed of suppliers, com-

[28] The chronology of development of the various types of simulation models is more obscure than we may have inferred. Analogue models, in terms of charts and equations, have been used in both the social and the physical sciences for many years. Break-even charts which are commonly used by businessmen are geometric analogues, and the marginal analysis charts, so commonly used in teaching elementary economics, are analogue models.

petitors, and customers.[29] Consider, also, the time and effort which would be involved in a physical simulation which attempted to trace the effects of operation of the model over a simulated time period of five or six years.[30]

In spite of these many and important advantages, there is one serious disadvantage. Unless the analogues of both the model and the environment are reasonably true representations of the real-world situation, the observed results might produce disappointing or even disastrous effects. Hence, in order to take advantage of simulation research, for practical purposes it is necessary to do very extensive research, by one or more of the other techniques, to gather the data required to build realistic analogues. Therefore, although the simulation method commands great theoretical interest, its value in complex problem solving is limited. Physical simulations, by contrast, may often be eminently useful in problem solving.

Most of the people who use the modern analogue simulation technique describe it as an experimental method. We disagree. The mathematical model is itself a straitjacket. Nothing can ever come out that was not put in, in the first place. The modern analogue simulation model, therefore, is essentially a logic machine. This, of course, does not mean that such models are useless. In very important research situations, when time is available for the construction of realistic models, and where substantial realism is achieved, great benefits may be derived from analogue simulation models, for in many situations the difficult problem is the logical deduction of results in extremely complicated models and environments. Hence, on both theoretical and practical grounds, we predict a great future for them. We do believe, however, that the method should be described as theoretical rather than experimental.

[29] R. M. Cyert and J. G. March ("Organizational Structure and Pricing Behavior in an Oligopolistic Market," *American Economic Review,* vol. 45, March, 1955, pp. 129–139) conducted a significant simulation of this general character. They analyzed the very old and extremely difficult problem of duopoly with both interesting and important results.

[30] Charles P. Bonini (*Simulation of Information and Decision Systems in the Firm,* Prentice-Hall, Inc., Englewood Cliffs, N.J., 1964) conducted an interesting and important analogue simulation in which 108 time periods were elapsed.

The *business game,* in many ways, is a simulation method. Business games must not be confused with game theory. In the latter, the object is to analyze situations in which the strategies of the players affect the outcome of the game. For example, the so-called game of dice is not a game, for the player bets against the odds and not against another player. In checkers, on the other hand, a true game is involved, for a player's correct strategy is determined by the move of his opponent. Much interest, in recent years, has attached to game theory, but most real-world problems are too complicated for present methods of analysis, and the theory has little practical application to complex problem solving.[31]

Business games, on the other hand, have present usefulness and great future promise. In general, a business game involves a description of a business situation which is presented to a number of different teams. Each team is required to react to the situation according to rules which are presented with the situation. The team reactions are forwarded to the umpires who score responses according to rules which are also established by the game. The umpires then feed new information to the teams, and the game process continues as before. Any number of repetitions and any number of new conditions may be presented as the game progresses. Results depend on the skill with which teams anticipate future "business conditions" and the skill with which they adjust their operations to them. As an executive training device, the method resembles role playing. As a system of research, it resembles both introspection and consultation with experts. The game-playing rule condition is suggestive of simulation, but the freedom of players to react in ways not contemplated by the rules suggests the observational method, or what some call the exploratory experiment. In any case, the business game can be adapted for use as a major research technique. If it is used to present a situation which is closely similar to a real complex problem faced by the researcher, it would

---

[31] The classic work in game theory was accomplished by J. von Neumann and O. Morgenstern (*Theory of Games and Economic Behavior,* Princeton University Press, Princeton, N.J., 1953). This book is somewhat more than difficult, but a briefer and much easier introduction to the theory is found in J. G. Kemeny, J. L. Snell, and G. L. Thompson, *Finite Mathematics,* Prentice-Hall, Inc., Englewood Cliffs, N.J., 1957.

almost certainly provide data for analysis, and it would probably shed light on the difficult areas of problem selection and alternative development.[32]

THEORETICAL RESEARCH

Definition of theoretical research

In each of the previous descriptions of research methodology, we have concerned ourselves primarily with procedures for gathering facts. We have often cautioned the reader that he should, in these research methods, pay strict attention to recording actual observations. The *interpretation* of facts is the proper function of theory. Hence theoretical research is concerned with the quest for understanding and the establishment of meaning which underlies the collected data. Understanding and meaning are established when causal relationships among facts are known, or reasonably well estimated.

Definition of a theoretical system

A theoretical system is an integrated body of facts on a particular subject, in which all of the facts are interrelated and in which the interrelationships contribute to mutual understanding. A theoretical system is an ordered set of facts, with their attached interpretations, which all contribute to a consistently meaningful whole.

A theoretical system begins with observations of facts in the real world. These are never absolute facts, but they are, at a given level of knowledge, the most probable facts at hand. These facts are gathered by one or more of the methods we have already described.

After the facts are at hand, general principles of their interrelationships are *induced*. This is accomplished by looking at the mass of observations as a whole and by trying to describe or explain the mass in a simple, abstracted form. As we contemplate all of our observations of lakes freezing over, for example, we induce the principle that lake freezing is caused by the arrival of Thanksgiving Day (a possible,

[32] An illustration of a business game is detailed in G. R. Andlinger, "Business Games—Play One," *Harvard Business Review*, vol. 36, March–April, 1958, pp. 115–125.

but false, induction). Induction, therefore, argues from the particular and specific (individual observations) to the general (unifying principles). Inductive reasoning has many pitfalls, but modern statistical techniques will, for the most part, circumvent them. Hence the primary tool which is used to establish scientific generalizations is the technique of statistical analysis.

When the scientific principles of the theoretical system have been established, a different kind of logic takes over. This is deductive analysis. The principal tools are those of mathematical logic. The aim of the deductive phase of theory building is to infer, from the established postulates that have been discovered by induction, theorems which contribute to the expansion of the system itself or to its usefulness in application.

The final phase of theory building is concerned with the comparison of deduced principles (theorems) with observations in the physical world. This step is necessary for system closure. We began with observations in the real world, and we come full circle to check our theoretical predictions against the facts of the real world. If the theorems produce predictions which are confirmed in observation, we have *presumptive evidence* that our original observations were correct, that our postulates which had been established by statistical induction are correct, and that our deductive analysis is correct.

In all theory construction, the primary aims are accuracy and completeness. The secondary aim is parsimony; that is, we wish to explain as many of the facts as possible in the real world with the fewest number of postulates. All students have seen and studied the theoretical system of Euclid (high school geometry). All students should have been considerably impressed by the tremendous number of theorems which were developed from a handful of axioms (postulates).

Inductive logic

The basic tool of modern scientific induction is the statistical method. Statistical inference is the study of principles for estimating the likelihood of the truth of fact. In this system, the truth is called a parameter, and a statistic is the estimate of the parameter. Hence, as we observed earlier, the average age of all students is a parameter, but the average age computed from a sample of 50 percent of the students is a statistic.

Now it is frequently impossible to observe and measure (or count) all of the facts of any given class—past, present, and future—and in such circumstances, one is forced to statistical estimation. These estimates should always carry with them measures of uncertainty concerning their validities. This is why statistics are normally reported in terms of their most probable values (arithmetic means, percents, correlation coefficients, etc.) but with attached estimates of error (standard errors, standard errors of estimate, levels of confidence, etc.). In using statistics, therefore, we recognize the uncertainty, more or less, of events which are predicted by their use.

The field of statistics, as most students know, is both wide and deep. Advanced statistical analysis should be left to experts, but understanding of basic principles must be achieved by all researchers and all complex problem solvers. Statistics is the tool which gives us our most valid scientific principles, and it is also the tool which tells us the degree of confidence we should place in those principles.

Deductive logic

All students are familiar with the operations of arithmetic, algebra, and geometry. Each of these is a system of deductive logic. Starting from sets of assumptions and definitions, deductive systems yield absolute statements of logical truth. This concept of absolute, logical truth is quite different from the concept of probable, existential truth. Logical conclusions are logically true, if conclusions are implied by the premises. Truth, in the world of existence, on the other hand, is always problematical, for all statements of fact are frank estimations.

All students study the principles of deductive logic—whether they know it or not. When they complete their courses in arithmetic, algebra, and geometry, they have followed precise, deductive procedures. All of these deductive systems are so obviously useful in business and engineering problem solving that there is no need for us to prove the statement or to dwell on it. Many students will have had additional courses in mathematics, programming, symbolic logic, set analysis, and other deductive systems which have, to those who know them, equal applicability. Hence, in this brief statement, no further argument is given. We simply observe that no matter how much mathematical or other training one gets in deductive logic, he will always be wishing he had more, for he will be forever bumping his head against the ceiling of his own knowledge. Researchers seem to be always operating at the outer limits of their logical capabilities. The moral, of course, is that students of business and engineering, while they still have time, should take as much training as possible in both statistics and mathematics, and whenever possible they should study both the classical and the symbolic logic as well.

The importance of theory to problem solving should be clear from its description, but a few of the important points bear emphasis. First, the knowledge we acquire, unless it is fitted into a theoretical frame of reference with other knowledge of a similar character, will be relatively useless for future application because one cannot relate isolated knowledge to future situations which may be quite similar in essence but very different in appearance. It is theory which reveals the essence. Second, isolated facts which are not associated with other facts will be quickly forgotten, and unremembered experience is no better than no experience at all.[33] Third, theory, in addition to providing hooks on which to hang new facts as they come along, itself provides inferences concerning the behavior of things, even when no observations have been made in previous, similar situations. This use of theory is extremely important in complex problem solving, for we view each problem as unique and, therefore, no opportunity has been presented, in the past, for observation. Hence we are constantly faced with the need to infer, on the basis of theory, what will happen in a current situation or as a result of a contemplated course of action.[34]

[33] This use of the idea of forgetting is different from our use of the term in Chapter 13. In the present use, it is more likely that the experience which is not related to earlier experience will be *imperfectly perceived*, and, therefore, it will not actually be received. Hence in most courses in memory training instruction emphasizes the need to associate facts which the subject wishes to remember with other facts which the subject cannot forget. Most American students, for example, remember the original date of the publication of Adam Smith (*The Wealth of Nations*, Richard D. Irwin, Inc., Homewood, Ill., 1963) to be the year (1776) of the American Declaration of Independence.

[34] The uses and procedures of theory in business research are the main subject of Rigby's excellent book (*op. cit.*).

OPERATIONS RESEARCH

In our opinion, operations research is not a separate and distinct method of research. Instead, it is a composite of all of the other techniques we have discussed. Moreover, the exact meaning of the term is not yet settled, even in the minds of many who most often use it, but at least a general idea can be formed and stated here.[35] Operations research is a broadly based, frequently interdisciplinary, approach to the solution of problems which do not, on the surface, quite fall into our classifications of either simple or complex. The problems undertaken seem to be complex problems which diligent effort can or should be able to simplify. Hence operations researchers are sometimes madly, but almost always earnestly, devoted to mathematical techniques, and they are unalterably and passionately devoted to quantification. They have achieved remarkable success in solving both military and civilian problems. For students whose interests lie in the fields of business and engineering, their most dramatic results, to date, have been in the field of linear programming.[36] Transportation, warehousing, machine utilization, cueing (queuing), forecasting, and all kinds of scheduling problems have been successfully analyzed. As we have stated, however, we do not classify operations research as a separate basic method because we are convinced that its approach is a composite of methods we have already described. Nevertheless, the work which has been and is being done by operations researchers

[35] The most reasonable definition we have seen is given by Russell L. Ackoff (ed.), (*Progress in Operations Research*, John Wiley & Sons, Inc., New York, 1961, pp. 3–34).

[36] Considering the short history of operations research (or at least the term itself), there is a large literature. We have already cited some of the best (Ackoff's *Progress in Operations Research*; Ackoff's *Scientific Method*; Churchman, Ackoff, and Arnoff; Miller and Starr, and Lindsay). In addition, the student will find the following to be valuable: Robert Ferber and P. J. Verdorn, *Research Methods in Economics and Business*, The Macmillan Company, New York, 1962, and Nyles V. Reinfeld and William R. Vogel, *Mathematical Programming*, Prentice-Hall, Inc., Englewood Cliffs, N.J., 1958. Of these, we believe Ackoff's *Progress in Operations Research* is most authoritative and comprehensive. For introductory purposes, we especially like Churchman, Ackoff, and Arnoff. It is slightly out of date, but we believe it is still the best introduction.

is significant, and its study should not be overlooked by people who are interested in research or in problem solving.

In our view, the complex problem-solving model presented in this book is an example of operations research. Our emphasis has been on the collection of facts, the measurement of facts, the classification of facts, and the clarification of relationships between and among facts. In all of these operations, we have constantly referred to the urgent need for the researcher to gather data from all available sources, especially from experts in other disciplines. We have tried to present an orderly scheme for coping physically and mentally with very large quantities of heterogeneous data. We have insisted on quantification by counting, measuring, or, if necessary, estimating problem variables. We have furnished a simple, easily understandable system for taking account of all known and suspected influences in the problem complex for making action decisions. Many other texts on operations research concentrate on the mathematical analysis of data. We have attempted to sail our ship into some of the less well-charted waters of fact-finding as it applies to complex problem solving. Our contribution has been intended to improve on current procedures for collection and identification of facts, for identification of problems and their interrelationships, and for selection of alternatives for analysis. We have also tried to apply operations research to all complex problems, whether or not their solutions can be cast in elegant mathematical forms. Our problem-solving model is useful for all kinds of complex problems, no matter how poor the data may be or how complex the problem is. The model, we feel, should be used by even the most erudite operations researcher, for it is a necessary preliminary to setting up the mathematical analysis, and it is a useful check on the results of mathematical conclusions. When one is abstracting from reality to mathematical model analysis, he can easily lose touch with the real world, and errors of fact or judgment can creep in without the analyst being aware of them. When this occurs, bizarre results may be obtained. Therefore operations researchers should use our model, or a variation on it, to check their results and be more confident that they are reasonable. Finally, it is believed that much of the resistance to operations research, in the workaday world of business, is caused by failure of operations researchers to speak a language that businessmen understand. Therefore the computational work, especially, should almost never be presented in the report which is made to business executives. Rather, the conclusions of the analysis should be carefully translated into a vocabulary and a frame of reference which are intelligible to the intended reader. This translation into lay language need be neither complete nor absolutely precise. It must, however, be meaningful, and if the report is not meaningful, it is often worthless.

Hence we claim to have contributed to operations research methodology, first, by concentrating our attention on the "dirty-work" aspects of research which are so often neglected, second, by generalizing the approach to make it applicable to all complex problem solving, third, by illustrating the use of common-sense analysis to check on mathematical solutions, fourth, by illustrating the translation of operations research results into the language of the businessman, and, fifth, by extending the range of application of the essential methods of operations research to the level of daily use by nonmathematically inclined, ordinary mortals. In any case, we hope some readers who are normally terrified by anything connected with mathematics will be agreeably surprised to learn that they have survived a trip through one of the most mathematics-laden disciplines of modern times. Returning to our main theme, however, we believe that operations research is and should be classified as a composite of all other kinds of research and not a separate research method in itself.[37]

METHODOLOGICAL RESEARCH

Another term which is often heard in connection with research is methodological research. Again, it is not a separate method. It is research which is conducted to appraise or to improve some other research method. It uses whatever research technique seems most appropriate to the task. We regard methodological research as one of the most important of all research approaches, and we regard this text as an example of methodological research which attempts to improve and extend the field of operations research.

[37] A first-rate, nontechnical example of operations research applied to a real business problem—and not simply a dissertation in theoretical mathematics—is available in Melvin Anshen, Charles C. Helt, France Modigliani, John F. Muth, and Herbert A. Simon, "Mathematics for Production Scheduling," *Harvard Business Review,* vol. 36, March–April, 1958, pp. 51–58.

REPETITIVE RESEARCH

Another kind of research is called repetitive. Still again, this is not a method but an approach. It uses whatever method was used in the original research.

Repetitive research is very common, indeed, in the physical sciences, and it should be used more often in business and economics. As soon as word is broadcast about an important scientific discovery anyplace in the world, other scientists, all over the world, rush into their laboratories to try to duplicate the reported results. It would, the scientists feel, be ridiculous to take one study and one man's skill as definitive for any important discovery. Hence, in science, repetitive research is common. In the social sciences, absolute repetition is usually impossible, for controls are very much more difficult to effect. Nevertheless, it is our opinion that many more closely approximate, repetitive studies should be made.

REPETITIVE RESEARCH WITH VARIATION

Even more common than repetitive research, whether in science or business, is the approach we call repetitive with variation. In this approach, the investigator wishes to use the same method that was used in the original, and he wishes to study the same problem. In addition, however, he wishes to extend the range of investigation of the experimental variable or to change one or more of the experimental variables. In the caveman-kitten experiment, for instance, the researcher might wish to repeat the experiment using a male dog instead of the original male cat, or he might wish to extend the experimental time period from five to fifty days. In either case, the new investigation has exceedingly high merit, for the second research is additive and represents not an isolated new area of fact but an orderly extension of a body of already accepted fact.

CONCLUSION

The reader who has come this far and who believes this chapter is too long might just as well not have read this book at all. For the student who complains that this chapter is the tail that wags the dog, the author replies that he wishes it could have been longer. The overview of research methods presented here is too brief and too shallow to be regarded as anything more than suggestive. Most readers should be inspired to seek more detailed instruction in formal research courses or in source materials on one or more of the methods suggested here.

chapter 15

USING THE PROBLEM-SOLVING MODEL

USING THE STANDING OPERATING PROCEDURE

The standing operating procedure (SOP) for complex problem solving is the application of the problem-solving model in all of its minute details and with full research of the facts which are necessary to support the analytical fine points. The SOP calls for great patience and considerable expenditure of time and effort.

However, as we observed at the beginning of the book, and as we have had occasion to repeat several times, the SOP cannot and should not be attempted for all complex problems that arise either in business or in personal life. Readers will observe that, in day-to-day decision making, problems present themselves in veritable torrents, and if the SOP were applied to each, dozens of new problems would pile up during the time the first was being solved. Hence, in practice, the business operator must be able to do two things. First, he must be able to select, from the multitude of problems that present themselves, those which will be given the full treatment of the SOP. Second, however, he must be able to dispose of the larger number of remaining problems by means of rapid problem-solving methods.

The question of when to use the SOP is not an easy one to decide. In some ways it is easier to state when not to use it. We would not use the SOP for choosing among action alternatives in times of emergency. In all problem solving, timeliness is a mighty ingredient of excellence. Therefore urgency of the need for action will frequently rule out use of the SOP. Second, we would not use the SOP for solving minor or superficial problems. The cost of full-scale problem solving is very high, and one cannot afford to spend the time and money unless the expected returns are equal to or greater than the cost.

In contrast, when there is plenty of time, and when the importance of the problem warrants it, the SOP should be used. Generally, the SOP will be used to solve the primary problems in each problem complex, while secondary problems will be solved by abbreviated methods. Now, inasmuch as primary problems lie at the root of hundreds and perhaps thousands of secondary problems, two conclusions may be drawn. First, there are relatively few primary problems, and, second, effective solution of primary problems will automatically dispose of many of the secondary problems which arise out of the primary difficulties.

Finally, there is one additional condition under which the SOP should be used. From time to time, but at fairly frequent intervals, the reader is urged to indulge himself in the full-scale application of the SOP. Unless one gives regular exercise to his problem-solving skills, he will get rusty on the technique itself. If this should occur, he will become less expert in his daily rapid problem-solving methods, for these are derived from and dependent on the SOP. In addition, he will be failing in his own professional development. One of the most important benefits to be derived from the use of the problem-solving model is the detailed knowledge it provides the analyst about his environment and ways to control it. Hence the use of the model is a formal discipline which forces growth of both the knowledge and the judgment which are the hallmarks of executive maturity.[1]

---

[1] An eloquent testimonial to the need for practice is given by Dr. Ben Eisman and Dr. Frank C. Spencer in *Time,* vol. 89, No. 9, February 26, 1965, p. 77. Discussing open-heart surgery, they observe that one United States surgeon who operates once a week on many of the world's toughest cases has a death rate below 5 percent, while twelve other surgeons who were technically qualified but lacked practice had a 30 percent death rate.

CONTROLLING URGENCY

Before we approach the subject of rapid problem solving, a few words should be said about the nature and control of urgency. It is, of course, important to recognize urgency, and we have referred to this many times. It is equally important, however, to learn that many, even most, problems which appear to be urgent can be, at least somewhat, delayed. Any delay at all permits at least a partial analysis before a decision is made.

The first step in controlling urgency is to recognize the danger of snap decisions. Everyone can recall times when he talked when he should have listened. Everyone can remember times when he wishes he had thought twice instead of having not thought at all. Everyone has regretted the next day some of the actions he took the day before.

After the need for cautious delay is recognized, the act of delay is usually easy. If the problem arises by way of a written communication, such as a letter or memorandum, there is no difficulty, for a written communication contemplates, at the very least, the routine delays of delivery. It is more difficult, but not really hard, to delay answering a telegram. In either of these two cases, the analyst simply refuses to reply until he has completed some kind of formal analysis.

When the communication is verbal, either face-to-face or over the telephone, delay is more difficult. Let's assume the situation described in the Hayden Tool Company case, except that Hayden is in his office at the time Keller threatens Becker. Let's also assume that Becker comes storming into Hayden's office, red in the face and breathing heavily. He rushes into the office, and, pounding on the desk, he declares, "If that SOB Keller isn't fired right now, I'm quitting."

Hayden is caught short, and unless he is careful he is likely to make the very same error which Becker made in the original version of the case. This, of course, would be very bad, but Hayden does not, in the present version of the case, have time for careful analysis. Therefore, what does he do?

He proceeds somewhat like this: "Holy Toledo, Karl, what the hell happened?" Whereupon Becker is slowed down, and he is given further opportunity to blow off steam. Becker describes the encounter in the shop. Hayden expresses his shock and bewilderment. He presses for more and more of the gory details, and he sympathizes with Becker. (By now Hayden has done enough of the analysis in his own mind to realize he can't afford to lose Becker.) He begins to ask questions and, as he proceeds, he continues his own analysis. As his understanding of the situation improves, his questions become more rhetorical and penetrating. Sooner or later, he will be discussing, not merely listening. Becker is discussing, not merely blowing his stack. Finally, and together, they explore the meaning of the incident rather than the incident itself. Before the interview is ended, they have, together, reconsidered the *mutually agreed* hasty decision, and they have formulated a constructive rather than a destructive action alternative. Before they have finished, the chances are very good that they will have written a few notes on paper, which we would recognize to be abbreviated versions of analysis sheets.

The results of Hayden's technique would have been these: He did make an immediate decision, in the sense that Becker was still in the office, but he made one which was carefully considered before action was taken. The important point is that Hayden did not send Becker away while he studied the problem. He used the very person who demanded action to help him complete a fairly detailed analysis.

Variations of this technique are as numerous as the situations in which problems arise. It is quite interesting and instructive to observe how other skilled people handle the demand for immediate action. Perhaps a few anecdotes will help the reader develop his skill.

The author was attending a banquet as a guest with a colleague. After dinner, a brief business meeting was followed by a serious speech by an invited, distinguished outsider. After the talk, the author was unexpectedly invited to "say a few words." In spite of his surprise, he was smart enough to avoid the trap of getting to his feet and running off at the mouth, without a prepared speech. The result was almost neutral. He probably didn't do his reputation much harm, but it's certain he didn't do himself any good. When his colleague was also invited to talk, he at least had had a warning that he might be called on. When he was, he rose, smiled, bowed, and waved his hand. He received an immediate ovation. Then he moved away from his place at the table, carefully replacing his chair; he walked slowly to the platform and on the way he stopped briefly to shake hands with an acquaintance. He made his way to the platform by taking the long way around. When he finally arrived at the speaker's stand, he looked around the room, smiled, and waved his hand again. He received another round of applause. He then told the longest, oldest joke we have ever heard. The audience clapped again. When he finally began his speech, he had probably consumed ten full minutes, but no one minded. All during that time, he had been sorting out his thoughts and organizing his speech. What he said was both interesting and appropriate, and within a month he was invited to join the club.

On another occasion, the author was employed by the allied occupation forces in Japan. His particular job at one time was the writing of a draft of the city government section of the Local Autonomy Act, and one of the requirements was the production of a document which would be acceptable to both the allied powers and the Japanese people. In preparing the paper, therefore, he was in daily conference with a member of the Japanese Diet. During the negotiations, whenever we asked a question our interpreter would repeat it in Japanese to the senator's interpreter, and the senator's interpreter would repeat the question, also in Japanese, to him. The senator then answered the question in Japanese to his interpreter, his interpreter repeated the answer to our interpreter, in Japanese, and our interpreter translated the answer into English. Needless to say, negotiations proceeded rather slowly. After many weeks of negotiation, we happened to meet the senator one Saturday afternoon on the Ginza. (This is the main shopping street in Tokyo.) We greeted him in English, and he replied in excellent English. We then fell to chatting, very easily, in English. When we finally brought up the subject of the tortuous negotiations with the interpreters, the senator stated his reasons for the procedure. He pointed out that we had enough advantage on our side, and, at the very least, he wanted to think over our questions carefully before giving his responses.

To sum up our point, let us repeat: Most situations are not of absolutely immediate urgency. If they are not, find ways to delay long enough to do at least some kind of an analysis. In the choice of delay tactics, select one which will not antagonize the person demanding immediate action. Naturally, do not delay so long, however, as to become guilty of default.

RAPID PROBLEM-SOLVING TECHNIQUES

The techniques for rapid problem solving are abbreviations and adaptations of the SOP, and some attention must be given to each step in the problem-solving model. Selecting the problem is still the most important step, for until the problem for analysis is chosen, one cannot even tell whether a full-scale or an abbreviated treatment will be appropriate. Similarly, the facts of the situation retain their significance in rapid problem solving, for without at least some of the facts no problem can be even recognized, let alone solved.

Once the main facts are established and the appropriate problem is stated, in emergency situations of great urgency or when problems of minor importance are involved, one may proceed as he does in business case analysis, without extensive research, to analyze the facts, to select alternative courses of action, to weigh the pros and cons of each alternative, to select the most favorable alternative from those considered, and to plan its execution. The amount of time and effort one devotes to each step depends on the importance of the problem and the time available for selecting a course of action.

In rapid problem solving, the weighing of advantages and disadvantages is done somewhat differently from the manner employed in the SOP. If an advantage and a disadvantage, for a given alternative, have approximately equal significance, eliminate them both. For the payoffs which are left, give a rating of 10 for the most important. By comparison with the most important, give each of the remaining payoffs suitable relative ratings. In completing this step, *be sure to use ratings and not rankings*. With ten payoffs, for example, we might have ratings of 10, 6, 6, 5, 5, 5, 3, 2, 1, 1. These ratings would mean that the first is twice as important as any of the three with ratings of 5, and it is ten times as important as either of the two which are rated 1.

In further consideration of this step, it is necessary to use the same scale-of-importance yardstick for evaluating all of the alternative actions under consideration. Therefore the top rating of 10, which will be given to the most significant payoff, may appear as either a pro or a con under any of the alternatives. Finally, in estimating the importance of a payoff, it is necessary to take simultaneous account of the chances that the payoff will materialize. This is to say that, in rapid analysis, no separate consideration is given to the probability that the event will occur. The certainty value and the probability of occurrence are judged concurrently, and a single value, from 0 to 10, is given to each payoff. When this is accomplished, with the usually few number of payoffs and the small, whole-number values, figures can be added rapidly in one's head, and the best alternative can be quickly discovered.

Even when rapid analysis is required, some thought must be given to implementation. One should never forget "Papworth's First Law": "That which can go wrong will go wrong." [2] Think quickly about the things that could go wrong, and make mental estimates of the best ways to head off trouble.

The final steps in rapid problem solving are no different from those described in the SOP. After the analysis has been completed, whatever paper was used to arrive at the action decision must be placed in the tickler file for future review. "Tall oaks from little acorns grow," [3] and knowledge gained from little decisions is useful a thousand times over in making big ones. At the time of the decision, therefore, wrap up the analysis paper, and send it to the tickler file. If the decision was made on horseback, and no paper exists, write up the case, before the day is over, and suspend it for future review.

CONCLUSION

In our discussions of the case method and the problem-solving method of business instruction, we have observed that one of the primary goals is the development, by students, of the principles of business management. After examining many actual situations from the world of business, students are supposed to abstract the principles of good management. Our whole discussion of the role of judgment and our suggestions for improving it are logical extensions of this aim. We do, however, emphasize that one swallow does not make a summer, and we caution students against jumping to conclusions on the basis

[2] This quotation has the same status as the one stated on page 128.
[3] David Everett, from lines written for a school declamation, *The Oxford Dictionary of Quotations*, 2d ed., Oxford University Press, London, 1955, p. 202.

of single experiences.[4] All general conclusions, therefore, should be most tentatively drawn, and all principles should be subjected to constant check and recheck.

We conclude this book with a final word to the reader that he must personally assume full responsibility for his problem solutions. This involves two contrasting aspects. On the one hand, the problem solver's growth and progress toward higher levels of competence, reward, and recognition will be hastened by his capacity to learn from his own mistakes. This capacity depends, in large measure, on his willingness to recognize that problem-solving errors cannot be either swept under the rug or blamed on scapegoats. On the other hand, the problem solver must be prepared to live with the total consequences of his decision recommendations and implementations. This means he must be prepared to defend not only the technical correctness of his analysis and the effectiveness of his action recommendations but also the moral principles on which they are based. In complex problem solving, the repercussive effects of decisions are widespread and often inscrutable. It is difficult or impossible to know, therefore, where the effects of any action will end. Nevertheless, the problem solution must look to the depths of the action consequences and to the remote future as well. Honest errors of judgment can be excused, but one cannot justify any failure to examine or to rationalize the moral foundations on which all action decisions must rest.

[4] This is a warning against hasty generalization. It is one of the common fallacies of inductive logic. All problem solvers should instruct themselves on the subject of fallacy. One of the best nontechnical treatments is the very readable text by W. Ward Fearnside and William B. Halther, *Fallacy: The Counterfeit of Argument,* Prentice-Hall, Inc., Englewood Cliffs, N.J., 1959.

CASES IN COMPLEX
PROBLEM SOLVING

A. ELWYN COUNTY MEDICAL ASSOCIATION

On October 31, 1956, Ward Williams, a public relations counsel, received a visitor in his Kansas City office. The caller introduced himself as Dr. Charles Conquest, general medical practitioner and president of the Elwyn County Medical Association. The purpose of his call was to engage Mr. Williams to restore public confidence in the medical profession and its practitioners in Elwyn County. His description of conditions is given in the following summary prepared by Mr. Williams after completion of the interview:

For a period of five years, from the time of the opening of the Elwyn County General Hospital to May 16, 1955, staff membership was granted on application, without examination or investigation, to all doctors who were licensed by the State Board of Medical Examiners and who were residing and practicing in Elwyn County. Other practitioners such as chiropodists, osteopaths, chiropracters, and dentists were excluded from staff membership and from use of hospital facilities, regardless of whether they were licensed by state authorities.

On the 16th of May, 1955, the president of the Elwyn County Medical Association was informed by the Board of County Supervisors that, effective June 1, 1955, osteopaths were to be granted staff membership and permitted free use of all hospital facilities. Inasmuch as the hospital was owned, operated, and supported by the county, such a decision was unquestionably legal. Also, since the state recognized the profession of osteopathy and granted to doctors of osteopathy the right of ministering to the sick, either by drug or by surgical therapy, no legal action could be taken against individual practitioners.

At an emergency meeting of the Elwyn County Medical Association Executive Committee on the 20th of May, it was decided to appeal the decision and to request its recision. Contained in the request was a statement that failure to comply with the wishes of the medical association would result in withdrawal of all doctors of medicine from the staff. On May 30, reply was received from the county board of supervisors in which the request was denied, but it was hoped that the medical association would reconsider. It was pointed out, in the reply, that the hospital was a publicly owned institution, that osteopathic practitioners were duly licensed by the state, and that discrimination against them might be ruled illegal. It was further explained that the public who might prefer treatment by osteopaths were entitled to hospital facilities and that patients who had been denied this right were being denied equal treatment in a publicly owned institution.

Despite the high-sounding purposes of the county board of supervisors, it was well known to members of the medical association that two of the three members of the board of supervisors were closely connected, through family relationship, to practicing osteopaths. There was no doubt, moreover, that political pressure had been put on the third member through his business relationship with the father-in-law of another prominent osteopath. Finally, it was public knowledge that the osteopaths of Elwyn County had been waging a long propaganda and smear campaign against the doctors of medicine, and it was suspected that the osteopaths were being financially supported by the state osteopathic society which regarded the Elwyn County affair to be of great significance as a test case and as a precedent for further expansion of acceptance to hospital staffs throughout the state.

On May 30, the executive committee of the association rejected the reply of the board of supervisors, and on May 31, all doctors of medicine resigned from the hospital staff. Thenceforth, doctors of medicine treated patients in their offices or in the patients' homes, or, in great need, patients were sent to small private hospitals or to general hospitals outside the county. These conditions proved to be a severe hardship not only on medical practitioners but also on their patients. Facilities at the private hospitals were inadequate, space was very limited, and professional care by members of the sister professions was often lacking.

Although members of the association backed the executive committee in its decision to withdraw, complaints kept pouring into association headquarters. Physicians complained that they were not able to give their best services to patients, and some doctors claimed they were losing patients to osteopaths. Patients felt that, although they would prefer treatment by a doctor of medicine, if hospitalization were required, they would prefer to go to the county hospital and be treated by an osteopath. Many patients blamed the medical association for pigheadedness and for lack of democratic procedure. Although they might not desire treatment by an osteopath, they felt that inasmuch as the profession was recognized and licensed by the state, and since the hospital was owned by the county, and since recurring hospital deficits were made up from general tax funds, the medical profession should not force patients to choose treatment by doctors of medicine simply because they had exclusive use of the only adequate hospital facility in the county.

Despite these complaints, the medical association stood firm, and no doctor of medicine rejoined the county hospital staff. The dispute, however, did not rest there. Practically everyone in the county was up in arms. Most people felt that, in the dispute, the osteopaths were right. The osteopathic society added fuel to the fire. In full-page ads, in newspapers throughout the county, they told the story that the medical profession was attempting to maintain its high fee schedule by excluding all who were not members of their "union." In retaliation, the medical association bought space to belittle the training and professional qualifications of osteopaths, in general, and, in particular, to suggest dirty politics in their successful penetration of the county hospital. In the recriminations which followed, many old friends who disagreed parted company, and members of some families even quit speaking to each other. Hospital nurses, for the most part, resigned from the hospital, but laboratory technicians, with a few exceptions, stayed on. Pharmacists were over a barrel, and most of them tried to serve both camps.

After six months of operation, from the time of withdrawal of the medical staff, the hospital was in dire financial straits. Not enough patients were admitted even to begin to meet operating costs. Although the county expected an annual deficit, it was generally small and could be handled within the county budget. For the six-month period ending November 30, however, the deficit was ten times the budgeted amount, and something had to be done. To meet this emergency, the board of supervisors proposed a 1,000 percent increase in the then existing "business assets" tax. This proposal, however, had to be submitted to the electorate, and a special referendum was set for February 7, 1956.

When announcement was made of the decision of the board of supervisors, businessmen throughout the county were enraged. They lost no time in explaining to their customers that such a tax would immediately increase prices of all goods and services, and, therefore, the question on the ballot should be defeated. This action had the desired effect, and on the referendum, the proposal was defeated. At a meeting held the following day, the board of supervisors reached a new decision. A letter was sent to the president of the Elwyn County Medical Association. It informed him that, effective March 1, osteopaths would not be retained on or admitted to the hospital staff and would not be permitted the use of hospital facilities. The letter also invited doctors of medicine to rejoin the staff. Another letter was drafted to the president of the osteopathic society, informing him of the action taken and requesting his notification of members of his society.

At a meeting held on the 15th of February the executive committee of the county medical association agreed to end its boycott on the 1st of March, provided the intention expressed by the board of supervisors was carried out. When news of these negotiations was published, the storm broke all over again, but most people, for practical reasons, appeared to be reconciled. The changeover at the county hospital took place as scheduled, and although the propaganda of the osteopathic society was bitter and unabated, no further changes were made. Conditions, however, were far from those which had prevailed prior to the initial decision of the board of supervisors. Many patients had been permanently lost by doctors of medicine to osteopathic practitioners. Others, and this group contained a very large number, were suspicious of the fee schedules maintained by the medical profession. Still others were outraged by the undemocratic and bulldozing tactics of the medical people. Conditions seemed to be improving, but doctors had lost much of the prestige they once held, and they felt that all their actions were being unfairly scrutinized.

B. THE STUDENT'S PERSONAL PROBLEM

In training for complex problem solving, there is no substitute for experience in seeking original problems for analysis. Therefore every student should begin to acquire skill in the discovery and the analysis of complex problems in the real world. Primarily he should learn to recognize problem situations in the stream of events of the natural environment, and he should learn to extract from the environment the facts which will be necessary both for problem selection and problem solution.

Of all possible problems which might be chosen for investigation, the easiest to find and analyze are those contained in the experience of the analyst himself. Therefore the student is required to write up an original case in which he is or was a participant. After writing the case, the student is required to solve it. The exercise is completed by the preparation of a report, similar to that illustrated in Chapter 12, for the course instructor.

The following three cases are illustrations taken from student reports. These cases may also be used to test one's skill in solving problems which other people have encountered.

B-1. THE ATLANTIC PRINTERS [1]

The Atlantic Printers is located in east central Virginia in the village of Charlesville. The village has a population of about five

_____

[1] This case was submitted by Kenneth D. Kok. It is edited and reprinted with his permission.

thousand, and the total related district has a population of about ten thousand. The area is somewhat isolated, but the neighboring village of Kingville is the site of Eastern Virginia University which has an enrollment of slightly more than three thousand graduate and undergraduate students. The nearest large city is Cederton, at a distance of about one hundred miles.

In February, 1966, the Atlantic Printers is in the process of moving to a new location, still in the village of Charlesville. The plant is being enlarged, and the equipment is being modernized. The plan is to increase the firm's printing capability and to improve its efficiency.

The Atlantic Printers had been owned and operated for many years by the Pioneer Press of Richmond. Two years ago, the company was purchased by the former managers. The company produces books, school yearbooks, the *Spectator* (student newspaper of Eastern Virginia University), and a variety of small job-printing orders. The company also sells religious books and artifacts, on special order, to churches and Sunday schools.

Sales of religious books and artifacts last year totaled about $10,000, while aggregate sales came to almost $150,000. The average-sized order for religious articles, has been about $5. It is estimated that the office secretary spends about one-third of her time drawing up orders and handling them when they are received. The secretary is paid $60 per week. Mailing costs come to about 50 cents per order, and the index from which religious books are ordered costs $20 per year.

One of the great difficulties in the handling of religious books and artifacts is its interference with the handling of the printing business. Billing of printing orders, for instance, sometimes runs as much as ten days behind schedule.

The company management believes that the religious book and artifact business is unprofitable. It also interferes with the desire of management to create an image of a printing house exclusively. Management feels that, with the enlarged and more efficient printing capabilities, its main product line can be expanded, and efforts should be turned in this direction. On the other hand, there is no other local firm that handles religious books and artifacts, and customers who have been loyal to the firm for many years might be unhappy if the Alantic Printers discontinues these services.

B-2. THE LANDON STANDARD
SERVICE STATION [1]

Mr. Cook took over the Landon Standard Service Station on the day after Labor Day, 1963. This particular day was chosen because Mr. Hand, the former owner, wished to reap the benefits of the Labor Day weekend before leaving the station.

The town of Landon has a population of only about 100 in winter, but it swells to a considerable number in the summer because of the tourist business. The town is located on one of the largest lakes in the state, and good hunting and fishing are within easy reach. In addition, the station is located on one of the state's busiest highways.

The town has long been known for its large, old-fashioned hotel, but now the hotel is almost out of business. The lake has many summer homes, both in the town and outside it. The area also has been known as one of the highest priced resort areas in the state.

The gas station is a small one, and it has only one stall with an automatic lift. Alongside the station is a small shed which was originally used for storage, but it was later turned into living quarters for Mr. Cook. The land is approximately 100 feet wide on the highway, and it is about 75 feet deep. Although the station is quite old, as indeed the whole town is, it was, at the time Mr. Cook took it over, reasonably clean both inside and out.

Mr. Cook purchased the station for $10,000 to be paid as follows: $1,000 down, $1,000 in six months, $1,000 in a year, and $1,000 a year thereafter. The station was bought on a land contract, with Mr. Hand holding the contract. In addition to the land and buildings, gas pumps, storage tanks, and all equipment were included

---

[1] This case was submitted by Allen W. Cronk. It is edited and reprinted with his permission.

in the sale. This is different from most gas station deals, for usually the operator leases the real estate from a distributor.

There was only one other gas station in the nearby area, but it was located across the street within 200 yards. This station also handled a major gas and oil brand, and it was well established. Prior to the winter that Mr. Cook took over, both of the gas stations had closed for the winter. Mr. Hand had worked for a large station in a nearby town, and because of health reasons, the owner of the other station had spent each winter in Florida. However, when the competitor found out that Mr. Cook planned to stay open all winter, he decided to remain open, too.

In the fall, many people came up north for weekends and vacations. Of course, there wasn't as much traffic as there is during the peak summer months, but there was enough to yield a small profit, and Mr. Cook built up his inventory during this period.

Mr. Cook made more profit per gallon on gas than most station operators because he did not have to lease his station and equipment. Still, it is extremely difficult to make very much money on gas unless there is a large volume of business. Almost all of the profits come from oil changes, lubrications, car washes, and other services. In addition, some tires and batteries were sold on order, but neither were stocked.

September turned into October, the hunting season opened, and the weather remained good. There were still many cars on the road, and although business dropped off somewhat, there was still enough to make a small profit. Hours of operation were kept constant from 8:00 A.M. to 8:00 P.M., seven days a week, and this schedule was maintained through the winter.

The middle of November brought the deer hunting season and the last profitable surge of business for the year. After this, winter hit with a vengeance, and this was to be the worst winter in history. Starting in December, business fell off to practically nothing. There were only a few cars on the road, an occasional truck, and, of course, some local business.

The severe winter brought on another problem. The competitor down the street had a jeep with a snowplow on the front. He plowed out driveways and started cars on cold mornings—but only for owners who were regular customers of his. Hence, although many people disliked him and would have given some trade to Mr. Cook, they were forced into trading with the competitor because of the cold weather and the heavy snowfall.

Shortly after the first of the year, Mr. Cook was so short of cash that he was forced to buy gas in quantities as small as 200 or 300 gallons at a time. Luckily, the gasoline dealer went along with him. Also, at this time, rumors began to circulate that a limited access superhighway was to be built five miles west of Landon.

On the 1st of March, the second payment of $1,000 was due, but Mr. Cook had no money to pay it, and Mr. Hand was demanding immediate payment. Mr. Cook attempted to borrow money to keep Mr. Hand happy, but he was not able to negotiate a loan.

About the middle of March, although he had not paid Mr. Hand, Mr. Cook was still in control of the station. At this time, he was offered a job that would last about two months. With Mr. Hand's expression of a willingness to wait two months, Mr. Cook closed the station and took the job. He believed he would make enough money to open the station again, in good shape, about the end of May.

The middle of May arrived, and although Mr. Cook had saved some money, he did not have enough to pay Mr. Hand and to fill up the tanks. About this time, Mr. Cook was offered a permanent job in a city 200 miles away.

B-3. THE KAIBOR ARMAMENT SCHOOL [1]

In 1960, Bob Owens, a technical representative (tech rep) from the Allied Equipment Corporation, was assigned to the Middle Eastern Assistance Group (MEAG) under the direction of the United

[1] This case was submitted by Dale Ball. It is edited and reprinted with his permission.

States Air Force (USAF) in Toki, Kaibor. Bob was reassigned to an armament school at a Kaibor Air Force (KAF) base in the Kaibor village of Boku. He understood his duties would be to establish a capacity, within the KAF, to install, maintain, and repair components of the LB-6 and LB-7 fire-control systems for jet-fighter aircraft. He was also assigned to determine KAF individual and group needs and to evaluate the effectiveness of training that was being conducted in the armament school.

When Bob arrived at Boku, he observed the following: The armament school is headed by a Kaibor colonel, Nuri Ucari, and it has three sergeants who are the school instructors. The school building is a Quonset hut with offices located downstairs and with classrooms and equipment upstairs. The school has been in operation for about ten years, and the present instructors have been teaching there for about five years.

Colonel Ucari speaks very poor English, and the instructors know only a few words of English. The colonel has little to do, and he spends most of his time trying to improve his English because he believes this will help in gaining further promotions. Normally, tech reps are provided with interpreters by the USAF, but Bob did not have one permanently assigned to him at Boku.

The equipment at the school is old, and many of the systems are not operational. The spare parts inventory is located in a dusty, small room on the second floor, and it is lighted by only one bulb and a dirty, small window. There are no inventory records, and much of the inventory is composed of equipment which had been salvaged from nonoperational fire-control systems. The repair shop is also located in this small room, and it consists of a table, a soldering iron, some test equipment (mostly inoperative), and tools scattered throughout the area.

The USAF has an office on the KAF base. It is headed by Major Pratt, and he is assisted by a staff of two officers and one sergeant. It is Major Pratt's responsibility to coordinate work between the USAF and both the tech reps and the KAF. Bob's immediate supervisor is Captain Flint who has been recently assigned and who is not familiar with fire-control systems. The KAF was under the impression that all tech reps would be directly under its control, but Captain Flint maintained otherwise. As a consequence, there were a number of heated arguments between the USAF and the KAF concerning the supervision of the tech reps. Finally, it was decided that the USAF would control the tech reps, and the KAF would use them as advisers with no direct supervision over their activities. Colonel Ucari was involved in these discussions, and he still feels that the KAF should have control.

Tech reps are paid by their individual American companies, but they are also paid monthly salaries by the USAF. For Bob, the total salary is about $1,000 per month, and if he works overseas for a continuous period of eighteen months, he will be exempt from paying the United States personal income tax. This would amount to about $2,500 in tax rebates.

Bob took about a week to familiarize himself with the facts as presented here. He has been told to advise the KAF whenever he is requested to do so, but he has not been asked for advice, and he has not been given any other work to do. He is annoyed, and he feels guilty about being paid for doing nothing.

C. THE STUDENT'S ORIGINAL CONSULTING CASE

Training in complex problem solving is not complete until the student has accomplished his first consulting job as a complex problem solver. Therefore students are required to do field research and to find businessmen who have problems and who are willing to talk about them. The individual student must find a businessman with a problem, get the facts, select the problem, analyze the problem, and write a report to his principal with an information copy to the instructor.[1]

The following three cases are examples of materials collected by students.

C.1.   THE BRANDT BAKERY[2]

The Brandt Bakery is located in a community of 20,000 in southern Minnesota. The town serves as a shopping center for a large, rich, farming area. The owner, Oscar Brandt, has been in business in

[1] The Harvard Business School recognizes the educational value of case collecting and case writing. ("Case Development at the School," *Harvard Business School Bulletin,* vol. 41, no. 1, January–February, 1965, p. 9.) Training in case solving is excellent, says the article, but "an equally important management asset is the ability to seek out the data, select relevant facts, and present them in a clear, concise, complete, and persuasive manner."

[2] This case was submitted by Stanley J. Graves. It has been edited and reprinted with his permission.

the same location for over thirty years, and he is a leading citizen of the community.

The shop is a two-story, brick building. The main production area is on the first floor, at the rear of a small retail sales front. The second floor is used for storage only. On one side of the building is a loading dock to serve the eight wholesale trucks which cover the small towns within a radius of 50 miles.

Mr. Brandt employs eight drivers who act as route salesmen, three female clerks in the retail store, one master baker, two journeymen bakers, three assistant bakers, three pot cleaners, one wrapper-boxer, and two wholesale order packers, or a total of twenty-three employees.

The sales of the business show a marked seasonal trend. Sales during July, August, and September are three times those during December, January, and February and twice those during the other six months of the year. The seasonal nature of the business is caused by the unwillingness of farm women to bake during the hot summer months and by the increased sales to restaurants which serve tourists in the summer.

Mr. Brandt is, himself, a master baker, and he helps out in any capacity when he is needed. Pete Peterson, the master baker, was trained at Dunwoody Institute, and when he came to work for Brandt, eight years ago, he was thirty years old, and he had had ten years' baking experience. He was employed as a journeyman baker and, five years ago, was promoted to master baker.

During the last three or four years, Mr. Brandt has relaxed his own efforts a bit. The baking business is very hard work, and Brandt feels that he has earned the right to ease off a little. As a consequence, he has come to turn more and more of the management of the business over to Pete. Until recently, this decision has worked out very well. Pete's salary has been increased, and Brandt has been constantly pleased with Pete's work. Pete has shown a real interest in his work and in the welfare of the bakery. He is on salary, but he has consistently worked overtime many hours during the busy season. He has always taken his vacation in the wintertime. He has been a good boss, and the men have responded well to his supervision. Pete has always spoken enthusiastically about the baking business, and he has, on many occasions, encouraged younger men to enter the trade.

Brandt has shown his appreciation of Pete by giving him ever-increasing authority and responsibility. He is one of the highest paid, nonowner workers in the town. On one occasion, Mr. Brandt co-signed a mortgage so that Pete could buy a house, and Brandt has cosigned three automobile purchase contracts.

Three months ago, Pete's attitude toward his job and the business took a complete turn for the worse. He appears to have lost all interest in the business. One day, he reported by telephone that he was ill, and he did not come to work. Brandt learned later, however, that Pete had spent the day playing cards in the back room of an out-of-town tavern. Also, Pete has taken to a strict eight-hour day, and he no longer automatically volunteers to work overtime, even when he is desperately needed. During his working day, Brandt has noticed that Pete sometimes stops in the middle of whatever he is doing and stares into space. He appears to be off in another world, but he suddenly recovers and picks up his work where he had left off.

Pete is still pleasant to the other employees, but he doesn't seem to care what they do. His supervision has relaxed to the point where Brandt himself has frequently found it necessary to interfere directly in the supervision of the men. Pete has lost his enthusiasm for the baking business, and he has told two or three of the younger men they would be crazy to get into it or to stay in it. He talks quite frequently about how well his younger brother, whom he sent through college, is doing in the Twin Cities.

One of the younger men, a journeyman baker, who is also a graduate of Dunwoody and who is in charge of sweet-goods production, has shown great interest in the business. He is on straight wages, but he gets time and a half for overtime. He volunteers in emergencies to help out in any way he can. He looks, in fact, like Pete looked until three months ago.

Mr. Brandt is sixty-two years old. He has no children, and he has sufficient money for an immediate retirement. He has had a number of opportunities to sell his business at a fair price, and he believes he could sell within a month or two at any time. He has never, however, given any thought to selling the business because he had assumed he would work out a time-sale deal with Pete when the day to retire arrived. He has not, however, ever discussed such a deal with Pete, and Pete has never approached him on the matter.

C-2. PENINSULA AIR SERVICE[1]

The Peninsula Air Service has its home office in Marquette, Michigan. It is in the business of operating an aerial photography and oil painting service. Primarily, it sells oil-painted aerial photographs to farmers.

The general procedure is to take aerial photographs of farmhouses during the summer months. Photographs are then processed, painted, and sold throughout the year. The firm is composed of four employees, two of whom are salesmen working on mileage expenses and commission. The third member of the firm is the founder and owner, and the fourth is a girl who is hired full time to process the film in the Marquette home office. The company owns the plane and all of the photographic equipment. The owner himself flies alone and does all the picture taking.

Last year (1964), the firm had gross sales of $25,000, and expenses were broken down as follows:

Salesman number 1	$ 6,000
Salesman number 2	1,500
Mileage paid to salesmen	1,250
Operating expense	10,000
Profit	6,250

Operating procedure

Pictures of farms in some given area are taken during the summer. There are fifty pictures to a roll and about ten rolls a day are shot. These pictures are then processed and printed to 5 x 7 proofs.

[1] This case was prepared by Rodger D. Peters. It is edited and reprinted with his permission.

At this point, the salesmen take the proofs and make direct contacts with the farmers involved. They show the black-and-white proofs and some already painted samples to the prospects. If the farmer decides to buy, the salesman notes the colors needed on the proof and returns it to Marquette where the picture is taken to a studio to be painted. The salesman later delivers the finished painting to the farmer.

Product

The product is the painting which can be purchased in three sizes. The largest is 16 x 24 inches, and it sells for $66. The black-and-white proofs are of little value, and they are sometimes left behind in the hope that the farmer will change his mind and buy a painting.

Sales method

The present marketing method is limited to commission salesmen who make approximately fifty calls a week. To cover costs, a salesman must get $200 sales out of every roll of film (i.e., fifty pictures). This works out to two or three sales a day, or about ten per week, and ten per roll of film. At present, salesmen are averaging about $300 sales per roll, or fifteen sales per roll.

The sales approach is to use the farmer's pride as the key to selling. There appears to be no specific target to be aimed at, and no trends in terms of such things as income, type of farming, size of farm, or age, have been noticed among those who buy the paintings. The salesmen do say, however, that after they have been in the area for a while, it is easier to sell because the word of their coming seems to spread.

The better of the two salesmen made $6,000 last year, and he worked an average of four days per week.

Competition

There is little knowledge of competition in any given area. It is known, however, that on occasion someone with a similar product has been through before. When salesmen run into this situation, however, they still make all normal stops for the two following reasons:

1. They have usually been able to sell even when someone else has been through the area.
2. They need to get $200 per roll of film to cover costs.

New products

On occasion, when flying over a motel or lodge, or place of business, the photographer takes pictures of them. These business establishments sometimes buy the pictures for advertisements (i.e., postcards or brochures). The postcard and brochure business is the only repeat business the firm has ever experienced and, up to the present time, it has been negligible.

Future prospects

The company has almost no repeat business, and areas near the city of Marquette have all been covered. As prospect areas become further removed from Marquette, the cost of selling, with present salesmen located in Marquette, becomes excessive, for salesmen will have to remain on the road overnight, and further allowances for food and lodging will have to be made. Hence the owner is considering a direct mail-order operation which would eliminate salesmen altogether.

C-3. TONY'S [1]

Background

Tony's is presently a three-division company which developed from a restaurant and bar business begun thirty-five years ago. Pres-

[1] This case was submitted by Ralph L. Merklin. It is edited and reprinted with his permission.

ent divisions include the restaurant and bar, the canning operation, and the frozen foods division. The canning division is currently packing two types of spaghetti sauces, while the frozen foods division is marketing three types of pizza, all of the same size.

In 1963, the canning company had gross sales of $20,900. These sales were generated from an area consisting of Michigan's Upper Peninsula, west of Marquette County, and a small account in Detroit.

History and organization

In 1922, Tony De Angeles took over a bar in Legrand, Michigan. He added a restaurant shortly thereafter. His brother entered the business, and a partnership was established which lasted until October, 1963. At that time, Tony purchased his brother's half of the business.

During the partnership, in 1950, the brothers began the canning company for the purpose of selling spaghetti sauces commercially. The idea stemmed from the fact that customers were demanding the sauces for takeout in the restaurant.

As the restaurant and canning business grew, Tony's sons Dale and Pete, along with their mother, joined in the operation of the business. The new members worked in many different positions. After Tony bought out his brother's half of the business, the firm was organized as a partnership between Tony and his wife. Each of the two sons was to receive monthly salaries and 25 percent shares in net profits. Mr. and Mrs. De Angeles were under the same arrangement.

The sons, Dale and Pete, were to handle the bar business. Dale, who had been working with his father since he was fifteen, also aided in the spaghetti-canning process and managed the restaurant at times. Pete, who had three years training in accounting, did part of the book work. Mrs. De Angeles kept the daily books and was in charge of the waitresses in the restaurant. Tony did all of the sauce preparation, a majority of the canning, and all of the purchasing for the entire business. In examining the daily time that each member of the family devoted to the business, it was noted that Tony spent about fourteen hours a day, Mrs. De Angeles spent approximately six hours, and Dale and Pete spent about twelve hours each. It was also noted that, at the present time, Tony De Angeles is sixty-two years old.

Finance and control

After the company was formed into the present partnership, the books for the two operations, canning and the restaurant-bar, were merged so that there was a lone sales figure and one net profit. Pete felt this would save time, and he believed it was unnecessary to keep track of the separate operations because they were both profitable.

Balance sheets and income statements are unavailable at this time because they are under review by the firm's accountant. However, it is possible to get some idea of sales and profitability of the canning business from Exhibits I and II.

For the canning business, there is little or no storage space. Therefore, purchasing of food ingredients is done on a weekly basis. Other items such as cartons, labels, and cans are purchsed monthly or bimonthly. All basic ingredients are purchased from a large, local fruit and produce wholesaler who is a close friend of Tony's. The meat is purchased from local suppliers on a best-price basis. Cans, labels, and cartons are all purchased from separate individual sources. The size of the canning operation does not give the company any leverage in buying supplies.

EXHIBIT I SAUCE PRICES PER CASE TO WHOLESALERS AND RETAILERS

Meatless Sauce	Retailers	Wholesalers
Number 303 can	$12.00	$10.75
Number 10 can		15.00

Sauce with Meat	Retailers	Wholesalers
Number 303 can	$13.75	$12.75
Number 1 can	8.25	7.50
Number 10 can		18.00

EXHIBIT II   COMBINED SAUCE SALES AND PROFIT

Year	1959	1960	1961	1962	1963
Sales	$15,470	$15,575	$17,725	$19,300	$20,965
Net profit	775	1,390	205	(15)	2,525
Profit as percent of sales	5 percent	8.9 percent	0.12 percent	(0.8 percent)	12.1 percent

Products and production

The canning operation currently produces two types of spaghetti sauce: meat-containing and meatless. Meat-containing sauce is packed in two can sizes—number 10 and number 1. The number 10 can is sold to various institutions in the local area. The meatless sauce is packed in number 303 cans. Cost/case to wholesalers and retailers is shown in Exhibit II. This exhibit shows there has been a continuous increase in sales, but the present output is limited to only nineteen cases per day. This is because it is carried out in the basement of the family home, and it is limited by both time and equipment. Production is not tailored to fit the number and size of orders but to the amount of time Mr. De Angeles can devote to preparation of the sauce. This is normally two days a week. The canning operation is frequently behind in its order-filling. In fact, there have been numerous occasions when large orders have never been filled. One example of not filling a sizable order occurred recently. A large independent grocers' association placed a sizable order, but Mr. De Angeles decided it was time to take a vacation, and the order was never filled.

Mr. De Angeles has an established policy that his product will contain nothing but the finest grade meat and the best of other ingredients. As a consequence, the sauce is higher priced than most competitive sauces on the local store shelves.

Competitive position

If the market is divided into high- and low-priced sauces, Tony has no true competition. If the market is considered as all spaghetti sauce being retailed in Tony's market area, however, the company has two major competitors. They are both nationally advertised brands. Because of limited production, no investigation has ever been made of Tony's market penetration, and there has been no estimate of the percent of the market Tony could take if he were to expand operations.

Sales and promotion

The present distribution area has already been outlined. Sales in this area are made, primarily, through a single wholesaler and direct to local retailers. There is also a limited amount of "backdoor business" in which customers buy directly at the restaurant. An attempt has been made to discourage this business, for it cuts into the amount of the product which can be sold to the wholesaler and the retailers.

The company uses no salesmen. All sales are based strictly on a demand which has been drawn through word-of-mouth channels. The wholesaler has approached Tony and has asked if he could be his sole distributor. There has been no advertising—even at the point of sale. The cans are simply placed on the store shelves, and they are placed next to brands which are nationally known and lower priced.

Information is not available on case sales in areas where the sauce is distributed. It is suspected, however, that the greatest volume, on a population basis, is in Baraga County where the Tony name is well known. Little is known about the cost of sales, for there has been no cost control in the entire history of the company. The information presented in Exhibit II indicates that the return on investment is variable, but not much reliance should be placed on these figures.

Tony De Angeles and the future

Mr. De Angeles is, in many ways, a typical Italian entrepreneur. After arriving in America, as a boy, he received a third-grade education and worked as a shoe-shine boy until he was seventeen years old. Through a fellow Italian acquaintance, and with his savings, he purchased the bar business in Legrand. The bar business led his Italian instincts to a favorite pastime—cooking. In the bar, he established a free lunch counter, and this eventually developed into a restaurant.

Over the years, the business has had many ups and downs. These originated both within the family and outside it. Through extremely long hours and hard work, however, Tony has developed a business which is presently valued at approximately $100,000. Tony's relationship with his sons has been one of hesitant delegation of authority. He does not appear confident that his sons are capable of assuming control of the business.

In developing his cooking skills over the years, Tony has formulated spaghetti and pizza sauces which many have attempted, unsuccessfully, to emulate. These sauces are considered sufficiently good by competitors and other manufacturers of canned goods for Tony to have been offered business propositions several times in the past fifteen years. However, he has deemed none of these of an acceptable quality.

There have been at least two cases where prominent local businessmen have approached him with offers to establish a corporation, to provide the capital, and to give him 51 percent of the voting stock. All that would be required of him would be his formulas and his establishment of quality control. Until now, Tony has rejected these offers, for he has feared that these men would eventually gain control of the business. This, he believes, would come about through his lack of education and lack of business knowledge.

When Mr. De Angeles was asked about his future objectives, he replied, "I'm almost sixty-two years old, and I want to take it easy. I would like to sell the canning formulas and keep the frozen pizza business." He made no statement about his intentions regarding the restaurant-bar.

More specific future plans of the company include the establishment of a cost control system. This is presently being worked out between Mrs. De Angeles and their CPA. Another plan is to examine what might be done with the canning division to make it more profitable and less of a burden on Tony. Otherwise, the family plans to keep the business operating along the present lines.

APPENDIXES

THE COMPLEX PROBLEM-SOLVING MODEL

1. Statement of the problem
2. Statement of the facts
3. Statement of alternative courses of action
4. Advantages and disadvantages of alternatives
5. Evaluation of advantages and disadvantages
6. Estimate of likelihood of occurrence of advantages and disadvantages
7. Selection of the best alternative
8. Implementation of the decision
9. Filing the problem solution
10. Comparing expected with actual results of the decision

CHECKLIST FOR SELECTING THE PROBLEM

1. List all problems, both observed and suspected.
2. Rate each problem according to ease of solution.
3. Set deadlines for solving urgent problems.
4. Establish problem hierarchies in terms of primacy or dependency.
5. Do partial analyses of a couple of easy problems.
6. Do partial analyses of a couple of urgent problems.
7. Do partial analyses of all primary problems.
8. In general, solve primary problems first.

9. If primary problem solving and implementing delays urgent problem solution beyond indicated deadlines, solve urgent problems first.
10. If urgent problems are solved first, be sure solutions are consistent with expected solutions to primary problems.

appendix C
CHECKLIST FOR GETTING THE FACTS

1. Using immediately available facts, make a preliminary analysis of the situation.
2. From this analysis, using personal judgment, make a preliminary selection of the problem to be solved.
3. From the preliminary analysis and from the preliminary definition of the problem, list the additional facts needed or desired.
4. Using appropriate research techniques, discover as many of the desired facts as time and money allow.
5. Using the presently available facts, recheck the definition of the problem, and if redefinition is required, repeat steps 3 and 4.
6. Using the now available facts, write up the situation in the form of a case. As far as possible and convenient, present events in chronological order.
7. Research additional facts, as needed, to close the gaps which have appeared in the written case.
8. Have the written case reviewed by a competent analyst who is not personally involved in the case.
9. Research additional facts requested by the independent analyst.
10. When time or money runs out, assume additional facts as necessary to complete the analysis.

appendix D

CHECKLIST FOR SELECTING ALTERNATIVE COURSES OF ACTION

---

1. Choose not less than three nor more than seven alternatives.
2. Select one alternative from each of the two extremes on the alternative spectrum.
3. Select another from a position near the center of the spectrum.
4. Select additional alternatives, as time and money allow, from spectrum positions midway between those already selected.

appendix E

PROCEDURE FOR LISTING ADVANTAGES AND DISADVANTAGES

---

1. Prepare as many analysis sheets as alternatives being analyzed.
2. At the top of analysis sheets, enter the specific alternatives, one to a page.
3. Beginning with advantages of the first alternative, list ideas as rapidly as possible.

4. Using the brainstorming–head-shrinking technique, strive for quantity of ideas.
5. While listing, avoid all temptations to judge the quality of ideas being generated.
6. After ideas on advantages for the first alternative stop flowing, repeat the procedure for the disadvantages of the first alternative.
7. Repeat the listing process for all of the alternatives.
8. Return to the first alternative, and repeat the entire operation for all alternatives.
9. Set the work aside and return to it later. Then, repeat the listing process once more for each alternative.

appendix F
PROCEDURE FOR EVALUATING ADVANTAGES AND DISADVANTAGES

1. Revise lists of advantages and disadvantages for clarity and unity.
2. Eliminate duplications within lists.
3. Examine items to assure that entries lie on the correct sides of the ledgers.
4. Determine whether advantages under one alternative are also advantages under one or more of the others.
5. Determine whether disadvantages under one alternative are disadvantages under one or more of the others.
6. Determine whether advantages under one alternative are disadvantages under one or more of the others.
7. Determine whether disadvantages under one alternative are advantages under one or more of the others.
8. Eliminate insignificant items from all lists.
9. Prepare fresh analysis sheets.
10. Assign dollar values to all advantages and disadvantages.
    a. Start with easy items to establish reference points for valuation.

b. Proceed with medium-difficult items to establish more reference points.

c. Finish with the very difficult items by reference to already valued items.

d. Whenever possible, use simple problem-solving techniques to establish dollar values.

e. Assign values to items on the assumption that predicted payoffs are absolutely certain.

11. Estimate the likelihood of occurrence for each payoff.

12. Multiplying certainty values by probabilities of occurrence, compute adjusted values for each advantage and each disadvantage for all alternatives.

REFERENCES

The following is not a bibliography. It is a listing of books and articles which have been cited in the text. A complete bibliography would run to several hundred pages. Interested readers, if they follow the procedures outlined in our discussion of library research, will have no difficulty in finding large quantities of additional literature on each of the many subjects discussed in the text.

ACKOFF, RUSSELL. L. (ed.), *Progress in Operations Research,* John Wiley & Sons, Inc., New York, 1961.

———, *Scientific Method: Optimizing Applied Research Decisions,* John Wiley & Sons, Inc., New York, 1962.

ADENAUER, KONRAD, "Quotable Quotes," *Reader's Digest,* March, 1965, p. 78.

ANDLINGER, G. R., "Business Games—Play One," *Harvard Business Review,* March–April, 1958, pp. 115–125.

ANGELL, ROBERT C., and RONALD FREEDMAN, "The Use of Documents, Records, Census Materials, and Indices," chapter 7 in Leon Festinger and Daniel Katz (eds.), *Research Methods in the Behavioral Sciences,* The Dryden Press, Inc., New York, 1953.

ANSHEN, MELVIN, CHARLES C. HELT, FRANCE MODIGLIANI, JOHN F. MUTH, and HERBERT A. SIMON, "Mathematics for Production Scheduling," *Harvard Business Review,* March–April, 1958, pp. 51–58.

AWAD, ELIAS N., *Business Data Processing,* Prentice-Hall, Inc., Englewood Cliffs, N.J., 1965.

BACH, GEORGE LELAND, *Economics,* 4th ed., Prentice-Hall, Inc., Englewood Cliffs, N.J., 1963.

BERRIEN, F. K., and W. H. BASH, *Human Relations,* Harper & Row, Publishers, Incorporated, New York, 1957.

BONINI, CHARLES P., *Simulation of Information and Decision Systems in the Firm,* Prentice-Hall, Inc., Englewood Cliffs, N.J., 1964.

BROSS, IRWIN D. J., *Design for Decision,* The Macmillan Company, New York, 1953.

BURKE, ROGER M., "What I Am Learning at HBS," *Harvard Business School Bulletin,* June, 1958, p. 19.

BURSK, EDWARD C., *Text and Cases in Marketing,* Prentice-Hall, Inc., Englewood Cliffs, N.J., 1962.

CALHOON, RICHARD P., E. WILLIAM NOLAND, and ARTHUR M. WHITEHILL, JR., *Cases on Human Relations in Management,* McGraw-Hill Book Company, New York, 1958.

CAMPBELL, A. ANGUS, and GEORGE KATONA, "The Sample Survey: A

Technique for Social Science Research," chapter 1 in Leon Festinger and Daniel Katz (eds.), *Research Methods in the Behavioral Sciences,* The Dryden Press, Inc., New York, 1953.

CHURCHMAN, C. WEST, RUSSELL A. ACKOFF, and E. LEONARD ARNOFF, *Introduction to Operations Research,* John Wiley & Sons, Inc., New York, 1957.

CLAUSWITZ, KARL VON, *On War,* Combat Forces Press, Washington, D.C., 1953.

COLLINS, ORVIS F., and DAVID G. MOORE, with DARAB UNWALA, "The Enterprising Man and the Business Executive," *Business Topics,* Michigan State University, East Lansing, Mich., Winter, 1964, pp. 19–34.

COMAN, E. T., *Sources of Business Information,* Prentice-Hall, Inc., Englewood Cliffs, N.J., 1949.

CONNELL, CHARLES F., and ROBERT L. KAHN, "The Collection of Data by Interviews," chapter 8 in Leon Festinger and Daniel Katz (eds.), *Research Methods in the Behavioral Sciences,* The Dryden Press, Inc., New York, 1953.

COOMBS, CLYDE H., "Theory and Methods of Social Measurement," chapter 11 in Leon Festinger and Daniel Katz (eds.), *Research Methods in the Behavioral Sciences,* The Dryden Press, Inc., New York, 1953.

CYERT, R. M., *and* J. G. MARCH, "Organizational Structure and Pricing Behavior in an Oligopolistic Market," *American Economic Review,* March, 1955, pp. 129–139.

DRUCKER, PETER F., *The Practice of Management,* Harper & Row, Publishers, Incorporated, New York, 1954.

EATON, PAUL W., Private communication, February, 1965.

EISMAN, BEN, and FRANK C. SPENCER (re Open Heart Surgery), *Time,* vol. 85, no. 9, February 26, 1965, p. 77.

EVERETT, DAVID, (re Tall Oaks), *The Oxford Dictionary of Quotations,* 2d ed., Oxford University Press, London, 1955, p. 202.

FEARNSIDE, W. WARD, and WILLIAM B. HALTHER, *Fallacy: The Counterfeit of Argument,* Prentice-Hall, Inc., Englewood Cliffs, N.J., 1959.

FEDERAL ELECTRIC COMPANY, *A Programmed Introduction to PERT,* John Wiley & Sons, Inc., New York, 1963.

FERBER, ROBERT, *Statistical Techniques in Market Research,* McGraw-Hill Book Company, New York, 1949.

——— and P. J. VERDORN, *Research Methods in Economics and Business,* The Macmillan Company, New York, 1962.

FESTINGER, LEON, "Laboratory Experiments," chapter 4 in Leon Festinger and Daniel Katz (eds.), *Research Methods in the Behavioral Sciences,* The Dryden Press, Inc., New York, 1953.

———, *A Theory of Cognitive Dissonance,* Stanford University Press, Stanford, Calif., 1957.

FINKNER, A. L., "Methods of Sampling for Estimating Commercial Peach Production in North Carolina," *North Carolina Agricultural Station Technical Bulletin 91,* Raleigh, 1950.

GLOVER, JOHN DESMOND, and RALPH M. HOWER, *The Administrator,* Richard D. Irwin, Inc., Homewood, Ill., 1963.

HANSEN, HARRY L., *Marketing,* Richard D. Irwin, Inc., Homewood, Ill., 1961.

HARVARD BUSINESS SCHOOL, "Case Development at the School," *Harvard Business School Bulletin,* January–February, 1965, p. 9.

HAUSER, P. M., and W. R. LEONARD, *Government Statistics for Business Use,* John Wiley & Sons, Inc., New York, 1946.

KATZ, DANIEL, "Field Studies," chapter 2 in Leon Festinger and Daniel Katz (eds.), *Research Methods in the Behavioral Sciences,* The Dryden Press, Inc., New York, 1953.

KEGEL, CHARLES H., and MARTIN STEVENS, *Communication,* Wadsworth Publishing Co., Inc., San Francisco, 1962.

KEMENY, J. G., J. L. SNELL, and G. L. THOMPSON, *Finite Mathematics,* Prentice-Hall, Inc., Englewood Cliffs, N.J., 1957.

KEREKES, FRANK, and ROBLEY WINFREY, *Report Preparation,* Iowa State College Press, Ames, 1951.

KINDALL, ALVA F., *Personnel Administration,* Richard D. Irwin, Inc., Homewood, Ill., 1961.

KISH, LESLIE, "Selection of the Sample," chapter 5 in Leon Festinger and Daniel Katz (eds.), *Research Methods in the Behavioral Sciences,* The Dryden Press, Inc., New York, 1953.

KOONTZ, HAROLD, "The Management Jungle," *Journal of the Academy of Management,* December, 1961, p. 174.

LAWRENCE, PAUL R., and JOHN A. SEILER, *Organizational Behavior and Administration,* Richard D. Irvin, Inc., Homewood, Ill., 1965.

LIKERT, RENSIS, "Measuring Organizational Performance," *Harvard Business Review,* March–April, 1958, pp. 41–51.

————, *New Patterns in Management,* McGraw-Hill Book Company, New York, 1961.

LINDSAY, FRANKLIN A., *New Techniques for Management Decision-Making,* McGraw-Hill Book Company, New York, 1958.

LUCK, DAVID J., HUGH G. WALES, and DONALD A. TAYLOR, *Marketing Research,* 2d ed., Prentice-Hall, Inc., Englewood Cliffs, N.J., 1961.

MACHIAVELLI, NICCOLÒ, *The Prince,* The Harvard Classics, vol. 36, P. F. Collier & Sons, New York, 1910.

MARQUIS, D. G., "Individual Responsibility and Group Decisions Involving Risk," *Industrial Management Review,* vol. III, 1962, pp. 8–23.

MEDDLETON, DANIEL J., PHILIP S. MCVITTIE, and ALAN R. PATTERSON, *A Survey of Chronic Illness in the Copper Country,* Department of Business and Engineering Administration, Michigan Technological University, Houghton, Michigan, 1964.

MILLER, DAVID W., and MARTIN K. STARR, *Executive Decisions and Operations Research,* Prentice-Hall, Inc., Englewood Cliffs, N.J., 1964.

MUNN, NORMAN L., *Introduction to Psychology,* Houghton Mifflin Company, Boston, 1962.

NETER, JOHN, and WILLIAM WASSERMANN, *Fundamental Statistics,* Allyn and Bacon, Inc., Boston, 1961.

NEUMANN, J. VON, and O. MORGENSTERN, *Theory of Games and Economic Behavior,* Princeton University Press, Princeton, N.J., 1953.

REINFELD, NYLES V., and WILLIAM R. VOGEL, *Mathematical Programming,* Prentice-Hall, Inc., Englewood Cliffs, N.J., 1958.

REMINGTON, LAWRENCE J., Private communication, February, 1965.

RIGBY, PAUL H., *Conceptual Foundations in Business Research,* John Wiley & Sons, Inc., New York, 1965.

RIM, Y., "Leadership Attitudes and Decisions Involving Risk," *Personnel Journal,* vol. IV, 1965, pp. 423–430.

ROETHLISBERGER, F. J., and W. J. DICKSON, *Management and the Worker,* Harvard University Press, Cambridge, Mass., 1939.

RUSSELL, FREDERIC A., and FRANK H. BEACH, *Salesmanship,* McGraw-Hill Book Company, New York, 1959.

RUSSELL, JACK, "A System of Sales Analysis Using Internal Company Records," *Journal of Marketing,* April, 1950, p. 676.

SCHLAIFER, ROBERT, *Probability and Statistics for Business Decisions,* McGraw-Hill Book Company, New York, 1959.

SCHNELLE, KENNETH E., *Manpower Resources in a Tight Labor Market,* Minnesota State Employment and Security Division, St. Paul, 1952.

SILK, LEONARD S., *The Education of Businessmen,* Committee for Economic Development, New York, 1960.

SIMON, HERBERT A., *Administrative Behavior,* 2d ed., The Macmillan Company, New York, 1957.

SMITH, ADAM, *The Wealth of Nations,* Richard D. Irwin, Inc., Homewood, Ill., 1963.

STAGNER, ROSS, "Resolving Top-level Managerial Disagreements," *Business Topics,* Michigan State University, Winter, 1965, pp. 15–22.

TERRY, GEORGE R., *Marketing: Selected Case Problems,* Prentice-Hall, Inc., Englewood Cliffs, N.J., 1956.

THUESEN, H. G., *Engineering Economy,* Prentice-Hall, Inc., Englewood Cliffs, N.J., 1957.

TREI, ALAN P., "What I Am Learning at HBS," *Harvard Business School Bulletin,* June, 1958, p. 20.

VARELA, JACOBO A., "Why Promotions Cause Trouble, and How to Avoid It," *Personnel,* November–December, 1964, pp. 17–21.

WARNER, W. LLOYD, and J. O. LOW, *The Social System of the Modern Factory,* Yale University Press, New Haven, Conn., 1947.

WATSON, EDWARD T. P., "Diagnosis of Management Problems," *Harvard Business Review,* January–February, 1958, pp. 69–76.

WERNER, EDWARD E., "One Variation of the Use of the Case Method in Marketing," *Collegiate News and Views,* South-Western Publishing Company, Cincinnati, October, 1959, pp. 5–8.

WERNETTE, J. PHILIP, "The Theory of the Case Method," *Michigan Busi-*

ness Review, University of Michigan, Ann Arbor, Mich., January, 1965, pp. 21–24.

WOODWORTH, ROBERT S., *Experimental Psychology,* Holt, Rinehart and Winston, Inc., New York, 1938.

World Almanac and Book of Facts, Newspaper Enterprise Association, 1966, pp. 705–718.

INDEX

INDEX